# 1001
# RHYMES &
# FINGERPLAYS

**Compiled fr**  **ne® Publications**

DATE DUE

## Illustrated by Gary Mohrmann

Published by Totline® Publications
an imprint of

**McGraw-Hill
Children's Publishing**

## Credits

Compiled from the best of Totline® Publications
Cover Design: Brenda Mann Harrison
Cover Illustration: Larry Countryman
Inside Illustrations: Gary Mohrmann
Executive Editor: Kathleen Cubley
Editors: Gayle Bittinger, Elizabeth McKinnon, Jean Warren, Miriam Bulmer, Kris Fulsaas
Editorial Assistant: Erica West
Page Design and Production: Sarah Ness
Art Manager: Jill Lustig
Production Manager: Jo Anna Brock

Many of the original rhymes and fingerplays in this book have been adapted from other Totline® sources. Most of the traditional fingerplays, including action directions, are adapted versions of those found in an early edition of *Ring A Ring O'Roses*, published by the Flint Public Library, Flint, MI.

*McGraw-Hill*
*Children's Publishing*

A Division of The **McGraw·Hill** Companies

Published by Totline® Publications
An imprint of McGraw-Hill Children's Publishing
Copyright © 1994 McGraw-Hill Children's Publishing

Send all inquiries to:
McGraw-Hill Children's Publishing
3195 Wilson Drive NW
Grand Rapids, Michigan 49544

All Rights Reserved • Printed in the United States of America

Library of Congress Catalog Number: 93-060788

*1001 Rhymes and Fingerplays*
ISBN: 0-911019-65-0

2 3 4 5 6 7 8 9 MAZ 07 06 05 04 03

# Introduction

*1001 Rhymes and Fingerplays* is the ultimate language resource for parents and teachers of young children.

No more searching through numerous books for the perfect rhyme or fingerplay! With *1001 Rhymes and Fingerplays*, you can easily find the perfect poem for storytime or for introducing a special topic.

Rhymes and young children seem to go together. Rhymes provide rich opportunities for children to develop listening and memory skills. When rhymes are appropriate and repetitious, young children experience early success, thereby increasing their self-esteem and general language knowledge.

Rhymes are great for together times and storytimes, but Totline rhymes can be much more. Creative parents and teachers can easily turn these rhymes into learning games, flannelboard fun, and movement opportunities.

Children love fingerplays, therefore we have provided action directions to accompany the rhymes wherever possible.

*1001 Rhymes and Fingerplays* is arranged by general themes. If you are looking for a particular rhyme or a rhyme about a specific topic, you can check the first-line index or the subject index.

We believe that this versatile book will become one of the most used in your library of children's literature. We wish you many happy rhyme and fingerplay experiences!

# Contents

## Me & My Community

## Nature

## Plants & Foods

## Weather

## Earth & Sky

# Celebrations & Special People

## Holidays

## Special Days

## Special People

# Me & My Community

## Growing Every Day

When I was very, very small,

I could only crawl and crawl.
> *(Crawl.)*

Now I'm growing up so tall,

I can run and catch a ball.
> *(Pretend to catch ball.)*

I am growing every day,

Getting bigger—every way.
> *(Stand tall.)*

*Gayle Bittinger*

## When I Was One

When I was one, I was so small,
> *(Hold up one finger.)*

I could not speak a word at all.
> *(Shake head.)*

When I was two, I learned to talk,
> *(Hold up two fingers.)*

I learned to sing, I learned to walk.
> *(Walk in place.)*

When I was three, I grew and grew.
> *(Hold up three fingers.)*

Now I am four, and so are you!
> *(Hold up four fingers, then point to other person.)*

*Adapted Traditional*

## I Am in Between

Giraffes are tall,
> *(Hold hands high.)*

Monkeys are small,
> *(Hold hands low.)*

And zebras are in between.
> *(Hold hands at waist level.)*

Grownups are tall,
> *(Stand on tiptoe.)*

Babies are small,
> *(Crouch low.)*

And I am in between!
> *(Stand, then point to self.)*

*Vicki Shannon*

## I Measure Myself

I measure myself from my head to my toes,
> *(Do actions as rhyme indicates.)*

I measure my arms, starting here by my nose.

I measure my legs and I measure me all,

I measure to see if I'm growing tall.

*Adapted Traditional*

## See How I Am Now

Sometimes I am tall,
  *(Stand tall.)*
Sometimes I am small.
  *(Crouch low.)*
Sometimes I am very, very tall,
  *(Stand on tiptoe.)*
Sometimes I am very, very small.
  *(Crouch and hug self.)*
Sometimes tall,
  *(Stand tall.)*
Sometimes small.
  *(Crouch low.)*
See how I am now.
  *(Stand normally.)*

*Adapted Traditional*

## I Am Growing

I'm growing here, I'm growing there,
  *(Point to head, then feet.)*
I am growing everywhere.
  *(Point to different parts of body.)*
I see someone who's growing too,
  *(Cup hand above eye.)*
Who could it be? Yes, it's you!
  *(Point to other person.)*

*Adapted Traditional*

## I Can

I can swim in the water,
  *(Pretend to swim.)*
I can climb a tree.
  *(Pretend to climb.)*
I can jump up high,
  *(Jump once.)*
I'm glad I'm me!
  *(Nod head and smile.)*

*Vicki Shannon*

## All by Myself

There are many things I can do
All by myself.
  *(Point to self.)*
I can comb my hair and lace my shoe
All by myself.
  *(Pretend to comb hair and lace shoe.)*
I can wash my hands and wash my face
All by myself.
  *(Pretend to wash hands and face.)*
I can put my toys and blocks in place
All by myself.
  *(Pretend to arrange objects.)*

*Adapted Traditional*

## Things I Do

I run fast,
> *(Run in place.)*

I walk slow.
> *(Walk in place.)*

I bend down

And touch my toe.
> *(Bend and touch toe.)*

I look up,
> *(Look up.)*

I look down.
> *(Look down.)*

I make a face

Just like a clown.
> *(Make a funny face.)*

*Vicki Shannon*

## Mirror, Mirror

I look in the mirror and who do I see?

A very wonderful, special me!
> *(Point to self.)*

With sparkling eyes all shiny and bright,
> *(Point to eyes.)*

My smile shows my teeth, all pearly white.
> *(Smile and point to teeth.)*

It certainly is great to be

This very wonderful, special me!
> *(Hug self.)*

*Ann M. O'Connell*

## What Do I See?

I look in the mirror

And what do I see?
> *(Look in mirror.)*

My smiling face

Reflected perfectly.
> *(Smile.)*

*Gayle Bittinger*

## A Reflection

A reflection is like a picture,

But it's not one you can keep.

You can see one in a mirror,

Or in some water deep.

You can see one in a window,

Or the bottom of a pan.

Why don't you try to see yours?

I just know you can!

*Diane Thom*

## Everybody Makes Mistakes

Everybody makes mistakes—

People like me and you.
*(Point to self, then others.)*

Just say you are sorry,

It's what you need to do.
*(Nod head.)*

Grandmas make mistakes,

Grandpas do too.
*(Gesture to right, then left.)*

Everybody makes mistakes—

People like me and you.
*(Point to self, then others.)*

Repeat, each time letting your children substitute
other words for *grandmas* and *grandpas*.

*Jean Warren*

## One Time I Made a Big Mistake

One time I made a big mistake—
*(Act out rhyme, using hand for bird.)*

I forgot to lock the door

Of my little parakeet's cage,

And she hopped down on the floor.

She flew up to the curtains,

She flew across my bed.

She flew around the house,

Then landed on my head.

She flew around in circles,

Not knowing where to land.

Finally she decided

To land upon my hand.

And very, very carefully,

I placed her in her home,

Then quickly shut the door.

At last, she could not roam.

Everybody makes mistakes,

I know that this is true.

But, next time, I will try

To remember what to do!

*Jean Warren*

## Being Proud Is Okay

Being proud is okay,
Bragging is not.
It's okay to tell someone
What you like a lot.

I am proud of _____ ,
And of _____ too.
I am proud of _____ .
How about you?

When someone starts to brag,
They make others feel bad.
Just remember not to brag,
So others can be glad.

*Jean Warren*

## An Example of Bragging

An example of bragging
Is to say that you're the best.
Just remember that life
Is not a great big test.

We all are good
At many, many things.
Just be happy that
They are not the same things.

So if you like to dance,
And know that you are good,
Just enjoy your dancing,
And be proud, like you should!

As you recite the rhyme for each of your children,
substitute an appropriate action word for *dance*.

*Jean Warren*

## Yes, I Know

Yes, I know I am unique,
From my head down to my feet.
　　*(Point to head, then feet.)*
Yes, I know I am worthwhile,
I can see it in your smile.
　　*(Smile.)*
Yes, I know I am okay,
I can tell by what you say.
　　*(Point to mouth.)*
Yes, I know I'm loved so much,
I can feel it in your touch.
　　*(Hug self.)*

*Jean Warren*

## Everybody Has a Name

Everybody
Has a name.
Some are different,
Some, the same.

Some are short,
Some are long.
All are right,
None are wrong.

My name is Andrew,
It's special to me.
It's exactly who
I want to be!

Each time you recite the rhyme, let one of your
children substitute his or her name for *Andrew*.

*Jean Warren*

## Special Me

Special me, special me,
*(Point to self.)*
How I wonder what I'll be.
*(Rest chin on hands.)*
In the big world I can be
*(Form circle with arms.)*
Anything I want to be.
*(Nod head.)*

*Kristine Wagoner*

## What I Do Best

What thing can you do the best?
Help us all so we can guess!
Can you lead or can you read?
Can you sing or pump a swing?
Tell us now, oh, tell us, do.
Please, oh, please give us a clue!

*Janice Bodenstedt*

## Fuzzies

Everybody has a lot
Of fuzzies deep inside.
And when you're nice to others,
Your fuzzies cannot hide.

Pretty soon they pop out
Into your open hand.
Then they start to jump out—
Where will your fuzzies land?

Everyone loves fuzzies,
Because they come from you.
They make others feel so warm,
And loved a whole lot too.

Don't worry about your fuzzies,
They tend to multiply.
Every time you give one,
You get lots more inside.

Fuzzies are so special,
They feel so good to you.
Just remember to help your friends,
So they'll have fuzzies too.

*Jean Warren*

## Ten Little Fingers

I have ten little fingers,
*(Hold up ten fingers.)*
And they all belong to me.
*(Point to self with thumb.)*
I can make them do things,
*(Wiggle fingers.)*
Would you like to see?
*(Tilt head to one side.)*

I can put them up high,
*(Raise hands.)*
I can put them down low.
*(Lower hands.)*
I can make them hide,
*(Put hands behind back.)*
And I can fold them, so.
*(Fold hands in lap.)*

*Adapted Traditional*

## Fee, Fie, Fo, Fum

Fee, fie, fo, fum.
See my finger,
*(Hold up pointer finger.)*
See my thumb.
*(Hold up thumb.)*

Fee, fie, fo, fum.
Finger's gone,
*(Bend down pointer finger.)*
So is thumb!
*(Hide thumb in fist.)*

*Adapted Traditional*

## Marching Fingers

Up the hill, down the hill,
*(Raise hands, then lower them.)*
Marching they will go.
*(March hands.)*
When they're up, they're very high,
*(Hold hands high.)*
When they're down, they're low.
*(Hold hands low.)*
Ten little fingers marching,
*(March hands.)*
Marching in a row.

*Adapted Traditional*

## Where Is Thumbkin?

Where is Thumbkin? Where is Thumbkin?
*(Put hands behind back.)*
Here I am!
*(Bring one thumb forward.)*
Here I am!
*(Bring other thumb forward.)*
How are you today, sir?
*(Wiggle one thumb.)*
Very well, I thank you.
*(Wiggle other thumb.)*
Run away. Run away.
*(Put hands behind back.)*

*Adapted Traditional*

## Open, Shut Them

Open, shut them,
(*Do actions as rhyme indicates.*)
Open, shut them,
Let your hands go clap.
Open, shut them,
Open, shut them,
Put them in your lap.

Creep them, creep them,
Creep them, creep them,
Right up to your chin.
Open up your little mouth,
But do not let them in!

*Adapted Traditional*

## This Is My Right Hand

This is my right hand,
(*Hold up right hand.*)
I raise it high.
(*Stretch hand upward.*)
This is my left hand,
(*Hold up left hand.*)
I'll touch the sky.
(*Stretch hand upward.*)

Right hand, left hand,
(*Hold up right hand, then left hand.*)
Roll them round and round.
(*Roll hands.*)
Left hand, right hand,
(*Hold up left hand, then right hand.*)
Pound, pound, pound.
(*Pound with both fists.*)

*Adapted Traditional*

## Five Little Fingers

Five little fingers on one hand.
(*Hold up five fingers.*)
Two little feet on which to stand.
(*Point to feet.*)
Two little arms to hold up high.
(*Raise arms high.*)
Watch me reach up to the sky!
(*Raise arms even higher.*)

*Karen L. Brown*

## Five Fingers on Each Hand

I have five fingers on each hand,
(*Hold up fingers of both hands.*)
Ten toes on my two feet.
(*Point to toes.*)
Two ears, two eyes,
(*Point to ears, then eyes.*)
One nose, one mouth,
(*Point to nose, then mouth.*)
With which to gently speak.
(*Continue pointing to mouth.*)

My hands can clap, my feet can tap,
(*Clap hands, then tap feet.*)
My eyes can brightly shine.
(*Point to eyes.*)
My ears can hear,
(*Cup hands behind ears.*)
My nose can sniff,
(*Wiggle nose.*)
My mouth can speak a rhyme.
(*Point to mouth.*)

*Adapted Traditional*

## My Head

This is the circle that is my head,
> *(Form circle with arms.)*

This is my mouth with which words are said.
> *(Point to mouth.)*

These are my eyes with which I see,
> *(Point to eyes.)*

This is my nose that is part of me.
> *(Point to nose.)*

This is the hair that grows on my head,
> *(Point to hair.)*

And this is my hat that is colored red.
> *(Stand hands on top of head.)*

*Adapted Traditional*

## My Eyes

Here are my eyes,

One and two.
> *(Point to eyes.)*

I give a wink,

So can you.
> *(Wink eye.)*

When they are open,

I see the light.
> *(Open eyes wide.)*

When they are closed,

It's dark like night.
> *(Close eyes.)*

*Adapted Traditional*

## Funny Face

Here is my face,
> *(Make a face.)*

I give it to you.
> *(Turn to another person.)*

Pass it along,
> *(Have person make a face.)*

Now you're funny too!
> *(Smile.)*

*Jean Warren*

## Head and Shoulders

Head and shoulders,
> *(Point to named body parts.)*

Knees and toes.

Eyes and ears,

Mouth and nose.

*Adapted Traditional*

## Clap Your Hands

Clap your hands,
    *(Do actions as rhyme indicates.)*
Touch your toes.
Stamp your feet,
Wiggle your nose.

Clap your hands,
Touch your wrist.
Stamp your feet,
Make a fist.

Clap your hands,
Touch your hips.
Stamp your feet,
Smack your lips.

Clap your hands,
Touch your thighs.
Stamp your feet,
Blink your eyes.

*Dawn Thimm*

## My Hands Can Clap

My hands can clap,
    *(Clap hands.)*
My feet can tap.
    *(Tap feet.)*
My mouth can talk,
    *(Point to mouth.)*
My feet can walk.
    *(Walk in place.)*
My shoulders can shrug,
    *(Shrug shoulders.)*
My arms can hug.
    *(Hug self.)*
I can do so many things!
    *(Smile.)*

*Diane Thom*

## Wiggle Your Toes

Wiggle your toes, wiggle your toes,
    *(Do actions as rhyme indicates.)*
Wiggle them up and down.
Wiggle them fast, wiggle them slow,
Wiggle them all around.

*Additional verses*: Wave your hands; Stamp your
feet; Blink your eyes.

*Jean Warren*

## My Eyes Can See

My eyes can see,
*(Point to eyes.)*
My mouth can talk.
*(Point to mouth.)*
My ears can hear,
*(Point to ears.)*
My feet can walk.
*(Walk in place.)*

My nose can sniff,
*(Point to nose.)*
My teeth can bite.
*(Point to teeth.)*
My lids can flutter,
*(Flutter eyelids.)*
My hands can write.
*(Pretend to write.)*

*Adapted Traditional*

## Here Are My Ears

Here are my ears,

Here is my nose.
*(Point to ears, then nose.)*
Here are my fingers,

Here are my toes.
*(Hold up fingers, then point to toes.)*

Here are my eyes,

Both open wide.
*(Point to wide-open eyes.)*
Here is my mouth,

With white teeth inside.
*(Point to open mouth.)*

Here is my tongue

That helps me speak.
*(Point to tongue.)*
Here is my chin,

And here are my cheeks.
*(Point to chin, then cheeks.)*

Here are my hands

That help me play.
*(Hold up hands.)*
Here are my feet,

For walking today.
*(Walk in place.)*

*Adapted Traditional*

## I Wiggle

I wiggle, wiggle, wiggle my fingers,
*(Wiggle fingers.)*

I wiggle, wiggle, wiggle my toes.
*(Wiggle toes.)*

I wiggle, wiggle, wiggle my shoulders,
*(Wiggle shoulders.)*

I wiggle, wiggle, wiggle my nose.
*(Wiggle nose.)*

Now no more wiggles are left in me,
*(Shake head.)*

So I will be as still as I can be.
*(Sit still.)*

*Adapted Traditional*

## I'll Touch My Hair

I'll touch my hair,
*(Do actions as rhyme indicates.)*

My lips, my eyes,

I'll sit up straight

And then I'll rise.

I'll touch my ears,

My nose, my chin,

And then I'll sit

Back down again.

*Adapted Traditional*

## Tap Your Head

Tap your head,
*(Do actions as rhyme indicates.)*

Tap your toe.

Turn in a circle,

Bend down low.

Tap your nose,

Tap your knees.

Hands on your shoulders,

Sit down, please.

*Margery A. Kranyik*

## All Kinds of Families

There are all kinds of families that I see,

Some are two and some are three.
> *(Hold up two fingers, then three fingers.)*

Some are eight and some are four,
> *(Hold up eight fingers, then four fingers.)*

And some are more and more and more!
> *(Raise and lower all ten fingers.)*

*Jean Warren*

## Some Families

Some families are big,

Some families are small.

Some families are short,

Some families are tall.

Some families live close,

Some live far away.

But they all love each other,

In their own special way.

Some families are happy,

Some families are sad.

But they still love each other,

Even when they are mad.

Some families you are born to,

Some families you are not.

But however you joined,

You are loved a whole lot!

*Jean Warren*

## Dads and Moms Are Best

Teddy bears are nice to clutch,

To hold, to love, to feel, to touch.
> *(Hold and rock pretend teddy bear.)*

But dads and moms are best of all

To hug, to kiss, when you're real small.
> *(Hug self, then blow a kiss.)*

*Lois E. Putnam*

## Shopping

Come to the store with me,

Just down the street.
> *(Beckon with hand.)*

We don't need a car,

We can go on our feet.
> *(Walk in place.)*

Daddy wants cherries

And apples and steak.
> *(Rub tummy.)*

Mommy wants bread

And strawberry cake.
> *(Lick lips and say, "Mmmm.")*

Repeat, substituting other family names
for *Daddy* and *Mommy.*

*Adapted Traditional*

## Mother's Knives and Forks

Here are Mother's knives and forks,
*(Interlace fingers, palms up.)*
Here is Father's table.
*(Turn palms down, fingers still interlaced.)*
Here is Sister's looking glass,
*(Form peak with pointer fingers.)*
And here is Baby's cradle.
*(Form additional peak with little fingers and rock pretend cradle.)*

*Adapted Traditional*

## Family Music

Mother plays the violin,
*(Pretend to play instruments.)*
Father plays the flute.

Little Sister plays the horn,

Toot, toot, toot, toot, toot!

Repeat, substituting *Brother* for *Sister*.

*Adapted Traditional*

## Grandma's Glasses

These are Grandma's glasses,
*(Form circles around eyes with fingers.)*
This is Grandma's hat.
*(Stand hands on top of head.)*
This is how she folds her hands
*(Fold hands.)*
And puts them in her lap.
*(Place hands in lap.)*

Repeat, substituting other family names for *Grandma*.

*Adapted Traditional*

## Grandpa and Grandma

Grandpa is my buddy,

Grandma is too.

They always try to help me

With what I want to do.


They help me learn to hammer,
*(Pretend to pound nails.)*
They help me learn to sew.
*(Pretend to sew with needle.)*
They help me learn to play games,
*(Pretend to play cards.)*
And make my playdough.
*(Pretend to knead dough.)*


They always take the time

To explain how things go.

They always take the time

To explain how things grow.


Grandpa is my buddy,

Grandma is too.

They always try to help me

With what I want to do.

*Jean Warren*

## Five Little Children

Here are five little children,
*(Hold up five fingers.)*
Quite a happy few.
They do so very many things
That children like to do.

This little girl sets the table,
*(Point to little finger.)*
This little boy sweeps the floor.
*(Point to ring finger.)*
This little girl helps her mother
*(Point to middle finger.)*
By softly closing the door.

This little boy loves his daddy,
*(Point to index finger.)*
He brings in his paper too.
And this little tiny baby
*(Point to thumb.)*
Is ready to laugh and coo.

*Adapted Traditional*

## Kids on the Bed

Five little kids jumping on the bed,
*(Hold up five fingers.)*
One fell down and bumped his head.
*(Bend down thumb.)*
He fell off and rolled out the door.
Kids on the bed? Now there are four.

Four little kids jumping on the bed,
One fell down and bumped her head.
*(Bend down pointer finger.)*
She fell off and bruised her knee.
Kids on the bed? Now there are three.

Three little kids jumping on the bed,
One fell down and bumped his head.
*(Bend down middle finger.)*
He fell off, he's black and blue.
Kids on the bed? Now there are two.

Two little kids jumping on the bed,
One fell down and bumped her head.
*(Bend down ring finger.)*
She fell off, no more fun.
Kids on the bed? Now there is one.

One little kid jumping on the bed,
This is what his mother said,
"No more jumping, turn out the light.
Now it's time to say goodnight!"
*(Bend down little finger and say, "Goodnight.")*

*Adapted Traditional*

## How I Help My Family

I set the table—one, two, three.
*(Pretend to set table.)*
That's how I help my family.

I put my toys away—one, two, three.
*(Pretend to put away toys.)*
That's how I help my family.

Let your children take turns telling how they
help their families, using phrases such as
these: I weed the garden; I fold the laundry;
I feed the puppy.

*Jean Warren*

## I Help My Parents

I help my parents,
*(Nod head.)*
I sweep the floor.
*(Pretend to sweep.)*
I dust the table,
*(Pretend to dust.)*
I run to the store.
*(Run in place.)*

I help beat eggs
*(Pretend to beat eggs.)*
And sift flour for cake.
*(Pretend to sift flour.)*
Then I help to eat
*(Pretend to eat.)*
All the good things we make.
*(Rub tummy and lick lips.)*

*Adapted Traditional*

## Who Will Feed the Baby?

Who will feed the baby?
*(Make feeding motions.)*
Who will go to the store?
*(Make fingers run.)*
Who will cook the dinner?
*(Make stirring motions.)*
Who will clean the floor?
*(Make scrubbing motions.)*

Who will wash the clothes?
*(Pretend to wash clothes.)*
Who will cut the grass?
*(Pretend to mow lawn.)*
Who will wash the car?
*(Pretend to wash car.)*
Who will get the gas?
*(Pretend to steer car.)*

If everybody helps,

The work will soon be done.

Then there will be more time

For having lots of fun!
*(Raise arms and shout, "Hurray!")*

*Jean Warren*

## Friends Are Special

Friends are special,
> *(Do actions as rhyme indicates.)*
So make a few.
Smile and say,
"How are you?"

*Karen Leslie*

## Friends

I have a friend whose name is Jon,
And we have fun together.
We laugh and play and sing all day,
In any kind of weather.

Let your children take turns substituting a
friend's name for *Jon.*

*Ruth Miller*

## Love Your Friends

Love your friends, love your friends,
Love them all the time.
Show them that you care for them
By being good and kind.
> *(Hug self.)*

*Lori Gross*

## A Friend of Mine

Nicole is a friend of mine.

Yes, indeed, I like her fine!

Let each of your children say the
rhyme, substituting a friend's name
for *Nicole.*

*Louanne Hutcheson*

## I Will Be Your Friend

I will be your brand-new friend,
May our friendship never end.
I will help at work or play,
I will be there night or day.
You can always count on me,
For I am your friend, you see.
> *(Point to self, then to other person.)*

*Karen L. Brown*

## Making Friends

Making friends and keeping them,
*(Do actions as rhyme indicates.)*
You learn to help another.
Just keep in mind the best thing is
To always love each other.
Hug your neighbor next to you,
Shake another's hand.
If you're kind in all you do,
You'll always have a friend.

*Judy Hall*

## Friends Old and New

Making friends is fun to do,
You like me and I like you.
*(Point to others, then self, then others.)*
Friends are great, let's make a few,
Then we'll have friends old and new.
*(Nod head.)*

*Tami Hall*

## Show Your Love

Love your friends, love your friends,
Love them in this way—
Show them you care with a great big smile,
Every single day!
*(Smile.)*

*Jean Anderson*

## My Friends

My friends are gaily waving,
*(Have everyone wave.)*
Waving, waving.
My friends are gaily waving,
And I will wave at them.
*(Wave back.)*

My friends are sweetly smiling,
*(Have everyone smile.)*
Smiling, smiling.
My friends are sweetly smiling,
And I will smile at them.
*(Smile back.)*

*Adapted Traditional*

## We Play Together

I have a friend who lives near me,
*(Point to other person.)*
We play together happily.
We ride our bikes and throw a ball
*(Pretend to ride bike, then toss ball.)*
In winter, summer, spring, and fall.

*Karen Vollmer*

## A Friend Is Someone Special

A friend is someone special,
And do you know why?
A friend is someone special
On whom you can rely.

A friend will listen to you,
And help when he or she can.
A friend is kind and caring,
And always your biggest fan.

So when you find somebody
On whom you can depend,
You know at last that you
Have found yourself a friend.

*Jean Warren*

## Faraway Friends

Whether we live close

Or miles and miles apart,
*(Hold palms together, then apart.)*
You'll still be my friend.

I'll keep you in my heart.
*(Place hand on chest.)*

Whenever I get lonely,

Or want to talk with you,
*(Tilt head to one side.)*
I'll just send a little note.

Then you can send one too!
*(Make writing motions.)*

*Jean Warren*

## I'm a Happy Face

I'm a happy face,

Just watch me grin.

I've a great big smile

From my forehead to my chin
*(Put on a big smile.)*

When I'm upset

And things are bad,

Then my happy face

Turns to sad.
*(Turn smile into a frown.)*

*Jean Warren*

## I Look Like This

I look like this when I'm happy,
*(Make faces as rhyme indicates.)*
I look like this when I sigh.

I look like this when I'm sleepy,

I look like this when I cry.

I look like this when I'm angry,

I look like this when I'm sad.

I look like this when I'm curious,

And I look like this when I'm glad.

*Cathy B. Griffin*

## Feelings

Sometimes on my face you'll see
*(Point to face.)*
How I feel inside of me.
*(Point to chest.)*
A smile means happy, a frown means sad,
*(Smile, then frown.)*
And when I grit my teeth, I'm mad.
*(Grit teeth and frown.)*
When I'm proud I beam and glow,
*(Smile.)*
But when I'm shy, my head hangs low.
*(Bow head.)*

*Karen Folk*

## Me in the Mirror

I look in the mirror,
*(Cup hands above eyes.)*
And what do I see?
*(Shrug shoulders, palms out.)*
I see myself there,
*(Point outward.)*
Looking at me.
*(Point to self.)*

Do I have a happy smile?
*(Smile.)*
Or am I sad today?
*(Frown.)*
No matter how I'm feeling,
*(Tilt head to one side.)*
I'm terrific anyway!
*(Pat self on back.)*

*Beverly Qualheim*

## I Look in the Mirror

I look in the mirror,
*(Pretend to look in mirror.)*

And what do I see?

I see a happy face
*(Smile.)*

Smiling at me.

I look in the mirror,
*(Pretend to look in mirror.)*

And what do I see?

I see a sad face
*(Frown.)*

Frowning at me.

*Adapted Traditional*

## I Feel Real Sad

When mother leaves,
*(Frown.)*

I feel real sad.

When mother leaves,

I don't feel glad.

It's okay to feel real sad.

It's okay to not feel glad.

When it's storytime,
*(Smile.)*

I don't feel sad.

When it's storytime,

I feel real glad.

It's okay to feel real glad.

It's okay to not feel sad.

Let your children take turns
suggesting other first lines for
the two verses. Here are possible
examples: When my friends move;
When I'm sick; When it's my birthday;
When Grandma comes to visit.

*Jean Warren*

## It's Okay to Have a Cry

It's okay to have a cry,

And I'll even tell you why.
*(Nod, then point to others.)*

We feel better when we cry,

Go ahead, it's no lie.
*(Bring fists to eyes.)*

Boohoo, boohoo, it's what we do,

When we feel so very blue.
*(Pretend to cry.)*

Then ever so slowly, after a while,

Our tears turn back into a smile!
*(Smile.)*

*Jean Warren*

## It's Okay to Hug One Another

It's okay to hug one another,
Your friends and your teacher,
Your sister, your brother.
It's okay to hug real tight.
It just makes the world seem right.

It's okay to hug one another,
Your grandma, your grandpa,
Your father, your mother.
It's okay to hug real tight.
It just makes the world seem right.

Let your children suggest names of other people
in their lives to substitute for those in the rhyme.

*Jean Warren*

## Hug Me

All I want are hugs from you,
    *(Exchange hugs.)*
Hugs that last the whole day through.
Hugs just make me feel so good,
So hug me, hug me, hug me!

Give me lots of hugs today,
    *(Exchange more hugs.)*
Hugs that chase the blues away,
Hugs that last the whole day through.
Just hug me, hug me, hug me!

*Jean Warren*

## Words and Faces

Words and faces
    *(Make faces as rhyme indicates.)*
Can change places
They tell
How you feel.

Sometimes happy,
Sometimes sad.
Sometimes worried,
Sometimes mad.

Words and faces
Can change places.
They tell
How you feel.

Sometimes scared,
Sometimes glad.
Sometimes surprised,
Sometimes feeling bad.

*Jean Warren*

## We All Need Help

We all need help
So let's help each other.
We all need help,
Friend, sister, brother.

So if you see
That someone needs a hand,
Help them out,
If you can.

*Jean Warren*

## I Have a Friend Who Cannot See

I have a friend
Who cannot see,
But can play the spoons
Upon his knee.

I have a friend
Who cannot walk,
But can tell where you're from
By the way you talk.

I have a friend
Who cannot sing,
But can throw a ball
Through a tire swing.

We all have some good things,
We all have some bad.
We all then are special,
And that makes me glad.

*Jean Warren*

## My Friend

I have a friend
Who has a wheelchair.
She cannot walk
From here to there.

But she's a good singer,
While I sing off-key.
She's also real smart,
Like I'd like to be.

She lets me push her,
Sometimes down the hall.
When I'm a helper,
I feel ten feet tall.

We both can play lotto
And checkers too.
We both like to paint
And visit the zoo.

She's such a good friend
And now you know why.
She's very special,
But then, so am I.

*Jean Warren*

| Signing | Is | Fun |
|---|---|---|
|  |  |  |
| Index fingers of both hands, with palms facing each other, move in alternating circles toward body. An *i* handshape twists to right to add *-ing* for correct English grammar. | Right pinkie (*i* handshape) starts on lower lip and moves straight out. | Index and middle fingers of right hand (*h* handshape) touch nose, then move to index and middle fingers of left hand. Both hands are palms down. |

## Signing Is Fun

**Signing is fun** for everyone,
*(Sign phrase as illustrated.)*
Come sign today.

**Signing is fun** for everyone,
Hip, hip hurray!

*Jean Warren*

## Let's Sign

**Signing is fun,** wouldn't you say?
*(Sign phrase as illustrated.)*
**Signing is fun,** let's sign today.

**Signing is fun,** we'll sign this way.

*Jean Warren*

## Hats on Everyone

Hats on police officers,
Starchy and blue.
Hats on firefighters,
Shiny and new.

Hats on marchers
In a band.
Hats on astronauts
When they land.

Hats on farmers,
Made of straw.
Hats on artists
When they draw.

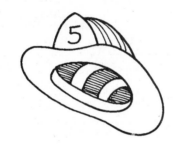

Hats on babies
Out in the sun.
Hats on almost
Everyone!

*Jean Warren*

## Caps for Sale

Caps for sale, caps for sale,
Caps upon my head.
    *(Touch head.)*
Caps for sale, caps for sale,
Yellow, blue, and red.

*Jean Warren*

## One, Two, Hats That Are New

One, two, hats that are new.
    *(Count on fingers.)*
Three, four, hats in a store.
Five, six, hats to do tricks.
Seven, eight, hats on the gate.
Nine, ten, hats on men.

*Jean Warren*

## Hats

Hats on people in the sun,
Hats on people on the run.
Hats on people in a band,
Hats on people on the sand.

Hats on people every day,
Hats on people when they play.
Hats on people at the fair,
Hats on people everywhere.

*Jean Warren*

## Carl the Clown's Hats

My name, boys and girls, is Carl the Clown.
I wear my hats all over town.
Each one has its own color name,
Which you can learn if you play my game.

Oh, here's a hat, and it is red.
It fits so nicely on my head.
Now when I wear my hat of yellow,
I'm told I'm quite a dandy fellow.

I hope you like my hat of blue.
I'll put it on now, just for you.
My purple hat is just for good.
I'd wear it always if I could.

I wear a white hat on a sunny day.
It looks quite nice, my friends all say.
I put on my green hat to go to the park,
But I take it off when it gets dark.

And when it's dark, I put on brown.
This hat is for a sleepy clown.
My orange and black hat is for Halloween night.
Yes, indeed, I'm quite a sight!

*Susan M. Paprocki*

## Mittens

Thumbs in the thumb place,
    *(Pretend to put on mittens.)*
Fingers all together.
This is the song
We sing in mitten weather.

When it is cold,
It doesn't matter whether
Our mittens are wool
Or made of finest leather.

*Adapted Traditional*

## Put on Your Mittens

Put on your mittens—it's cold, I fear,
    *(Pretend to put on mittens.)*
Now that winter snow is here.
    *(Hug self and shiver.)*
Play in the yard and when you're done,
    *(Pretend to make and toss snowballs.)*
Pull off your mittens one by one.
    *(Pretend to remove mittens.)*

*Barbara Paxson*

## Color Mittens

My poor little kitten lost her mitten

And started to cry, "Boohoo."
>*(Pretend to cry.)*

So I helped my kitten look for her mitten,
>*(Cup hand above eye and glance around.)*

Her beautiful mitten of blue.

I found a mitten just right for a kitten

Under my mother's bed.
>*(Pretend to peek under bed.)*

But, alas, the mitten was not the right mitten,
>*(Shake head.)*

For it was colored red.

I found a mitten just right for a kitten

Under my father's pillow.
>*(Pretend to peek under pillow.)*

But, alas, the mitten was not the right mitten,
>*(Shake head.)*

For it was colored yellow.

I found a mitten just right for a kitten

Under the laundry so clean.
>*(Pretend to peek under folded laundry.)*

But, alas, the mitten was not the right mitten,
>*(Shake head.)*

For it was colored green.

I found a mitten just right for a kitten

Inside my favorite shoe.
>*(Pretend to peek inside shoe.)*

And this time the mitten was just the right mitten,
>*(Nod head and smile.)*

For it was colored blue!

*Jean Warren*

## Mittens and Boots

These are our mittens,
>*(Pretend to put on mittens.)*

What are they for?

They keep our hands warm

When we go out the door.

And these are our boots.
>*(Pretend to pull on boots.)*

They will keep our feet dry

In piles of cold snow

When we play outside.

*Beverly Qualheim*

## Quiet Feet

Hickory, dickory, dock,

Let's put on our socks.
>*(Pretend to put on socks.)*

We'll walk around

Without a sound,
>*(Tiptoe.)*

When we put on our socks.

*Jean Warren*

## Stockings On

Deedle, deedle, dumpling,
>*(Walk in stocking feet.)*

Shoes all gone.

We went to town

With our stockings on.

Shoes all gone,

Stockings on.

Deedle, deedle, dumpling,

Shoes all gone.

*Adapted Traditional*

## Five Pairs of Shoes

Five pairs of shoes
*(Hold up five fingers.)*
In the shoe store.
Someone bought the red ones,
*(Bend down thumb.)*
Now there are four.

Four pairs of shoes
For all to see.
Someone bought the blue ones,
*(Bend down pointer finger.)*
Now there are three.

Three pairs of shoes,
Shiny and new.
Someone bought the yellow ones,
*(Bend down middle finger.)*
Now there are two.

Two pairs of shoes
Standing in the sun.
Someone bought the green ones,
*(Bend down ring finger.)*
Now there is one.

One pair of shoes,
Oh, what fun!
Someone bought the black ones,
*(Bend down little finger.)*
Now there are none.

*Jean Warren*

## Shining My Shoes

I spread some polish on my shoes,
*(Pretend to shine shoes as rhyme indicates.)*
Then I let it dry.
I brush and brush and brush and brush,
How those shoes shine! Oh, my!

*Adapted Traditional*

## Zipper Suit

My zipper suit is bunny brown,
The top zips up, the legs zip down,
*(Pretend to zip zippers.)*
I wear it every day.

Mommy bought it for me in town,
I zip it up, I zip it down,
*(Pretend to zip zippers.)*
And hurry out to play.

*Adapted Traditional*

## In My Pockets

The things in my pockets are lots of fun,
  *(Hold up five fingers.)*
I will show you one by one.

In my first pocket is a frog,
  *(Point to thumb.)*
I found him sitting on a log.

In my second pocket is a car,
  *(Point to index finger.)*
It can race off very far.

In my third pocket is a ball,
  *(Point to middle finger.)*
I can bounce it on a wall.

In my fourth pocket is a bunny,
  *(Point to ring finger.)*
She twitches her nose and looks so funny.

In my fifth pocket is a dog,
  *(Point to little finger.)*
He's a friend of my little frog.
  *(Touch little finger to thumb.)*

*Sue Schliecker*

## I Can Do It Myself

Hat on head, just like this,
  *(Do actions as rhyme indicates.)*
Pull it down, you see.
I can put my hat on
All by myself, just me.

One arm in, two arms in,
Buttons, one, two, three.
I can put my coat on
All by myself, just me.

Toes in first, heels push down,
Pull and pull, then see—
I can put my boots on
All by myself, just me.

Fingers here, thumbs right here,
Hands warm as can be.
I can put my mittens on
All by myself, just me.

*Adapted Traditional*

## Got My Toothpaste

Got my toothpaste, got my brush,
*(Hold up one pointer finger, then the other.)*
I won't hurry, I won't rush.
*(Shake head.)*
Making sure my teeth are clean,
*(Show teeth in a smile.)*
Front and back and in between.
*(Point as indicated.)*
When I brush for quite a while,
*(Pretend to brush teeth.)*
I have such a happy smile!
*(Smile.)*

*Frank Dally*

## A Toothbrush

Of all the things around the town,

A toothbrush is just right.
*(Hold up pointer finger.)*
Brush up and down and all around,
*(Make brushing movements with finger.)*
To keep your teeth so white.
*(Show teeth in a smile.)*

*Florence Dieckmann*

## Do You Brush Your Teeth?

Do you brush your teeth

After every meal you eat?
*(Pretend to brush teeth.)*
Is your smile so bright

It shines like a light?
*(Smile and point to teeth.)*
Do you open your mouth wide

So the dentist sees inside?
*(Point to open mouth.)*
Yes, I do!

How about you?
*(Smile and point to others.)*

*Diane Thom*

## I Brush My Teeth

I brush my teeth, I brush my teeth,
*(Do actions as rhyme indicates.)*
Morning, noon, and night.

I brush them, floss them, rinse them clean,

I keep them nice and white.

I brush them once, I brush them twice,

I brush them till they shine.

I always brush them up and down,

These precious teeth of mine!

*Stella Waldron*

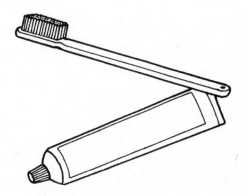

## So Good for You

Milk, fruits, and vegetables,

Meat and brown bread too.

Try to have some every day,
*(Pretend to eat.)*
They're so good for you!

*Elizabeth McKinnon*

## Good Foods

Milk, meat, bread, and fruit,

These will help me grow

To be strong and tall and well,
*(Show arm muscles and stand tall.)*
Healthy from head to toe!

*Barbara Robinson*

## Healthy Habits

Be sure to eat nutritious foods

To keep your body strong.
*(Pretend to eat.)*
Too much candy, junk, and pop

Can do your body wrong.

Be sure to get a lot of sleep

Each and every night.
*(Rest cheek on folded hands.)*
You'll feel good in the morning

When your nighttime's right.

Be sure to wash both your hands

And use a lot of soap.
*(Pretend to wash hands.)*
Don't give cold and flu germs

Any kind of hope.

*Susan M. Paprocki*

## Good Exercise

I stretch and stretch my arms out wide
   *(Do actions as rhyme indicates.)*
As if to make them longer.
I stretch and stretch and stretch and stretch,
For that will make me stronger.

I stretch and stretch my arms up high
As high as they will go.
I stretch and stretch and stretch and stretch,
For that will make me grow.

*Adapted Traditional*

## Stretching Fun

I stretch and stretch and find it fun
   *(Stretch arms high.)*
To reach and try to touch the sun.

I bend and bend to touch the floor,
   *(Bend and lower arms.)*
Till muscles in my legs get sore!

*Adapted Traditional*

## Reach for the Ceiling

Reach for the ceiling
   *(Do actions as rhyme indicates.)*
Touch the floor.
Stand up again,
Let's do some more.

Nod your head,
Bend your knee.
Shrug your shoulders
Like this, you see?

Reach for the ceiling,
Touch the floor.
That's all now,
There isn't any more.

*Adapted Traditional*

## Stretching High

Stretch, stretch, way up high,
   *(Do actions as rhyme indicates.)*
On your tiptoes reach the sky.
Wave to the bluebirds flying by.

Bend, bend, touch your toes,
Swing and sway as the north wind blows.
Waddle off like the duckling goes.

*Adapted Traditional*

## Washing Your Hands and Face

If you wash your hands and face every day,
*(Pretend to wash hands, then face.)*
If you wash your hands and face in this way,

Then your skin will have a glow

And everyone will know

That you wash your hands and face every day.

*Judy Hall*

## After My Bath

After my bath I try, try, try

To rub with a towel till I'm dry, dry, dry.
*(Pretend to rub body with towel.)*
Hands to dry, and fingers and toes,

And two wet legs and a shiny nose.
*(Point to named body parts.)*
Just think how much less time I'd take

If I were a dog and could shake, shake, shake!
*(Shake body.)*

*Adapted Traditional*

## Brush Your Hair

Brush your hair every day,
*(Do actions as rhyme indicates.)*
Give your hair a treat.

Part it, braid it, brush it back,

But always keep it neat.

Brush it once, brush it twice,

Keep it nice and clean.

Brush and brush the tangles out

And see the lovely sheen!

*Lynn Beaird*

## If You Cough

If you cough,
*(Do actions as rhyme indicates.)*
Or if you sneeze,

Cover your mouth,

If you please.

*Ruth Miller*

## Mr. Yuk

Mr. Yuk means no, no, no!
*(Shake head and pointer finger.)*
If you see him, go, go, go!
*(Run in place.)*
If you see him anywhere,
*(Cup hand above eye and look around)*
You will know that poison's there!
*(Frown and push away with hands.)*

*Priscilla M. Starrett*

## Color Balloons

I had a great big red balloon,
Until I let it go.
Now where, oh, where, I wonder,
Did my balloon blow?

I had a great big blue balloon,
The string I held so tight.
But when I opened up my hand,
My balloon flew out of sight.

I had a great big green balloon,
As pretty as could be.
But when I let go of its string,
It flew away from me.

I had a great big yellow balloon,
When I went out to play.
But when I wasn't watching,
My balloon just flew away.

Red balloon, red balloon,
Where can you be?
I see a red balloon
Up in the tree.

Blue balloon, blue balloon,
Where did you fly?
I see a blue balloon
Up in the sky.

Green balloon, green balloon,
Where can you be?
I see a green balloon
Under the tree.

Yellow balloon, yellow balloon,
Where did you fly?
I see a yellow balloon
High in the sky.

*Jean Warren*

## My Big Balloon

Here I have a big balloon,
*(Clasp hands.)*
Watch me while I blow.
*(Blow into hands.)*
Small at first, then bigger,
*(Form circle with fingers.)*
Watch it grow and grow.
*(Form larger circles with hands.)*

Do you think it's big enough?
*(Continue forming circles with hands.)*
Maybe I should stop.
*(Nod head.)*
For if I blow much longer,
*(Tilt head to one side.)*
My balloon will surely pop!
*(Clap hands once.)*

*Adapted Traditional*

## Pretty Balloons

Pretty balloons in the air,

Lots of colors everywhere.

Red and yellow, green and blue,

Can you see the colors too?

*Susan Burbridge*

## A Little Ball

A little ball,
*(Form circle with thumb and finger.)*
A bigger ball,
*(Form circle with hands.)*
A great big ball I see.
*(Form circle with arms.)*
Now let's count them.

Are you ready?

One,
*(Form circle with arms.)*
Two,
*(Form circle with hands.)*
Three.
*(Form circle with thumb and finger.)*

*Adapted Traditional*

## Bouncing Ball

I'm bouncing, bouncing everywhere,
*(Make bouncing movements.)*
I bounce and bounce into the air.

I'm bouncing, bouncing like a ball,

I bounce and bounce until I fall.
*(Drop to the floor.)*

*Adapted Traditional*

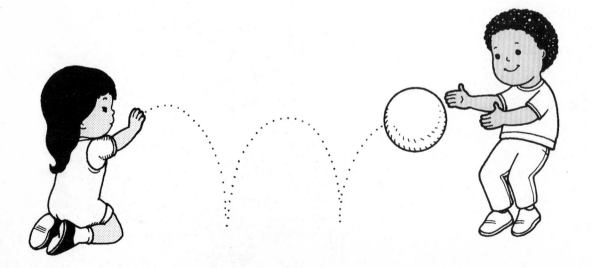

## Here Is a Ball

Here is a ball I keep on the shelf.
*(Do actions as rhyme indicates.)*
I can toss it and catch it
And bounce it myself.

Here is a ball that I toss to you.
Please catch it and toss it
Right back to me too.

*Adapted Traditional*

## My Little Doll

Look, I have a little doll,
*(Do actions with pretend doll.)*
It is lots of fun.
I can make it sing and dance,
And hop and sing and run.
Little doll, dance with me,
Dance round and round.
We will dance around the room,
And then we'll both sit down.

*Jean Warren*

## My Doll

This is how my doll walks,
This is how it walks, you see?
*(Walk, holding arms and legs stiff.)*
This is how my doll talks,
This is how it talks, you see?
*(Bend at waist, saying appropriate words.)*

*Adapted Traditional*

## Floppy Rag Doll

Flop your arms, flop your feet,
*(Do actions as rhyme indicates.)*
Let your hands go free.
Be the floppiest rag doll
You ever did see.

*Adapted Traditional*

## Jack-In-The-Box

Jack-in-the-box,
You sit so still.
*(Make fist with thumb inside.)*
Won't you come out?
Yes, I will!
*(Pop out thumb.)*

*Adapted Traditional*

## Jack, Jack

Jack, Jack, down you go,
Down in your box, down so low.
*(Crouch down.)*
Jack, Jack, there goes the top.
Quickly now, up you pop!
*(Jump up.)*

*Author Unknown*

## Wake Up, Jack-In-The-Box

Jack-in-the-box, jack-in-the-box,
    *(Make fist with thumb inside.)*
Wake up, wake up, somebody knocks.
    *(Knock on fist with other hand.)*

One time, two times, three times, four.
    *(Knock four times.)*
Jack pops out of his little round door.
    *(Pop thumb up out of fist.)*

*Adapted Traditional*

## Come Fly a Kite

Come fly a kite
And watch it sail
    *(Hold hand high.)*
Across the sky,
Waving its tail!
    *(Wave hand back and forth.)*

*Jean Warren*

## Kite Friends

One little kite in the sky so blue,
Along came another, then there were two.
    *(Hold up one finger, then two fingers.)*
Two little kites flying high above me,
Along came another, then there were three.
    *(Hold up three fingers.)*
Three little kites, just watch how they soar,
Along came another, then there were four.
    *(Hold up four fingers.)*
Four little kites, so high and alive,
Along came another, then there were five.
    *(Hold up five fingers.)*
Five little kites dancing 'cross the sky,
What a sight to see, way up so high!
    *(Dance all five fingers in air.)*

*Jean Warren*

## Kite, Kite

Kite, kite, soaring high,
    *(Do actions as rhyme indicates.)*
Reaching, reaching to the sky.
First you're high, then you're low,
Swooping, swirling, round you go.
Kite, kite, fine and free,
Dancing, dancing, just for me.

*Susan M. Paprocki*

## Five Shiny Marbles

Five shiny marbles lying on the floor,
*(Hold up five fingers.)*
One shoots away and that leaves four.
*(Bend down thumb.)*
Four shiny marbles I can plainly see,
One rolls off and that leaves three.
*(Bend down pointer finger.)*
Three shiny marbles, now just a few,
One spins away and that leaves two.
*(Bend down middle finger.)*
Two shiny marbles sparkling in the sun,
One wanders off and that leaves one.
*(Bend down ring finger.)*
One shiny marble looking for some fun,
Goes off to find the others and that leaves none.
*(Bend down little finger.)*

*Susan M. Paprocki*

## Puppet Clown

I'm a funny little puppet clown
When my strings move up and down.
*(Bend up and down at knees.)*
First, I stand up, then I fall down.
*(Stand straight, then drop to floor.)*
I'm a funny little puppet clown.

*Adapted Traditional*

## Teddy Bear, Teddy Bear

Teddy bear, teddy bear, turn around,
*(Do actions as rhyme indicates.)*
Teddy bear, teddy bear, touch the ground.
Teddy bear, teddy bear, reach up high,
Teddy bear, teddy bear, touch the sky.
Teddy bear, teddy bear, bend down low,
Teddy bear, teddy bear, touch your toe.

*Adapted Traditional*

## Dancing Teddy Bear

Pick your teddy bear up from the ground,
*(Do actions with pretend teddy bear.)*
Then go dancing all around.
Hold him high and hold him low,
As round and round and round you go.

*Jean Warren*

## My Wagon

I have a little wagon
*(Do actions as rhyme indicates.)*
I pull around with me.
I fill it with my toys
So everyone can see.

I love my little wagon,
Sometimes I jump inside.
Then I push with my two feet
And give my toys a ride.

*Jean Warren*

## Baby's Toys

Here's a ball for Baby,
Big and soft and round.
*(Form ball with hands.)*
Here is Baby's hammer,
See how she can pound.
*(Pound fist.)*

Here is Baby's music,
Clapping, clapping, so.
*(Clap hands.)*
Here are Baby's stuffed toys,
Standing in a row.
*(Hold up fingers.)*

Here is Baby's trumpet,
Toot-a-toot-a-toot.
*(Pretend to play horn.)*
Here's the way that Baby
Plays at peekaboo.
*(Hold fingers in front of eyes.)*

*Adapted Traditional*

## Mama's Little Baby

Mama's little baby a kiss can blow,
*(Blow a kiss.)*
And rub noses just like so.
*(Rub noses with baby.)*
Two little hands can clap, clap, clap,
*(Clap baby's hands together.)*
Ten little toes can tap, tap, tap.
*(Tap baby's toes.)*

*Karen L. Brown*

## I Can Make a Baby Smile

I can make a baby smile
When I tickle her toes.
*(Tickle baby's toes.)*
And I can make a baby laugh
When I tickle her nose.
*(Tickle baby's nose.)*

*Betty Silkunas*

## To Market, to Market

To market, to market,
*(Move baby up and down on knee.)*
To buy a fat pig.
Home again, home again,
Jiggety-jig.

To market, to market,
To buy a fat hog.
Home again, home again,
Jiggety-jog.

*Adapted Traditional*

## Peekaboo

Where are you hiding?
I can't see you.
*(Cover eyes with hands.)*
Are you near or far?
Peekaboo!
*(Uncover eyes.)*

*Pat Cook*

## Where Are You?

Where is Michael? Where is Michael?
There he is!  There he is!
*(Point to baby.)*
Will you come and play today?
Oh, look, he's gone away!
*(Cover face with hands.)*

Substitute your baby's name for *Michael*.

*Nancy Giles*

## I'm Hiding

I'm hiding, I'm hiding,
*(Place small blanket over baby.)*
And no one knows where,
For all they can see
Are my toes and my hair!

*Adapted Traditional*

## Knock, Knock

Knock, knock,
*(Tap on baby's forehead.)*
Peek in.
*(Cup hand above eye.)*
Open the latch,
*(Touch baby's nose.)*
And walk right in.
*(Put fingertip in baby's mouth.)*

*Adapted Traditional*

## The Way the Baby Grows

Five fingers on this hand,
*(Hold up baby's hand.)*
Five fingers on that.
*(Hold up baby's other hand.)*
A dear little nose,
*(Point to baby's nose.)*
A mouth like a rose,
*(Point to baby's mouth.)*
Two cheeks so tiny and fat.
*(Point to baby's cheeks.)*
Two eyes, two ears,
*(Point to baby's eyes, then ears.)*
And ten little toes.
*(Point to baby's toes.)*
That's the way the baby grows.
*(Hug baby.)*

*Adapted Traditional*

## Merry-Go-Round

Merry-go-round, merry-go-round,

We go riding all around.

First we're up, then we're down
*(Move baby up and down on knee.)*
We go riding all around.

Merry-go-round, merry-go-round,

We go riding all around.

Hold on tight! Don't fall down!
*(Gently lean baby to one side.)*
We go riding all around.

*Jean Warren*

## Pat-A-Cake

Pat-a-cake, pat-a-cake, baker's man,
*(Hold baby's hands and do actions indicated.)*
Bake me a cake as fast as you can.

Roll it and pat it and mark it with *B*,

And put it in the oven for Baby and me.

*Adapted Traditional*

## Rock-A-Bye, Baby

Rock-a-bye, baby, on the treetop,
*(Hold baby in arms.)*
When the wind blows, the cradle will rock.
*(Rock baby back and forth.)*
When the bough breaks the cradle will fall,
*(Continue rocking movements.)*
And down will come baby, cradle and all.
*(Rock baby down, then up again.)*

*Adapted Traditional*

## Nap Time

I've just come in from playing,

I'm tired as I can be.
*(Rub eyes, then do following actions.)*
I'll cross my legs and fold my hands,

I'll close my eyes so I can't see.

I will not move my body,

I'll be like Raggedy Ann.
*(Relax body and lie still.)*
My head won't move, my arms won't move,

I'll just be still, because I can.

*Adapted Traditional*

## Close Your Eyes

Now it's time for you to rest,

Close your eyes—do your best.
*(Close eyes.)*
I'll stay with you while you sleep today,

And when you awake, we'll go and play.

*Cindy Dingwall*

## Be Very Quiet

Shhh—be very quiet,
*(Do actions as rhyme indicates.)*
Shhh—be very still.

Fold your busy little hands,

Close your sleepy little eyes.

Shhh—be very still.

*Adapted Traditional*

## Ready for a Nap

Here is a baby, ready for a nap,
*(Hold up pointer finger.)*
Lay her down in her mother's lap.
*(Place finger on opposite palm.)*
Cover her up so she won't peep,
*(Fold hand over finger.)*
Then rock her till she's fast asleep.
*(Rock hand back and forth.)*

*Adapted Traditional*

## Nap Time Is Over

Hey, you sleepy heads, wake up,
*(Do actions as rhyme indicates.)*
You cannot sleep all day.

It s time to open up your eyes

So we can run and play.

Find your shoes and put them on,

We'll put your cot away.

We are rested from our nap,

And now we want to play.

*Frank Dally*

## Wee Willie Winkie

Wee Willie Winkie runs through the town,
*(Run in place.)*
Upstairs and downstairs in his nightgown,
*(Pretend to climb up, then down.)*
Rapping at the window, crying through the lock,
*(Pretend to knock, then hold fist up to mouth.)*
"Are the children in their beds? It's now eight o'clock!"

*Adapted Traditional*

## I'm Sleepy

I'm sleepy, oh, so sleepy,
*(Do actions as rhyme indicates.)*
Watch me stretch and yawn.
I'll close my eyes and just pretend
That daylight now has gone.

I'll breathe so softly, lie so still,
A little mouse might creep
Across the floor, because he thought
That I was sound asleep!

*Adapted Traditional*

## Go to Sleep

Go to sleep, go to sleep,
*(Do actions as rhyme indicates.)*
Rest your head, rest your feet.
Close your eyes, curl up tight,
Dream about the things you like.

*Jean Warren*

## Five Little Elves

Said this little elf,
"I'm tired as can be."
*(Point to thumb.)*
Said this little elf,
"My eyes can hardly see."
*(Point to index finger.)*
Said this little elf,
"I'd like to go to bed."
*(Point to middle finger.)*
Said this little elf,
"I want to rest my head."
*(Point to ring finger.)*
Said this little elf,
"Come climb the stairs with me."
*(Point to little finger.)*
One, two, three, four, five, they tiptoed
Just as still as still could be.
*(Tiptoe five fingers.)*

*Adapted Traditional*

## Night-Night Rhyme

Go to sleep, little toes,
    *(Point to body parts named.)*
You've worked hard all day.
Go to sleep, little legs,
You've run hard and played.

Go to sleep, little hands,
You're always so busy.
Go to sleep, little arms,
Being small isn't easy.

Go to sleep, little ears,
There's so much to hear.
Go to sleep, little mouth,
There's nothing to fear.

*Sharon Sweat*

## Go to Sleep Now

Go to sleep now,
No eyes peek now,
Close your eyes, close them tight.
Dreaming you will soon be,
Oh, the things that you will see
All through the night!

*Bobbie Lee Wagman*

## Unicorn Dream

One night I dreamed of a little white horse
That had a great big horn
Right in the middle of its head.
It was a unicorn!
I rode all night upon its back,
As I dreamed along.
But when the morning light appeared,
Poof! It was gone.

*Jean Warren*

## Little Shadow

There is a little shadow
    *(Do actions as rhyme indicates.)*
That dances on my wall.
Sometimes it's big and scary,
Sometimes it's very small.

Sometimes it's, oh, so quiet
And doesn't move at all.
Then other times it chases me
Or bounces like a ball.

I'd love to meet that shadow
Who dances in the night,
But it always runs away
In the morning light.

*Jean Warren*

## It Is Nighttime

It is nighttime, see the moon,
See it overhead.
That means just one thing—
It's time to go to bed.

Let's put on our pajamas
And brush our teeth just right.
Then we'll hop into our beds
And sleep all through the night.

Now it's morning, see the sun,
Shining down this way.
Time for all us sleepyheads
To start a brand-new day!

*Gayle Bittinger*

## Rise and Shine

Up, up, get out of bed,
        *(Do actions as rhyme indicates.)*
It's time to rise and shine.
I put my clothes on, brush my hair,
I'm looking mighty fine.

I'm ready now, it's breakfast time,
And I eat every bite.
I wash my face, then brush my teeth,
I've started my day right!

*Lynn Tarleton*

## Wake Up, Little Fingers

Wake up, little fingers, the morning has come,
        *(Slowly open fists.)*
Now hold them up, every finger and thumb.
        *(Hold fingers up straight.)*
Come jump out of bed, see how tall you can stand,
        *(Raise outstretched hands.)*
Oh my, you are such a wide-awake band.
        *(Clap hands once.)*
You have all washed your faces and you look so neat,
        *(Rub hands together, then fold them.)*
Now come to the table and let us all eat.
        *(Pretend to eat.)*
Now all you fingers run out to play,
        *(Wiggle and dance fingers.)*
And have a good time on this beautiful day!
        *(Smile.)*

*Adapted Traditional*

## First Day of School

Good morning, Lauren,

How are you?
> *(Shake hands.)*

I'm glad to meet you,

Others will be too.
> *(Smile.)*

Won't you come into the room?

There are lots of things to do!
> *(Beckon with hand.)*

Substitute the name of one of your children for *Lauren.*

*Kristina Carle and Nanette Belice*

## Making New Friends

Good day, everybody,
> *(Nod to others.)*

Good day, everybody,

Good day, good day, good day.

Smile, everybody,
> *(Smile at others.)*

Smile, everybody,

Let's chase the blues away.

Shake hands, everybody,
> *(Shake hands with others.)*

Shake hands, everybody,

Let's make new friends today.

*Adapted Traditional*

## I'm So Glad

I'm so glad that you are here,

I'm so glad you came.

I want to be your friend today,

What is your name?
> *(Child says name.)*

I'm so glad that you are here,

Now I know your name!

*Vicki L. Gilliam*

## Who Is Here Today?

Let's see who is here today,
> *(Do actions as rhyme indicates.)*

Who has come to join our play?

Everyone sit close at hand,

Say your name, then you can stand.

*Ellen Bedford*

## Counting Friends

How many friends are here today,

Here at school to work and play?

How many friends are here today?

Let's count them all right now.
> *(Count all together.)*

*Betty Silkunas*

## I'm a Little Helper

I'm a little helper,

Look at me,

I'm as busy

As I can be.

I put away the toys,

As you can see,

Now I'm ready for the circle.

Look at me!

*Betty Ruth Baker*

## Helpers

Helpers play and share their toys

With the other girls and boys.
*(Share a toy.)*

Helpers put their toys away,

Kind and happy words they say.
*(Put a toy on the toy shelf.)*

*Karen Vollmer*

## Helping Ashley

Here are Ashley's two white shoes,
*(Do actions as rhyme indicates.)*

Here is Ashley's truck.

Here are Ashley's blocks and books,

Here is Ashley's duck.


Let's help Ashley pick up her toys

And put them on the shelf.

So next time Ashley wants them,

She can find them by herself.

Substitute one of your children's names
for *Ashley*.

*Adapted Traditional*

## Being a Good Helper

Being a good helper
Is lots of fun to do.
It makes others happy,
And makes me happy too.

When the job is finished,
My friends say "Thank you."
And I say "You're welcome,
I'm glad I could help you."

*Diana Nazaruk*

## Helping

When I come in from outdoor play,
*(Do actions as rhyme indicates.)*
I take my boots off right away.
I place them by the door just so,
Then off my hat and mittens go.
I zip down my coat and snow pants too,
And hang them up when I am through.
I'm a helper, don't you see,
Helping's fun as fun can be!

*Adapted Traditional*

## Being Patient

Being patient means to wait,

Being patient I sometimes hate.
> *(Make a face.)*

I wait my turn and wait to share,

Sometimes I want to tear my hair!
> *(Pretend to tear hair.)*

But I know that I'll feel fine

When my friend is patient and the turn is mine.
> *(Nod head and smile.)*

*Barbara Butler*

## Say You're Sorry

It's not so easy to do good,

Sometimes we don't when we should.

But, say you're sorry when you're wrong,

Then you'll be happy all day long.

*Karen Leslie*

## We Have Rules

We have rules, we have rules,

Rules to keep us safe at school.

We use inside voices and walking feet,
> *(Point to mouth, then to feet.)*

We don't touch or bother the friends we meet.
> *(Hug self and shake head.)*

And when we're eating we stay in our seats,
> *(Sit and pretend to eat.)*

'Cause we have rules

At our school.

*Priscilla M. Starrett*

## Taking Turns

Back and forth, back and forth,
> *(Do actions as rhyme indicates.)*

On the swing I go.

This is how I take my turn,

Swinging fast and slow.

Back and forth, back and forth,

I think I'd better stop.

Now it's time to share this toy,

So off it I will hop.

Up and down, up and down,

On the bouncing horse I go.

This is how I take my turn,

Bouncing fast and slow.

Up and down, up and down,

I think I'd better stop.

Now it's time to share this toy,

So off it I will hop.

*Jean Warren*

## Being Generous

Being generous means to share
With every person everywhere.
Generous means to give with a smile.
You take your turn and, after a while,
Friends will then be generous too,
And share the things they have with you.

*Barbara Butler*

## Getting Along

We know how to get along
Every single day.
We take turns and share a lot
While we work and play.
    *(Nod head and smile.)*

*Kathy McCullough*

## I Will Be Loving

I will be loving
To my friends today,
I will be loving
In my own special way.

I will take turns
And share my playthings too.
I will be loving,
'Cause that's what good friends do.

*Linda Warren*

## Thank You, Thank You, Thank You

Thank you, thank you, thank you,
It's what I love to hear.
Thank you, thank you, thank you,
It really is quite clear.

When I hear "Thank you,"
It makes things all worthwhile.
When I hear "Thank you,"
It makes me want to smile.

I like to know that others
Appreciate what I do.
I just love to hear those words,
"Thank you, thank you, thank you!"

*Jean Warren*

## Be Kind

Be kind to one another,
Use magic words like these—
"Thank you" and "You're welcome."
And when you ask, say, "Please."

*Janet Harris*

## Two Magic Words

There are two magic words
That can open doors with ease.
    *(Pretend to open door.)*
Those two magic words
Are "Thank you" and "Please."
    *(Hold up one finger, then two fingers.)*

*Teri Muller*

# Cooperation

## Three Is More Fun

One, two, three—yes, siree,
   *(Hold up three fingers.)*
We're as happy as we can be.
   *(Nod head.)*
It's more fun than with two or one.
   *(Hold up two fingers, then one finger.)*
When there's three we get more done.
   *(Hold up three fingers.)*

*Jean Warren*

## We Share

We share all our blocks and toys
With the other girls and boys.
Crayons, scissors, paint, and glue,
Puzzles, books, the easel too.
We take turns because it's fair,
And we're happy when we share.

*Sue Brown*

## It's Fun to Work Together

Oh, it's fun to work together,

That's what I like to do.

Oh, it's fun to work together

When it's just us two.
   *(Hold up two fingers.)*

Oh, it's fun to work together,

Don't you all agree?

Oh, it's fun to work together

When we get to work with three.
   *(Hold up three fingers.)*

Oh, it's fun to work together,

It's fun with even more.

Oh, it's fun to work together

When we get to work with four.
   *(Hold up four fingers.)*

Oh, it's fun to work together,

All of us side by side.

Oh, it's fun to work together

When we get to work with five.
   *(Hold up five fingers.)*

Oh, it's fun to work together,

A very special mix.

Oh, it's fun to work together

When we get to work with six.
   *(Hold up six fingers.)*

*Jean Warren*

## Five Purple Polka Dots

Five purple polka dots sitting on the floor,
*(Hold up five fingers.)*
One crawled away and then there were four.
*(Bend down thumb.)*
Four purple polka dots got on their knees,

One tipped over and then there were three.
*(Bend down pointer finger.)*
Three purple polka dots stood on one shoe,

One fell down and then there were two.
*(Bend down middle finger.)*
Two purple polka dots started to run,

One stopped quickly and then there was one.
*(Bend down ring finger.)*
One purple polka dot rolled out the door,

When it disappeared there were no more.
*(Bend down little finger.)*

*Janet Hoffman*

## Color Surprises

I took a blob of red paint,
*(Do actions as rhyme indicates.)*
Then I took a blob of yellow.

I squished and swished them all around

As far as they would go.

My red and yellow began to change,

And much to my surprise,

I saw those colors turn to orange,

Right before my eyes!

I took a blob of red paint,

Then I took a blob of blue.

I squished and swished them all around

Like I was told to do.

My red and blue began to change,

And much to my surprise,

I saw those colors turn to purple,

Right before my eyes!

I took a blob of blue paint,

Then I took a blob of yellow.

I squished and swished them all around

As far as they would go.

My blue and yellow began to change,

And much to my surprise,

I saw those colors turn to green,

Right before my eyes!

*Cindy Dingwall*

## Colors for Painting

I know the colors for painting fun—
Green grass, a yellow sun,
An orange pumpkin, white snow,
A red rose, a black crow,
A blue mailbox, brown apes,
A pink pig, and some purple grapes.

*Ellen Bedford*

## Pretty Color Crayons

Pretty color crayons—
Red, green, and blue,
Orange, purple, and yellow—
I love them, yes I do!

*Jean Warren*

## Color Square Dance

Blues, step forward,
  *(Have those wearing named
   colors do actions as indicated.)*
Then turn around,
Walk back to your place
And jump up and down.

Reds, hop to the middle
And back again,
Find the yellows
And shake their hands.

Now, greens, you slowly
Turn around,
Clap your hands
And make a sound.

Do-si-do,
Around we go,
All the colors
Heel to toe.

*Jean Warren*

## Color Rhyme

If your clothes have any red,
*(Do actions as rhyme indicates.)*
Put your finger on your head.

If your clothes have any blue,
Put your finger on your shoe.

If your clothes have any green,
Wave your hand so that you're seen.

If your clothes have any yellow,
Smile like a happy fellow.

If your clothes have any brown,
Turn your smile into a frown.

If your clothes have any black,
Put your hands behind your back.

If your clothes have any white,
Stamp your feet with all your might.

*Jean Warren*

## Color Ribbons

I found a little ribbon
Lying on my bed.
It was a pretty ribbon,
Shiny, new, and red.

I found a little ribbon
Tied upon my shoe.
It was a pretty ribbon,
Shiny, new, and blue.

I found a little ribbon
Lying on my pillow.
It was a pretty ribbon,
Shiny, new, and yellow.

I found a little ribbon
On my washing machine.
It was a pretty ribbon,
Shiny, new, and green.

*Jean Warren*

## What Will I Wear to School Today?

What will I wear to school today,
Something old or something new?
What will I wear to school today?
Perhaps the color blue.
*(Point to something blue.)*

What will I wear to school today,
Something that covers my head?
What will I wear to school today?
Perhaps the color red.
*(Point to something red.)*

What will I wear to school today,
Something happy or something mean?
What will I wear to school today?
Perhaps the color green.
*(Point to something green.)*

What will I wear to school today,
Something wild or something mellow?
What will I wear to school today?
Perhaps the color yellow.
*(Point to something yellow.)*

What will I wear to school today,
Something dull or something bright?
What will I wear to school today?
Perhaps the color white.
*(Point to something white.)*

What will I wear to school today,
Something with hearts or a clown?
What will I wear to school today?
Perhaps the color brown.
*(Point to something brown.)*

What will I wear to school today,
Something that buttons in front or in back?
What will I wear to school today?
Perhaps the color black.
*(Point to something black.)*

*Jean Warren*

## Colors, We Love You

Purple, we love you,
Yes, we do.
Eggplants, grapes,
And violets too.

Blue, we love you,
Yes, we do.
Sky and lakes,
And bluebirds too.

Green, we love you,
Yes, we do.
Grass and trees,
And lettuce too.

Red, we love you,
Yes, we do.
Apples, berries,
And cherries too.

Orange, we love you,
Yes, we do.
Pumpkins, juice,
And carrots too.

Yellow, we love you,
Yes, we do.
Bananas, sun,
And lemons too.

*Jean Warren*

# Numbers

## Say a Little Number Rhyme

Say a little number rhyme,

Count numbers one by one.

Say a little number rhyme,

We've only just begun.

One, two, three, four, five,
 *(Count on fingers.)*
Six, seven, eight, nine, ten.

When we finish counting,

We'll start all over again.

*Judy Hall*

## I Can Count

One, two, three, and four.
 *(Count four fingers on one hand.)*
I can count even more.

Five, six, seven, and eight.
 *(Count four fingers on other hand.)*
My lady fingers stand up straight.

Nine and ten
 *(Make fists and hold up thumbs.)*
Are my two thumb men.

*Adapted Traditional*

## One, Two, Three

One, two, three, count with me.
 *(Count on fingers.)*
It's as easy as it can be—

Four, five, six, seven, eight, nine, ten.

Now let's count all over again.

*Judy Hall*

## Clap One, Two, Three

Clap, clap, clap your hands,
 *(Clap as rhyme indicates.)*
Clap them one, two, three.

The more you clap, the more we count,

So what will your count be?

One, two, three, four,

Five, six, seven.

The more you clap, the more we count,

Eight, nine, ten, eleven.

*Author Unknown*

## One, Two

One, two,

Sit up, please do.
*(Sit up straight.)*

Three, four,

Feet on the floor.
*(Place feet flat on floor.)*

Five, six,

Stir and mix.
*(Make stirring motions.)*

Seven, eight,

Close the gate.
*(Clap hands once.)*

Nine, ten,

Make a house for a hen.
*(Form roof shape with fingers.)*

*Adapted Traditional*

## Counting Rhyme

One, two, three, four, five,
*(Bend down five fingers, one at a time.)*
I caught a fish alive.

Six, seven, eight, nine, ten,
*(Hold up five fingers, one at a time.)*
I let it go again.

*Adapted Traditional*

## One Rap, Two Rap

One rap, two rap, three rap, four.
*(Rap fist as rhyme indicates.)*
Who's that rapping at my door?

Five rap, six rap, seven rap, eight.

Don't you think it's kind of late?

*Jean Warren*

## One Potato

One potato, two potato,
*(Count on fingers.)*
Three potato, four,

Five potato, six potato,

Seven potato, more.

Eight potato, nine potato,

Here is ten.

Now let's count

All over again.

*Adapted Traditional*

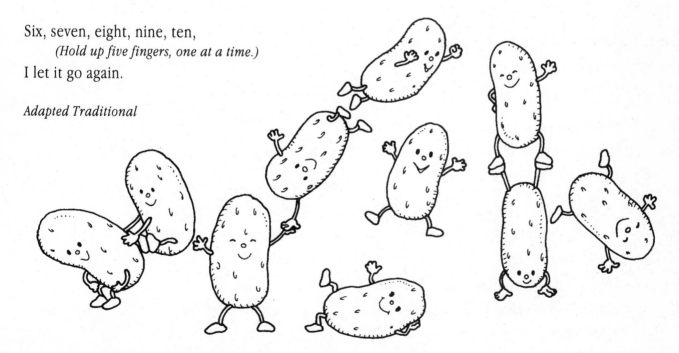

## Mother Hubbard Rhyme

Old Mother Hubbard went to the cupboard

To fetch her poor dog a bone.

But when she got there the cupboard was bare

And so the poor dog had none.
> *(Form a zero with fingers.)*

Old Mother Hubbard went to the butcher

To get a bone, all alone.

When she got home she put in the bone

And now her cupboard has one.
> *(Hold up one finger.)*

Old Mother Hubbard went to the butcher

For another bone, it's true.

When she got home she put in the bone

And now her cupboard has two.
> *(Hold up two fingers.)*

Old Mother Hubbard went to the butcher

To get another, you see.

When she got home she put in the bone

And now her cupboard has three.
> *(Hold up three fingers.)*

Old Mother Hubbard went to the butcher

And asked for just one more.

When she got home she put in the bone

And now her cupboard has four.
> *(Hold up four fingers.)*

*Jean Warren*

## Five Humpty Dumpties

Five Humpty Dumpties,
> *(Hold up five fingers.)*

And not one more.

One dropped to the ground,
> *(Bend down thumb.)*

And that left four.

Four Humpty Dumpties,

Cute as they could be.

One did a flip-flop,
> *(Bend down pointer finger.)*

And that left three.

Three Humpty Dumpties,

Just a lonely few.

Down went another,
> *(Bend down middle finger.)*

And that left two.

Two Humpty Dumpties,

Basking in the sun.

One got baked,
> *(Bend down ring finger.)*

And that left one.

One Humpty Dumpty,

A real egghead hero.

He took a mighty fall,
> *(Bend down little finger.)*

And that left zero.

*Susan M. Paprocki*

## Ten Little Candles

Ten little candles standing on a cake.
*(Hold up ten fingers.)*
"Whh! Whh!" Now there are eight.
*(Blow twice and bend down two fingers.)*

Eight little candles in candle sticks.
*(Hold up eight fingers.)*
"Whh! Whh!" Now there are six.
*(Blow twice and bend down two fingers.)*

Six little candles, not one more.
*(Hold up six fingers.)*
"Whh! Whh!" Now there are four.
*(Blow twice and bend down two fingers.)*

Four little candles, yellow and blue.
*(Hold up four fingers.)*
"Whh! Whh!" Now there are two.
*(Blow twice and bend down two fingers.)*

Two little candles, one plus one.

"Whh! Whh!" Now there are none.
*(Blow twice and bend down two fingers.)*

*Adapted Traditional*

# Shapes

## The Circle

The circle is a shape
That's easy to be found.
It has no corners on it
And is completely round.
*(Form circle with fingers.)*

*Author Unknown*

## What Is a Circle?

Now, what is a circle?
Where can it be found?
I know what it looks like,
It goes round and round.

It could be a Frisbee
Or the top of a cake.
It could be a pizza
Or a cookie we baked.

It could be the tire
On a brand-new car.
It could be a button
Or the lid of a jar.

Now, what is a circle?
Well, you'll have to guess.
A circle is something
A little like this.
*(Form circle with thumb and finger.)*

*Vicki Claybrook*

## A Square Is Its Name

Here's a shape that you should know.
   *(Form square with fingers.)*
A square is its name.
It has four corners and four sides
That measure all the same.

*Author Unknown*

## Sally the Square

When Sally the Square
Went to the fair,
She was all alone and blue.
Then she found a square cat
To be her friend,
And now the squares are two.

When Sally the Square
Went to the fair,
She was all alone, you see.
But she found a square cat
And then a square pig,
And now the squares are three.

When Sally the Square
Went to the fair,
She wanted to see more.
She found a square cat,
A square pig, then a duck,
And now the squares are four.

*Jean Woods*

## The Triangle

The triangle is a simple shape,
*(Form triangle with fingers.)*
I think you will agree.

Count its sides and corners,

And you will find just three.

*Author Unknown*

## I Am a Small Triangle

I am a small triangle,
*(Form triangle with fingers.)*
I have three sides, you see.

I also have three corners

That are just right for me.

*Rita Galloway*

## A Rectangle

This shape is called a rectangle,
*(Form rectangle with fingers.)*
It's found most everywhere.

It has four corners and four sides,

Sort of like a square.

But if you call this shape a square,

You would be very wrong.

Since two of its sides are short,

And two of them are long.

*Author Unknown*

## How Can You Tell?

This is a circle.
*(Point to a circle.)*
How can you tell?

It goes round and round,

No end can be found.


This is a square.
*(Point to a square.)*
How can you tell?

It has four sides,

All the same size.

*Jeanne Petty*

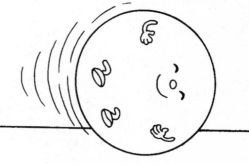

## Draw for Me

Draw a circle,

Round as can be.
> *(Draw circle in air.)*

Draw a circle

Just for me.
> *(Point to self.)*

Draw a square,

Shaped like a door.
> *(Draw square in air.)*

Draw a square

With corners four.
> *(Hold up four fingers.)*

Draw a triangle,

With corners three.
> *(Draw triangle in air.)*

Draw a triangle

Just for me.
> *(Point to self.)*

*Adapted Traditional*

## I Can Make a Shape

I can make a circle,

How about you?

Make a circle

Like I do.
> *(Form circle with fingers.)*

I can make a square,

How about you?

Make a square

Like I do.
> *(Form square with fingers.)*

I can make a triangle,

How about you?

Make a triangle

Like I do.
> *(Form triangle with fingers.)*

*Jean Warren*

## Shapes

Circles, rectangles, triangles, squares,

There are so many shapes out there.

Everywhere you look you'll see

Another shape. What will it be?

*Angela Wolfe*

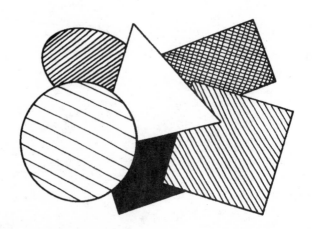

## My Clock

My clock is like a great big face

With hands that move from the little nose place.
*(Form circle with arms.)*

The hour hand moves very slow,

From one to twelve it must go.
*(Move right arm in a circle.)*

The hour hand won't say its o'clocks

Till the minute hand makes sixty tocks.
*(Move left arm in a circle.)*

*Ellen Bedford*


## Tick, Tock

Big clocks make a sound like

"TICK, TOCK, TICK, TOCK."
*(Move upright arm back and forth slowly.)*

Small clocks make a sound like

"Tick, tock, tick, tock."
*(Move upright arm back and forth faster.)*

And tiny little clocks make a sound like

"Tick, tock, tick, tock, tick, tock."
*(Move upright arm back and forth still faster.)*

*Adapted Traditional*


## See the Little Hand

Hickory, dickory, dock,

The time is one o'clock.

See the little hand

Point to one.
*(Demonstrate with a play clock.)*

Hickory, dickory, dock.


Hickory, dickory, dock,

The time is two o'clock.

See the little hand

Point to two.
*(Demonstrate with a play clock.)*

Hickory, dickory, dock.


Continue, naming hours up to twelve o'clock.

*Elizabeth McKinnon*


## Clock Hands

Hickory, dickory, dock,

The hands are on the clock.

One is long, the other's short,
*(Extend index finger, then thumb.)*

Hickory, dickory, dock.

*Judy Hall*

## Hickory, Dickory, Dock

Hickory, dickory, dock.

The mouse ran up the clock.
*(Run fingers up arm.)*

The clock struck one.
*(Clap hands once.)*

The mouse ran down.
*(Run fingers down arm.)*

Hickory, dickory, dock.

Hickory, dickory, dock.

The mouse ran up the clock.
*(Run fingers up arm.)*

The clock struck two.
*(Clap twice.)*

The mouse ran down.
*(Run fingers down arm.)*

Hickory, dickory, dock.

Continue, naming hours up to twelve.

*Adapted Traditional*

## With a Tick and a Tock

With a tick and a tock, and a tick and a tock,
*(Move upright arm back and forth rhythmically.)*

The clock goes round all day.

It tells us when it's time to work

And when it's time to play.

*Adapted Traditional*

## The Little Clock

I'm a little clock

Up on the wall.
*(Form circle with arms.)*

Here is my big hand,

Here is my small.
*(Hold out arms, one at a time.)*

If you listen carefully,

You will hear
*(Cup hand behind ear.)*

"Tick, tock, tick, tock"

In your ear.

*Judy Hall*

## My Little Watch

See my little watch right here?
> *(Form circle with thumb and finger.)*

Hold it closely to your ear.
> *(Hold circle up to ear.)*

Hear it ticking, ticking fast.
> *(Making ticking sounds with tongue.)*

It tells us when our playtime's past.

Substitute words such as *snacktime* or *quiet time* for *playtime*.

*Adapted Traditional*

## Count the Days

Come along and count with me,

There are seven days, you see.

Monday, Tuesday, Wednesday too,
> *(Count days on fingers.)*

Thursday, Friday, just for you.

Saturday, Sunday, that's the end.

Now let's say them all again.

*Judy Hall*

## Days of the Week

Sunday, Monday,

One, two.

Tuesday, Wednesday,

Half through.

Thursday, Friday,

What a glad day.

Then there's Saturday,

Just for you!
> *(Point to others.)*

*Barbara Dinart*

## Tall as a Tree

Tall as a tree,
    *(Raise arms high.)*
Big as a house.
    *(Stretch arms out wide.)*
Thin as a pin,
    *(Hold arms at sides.)*
Small as a mouse.
    *(Make self small.)*

*Author Unknown*

## Do You Suppose

Do you suppose a giant
Who is tall, tall, tall
    *(Stretch high on tiptoe.)*
Could ever be an elf
Who is small, small, small?
    *(Crouch down.)*
But the elf, who is tiny,
Will try, try, try
    *(Stand and raise arms.)*
To reach up to the giant,
Who is high, high, high.

*Adapted Traditional*

## Opposites

The opposite of left is right,
The opposite of day is night.
Now we come to short and long,
After that there's right and wrong.
Lost and found, sick and well,
How many opposites can you tell?

Heavy and light are not the same,
Don't you like our opposites game?
Next, I think of stop and go,
After that, high and low.
First and last, fast and slow,
How many opposites do you know?

*Mildred Hoffman*

## Soft Touches

I love soft things
Very much.
Soft things to feel,
Soft things to touch.

A feather pillow,
A furry muff,
A baby's cheek,
A powder puff.

My kitten's fur,
A gentle breeze,
A bedtime kiss,
I love all these.

*Adapted Traditional*

## "A, A," What Can I Say?

A, A, what can I say?
Just what can I say about the letter A?

Airplane and alligator start with an A.
Acorn and apple begin the same way.

Anchor and astronaut start with A too,
As do apron and acrobat, to name just a few.

Abracadabra begins with an A,
It's a magical word that I like to say.

Ant and ax both start with A.
Let's hear it for A! Hip, hip hurray!

*Susan M. Paprocki*

## "B" is for Butterflies

B is for butterflies in the air,
    *(Wave arms at sides.)*
B is for buttons found here and there,
    *(Point to buttons on clothes.)*
B is for bears found everywhere.
    *(Point to teddy bears.)*

*Jean Warren*

## "C" is Cool

Carrots, castles, candy canes,
Cucumbers and clouds with rain.
Cats and cookies, crayons too.
I think C is cool. Don't you?
    *(Tilt head to one side.)*

*Cathi Ulbright*

## Let's Dance for "D"

Let's dance for D, dance, dance, dance.
    *(Dance in place.)*
Let's drive for D, drive, drive, drive.
    *(Pretend to drive car.)*
Let's drum for D, drum, drum, drum.
    *(Pretend to beat drum.)*
Let's dive for D, dive, dive, dive.
    *(Make diving movements.)*

*Elizabeth McKinnon*

## What Do You See?

What do you see

That begins with *E*?

I see an egg,
  *(Form egg shape with fingers.)*
That's what I see.

Do you see something else

That begins with *E*?

I see an elephant,
  *(Stretch arms out wide.)*
Big as can be.

*Elizabeth McKinnon*

## "F's" Everywhere

*F*'s are here, *F*'s are there.

*F*'s are found everywhere.

Feathers and forks—

Footballs too—

And frogs and flags,

To name a few.

*Jean Warren*

## When I Look Around

When I look around I see
  *(Cup hand above eye and glance around.)*
Many things that start with *G*.

I see grass and girls galore,

I see gloves and so much more.

Won't you look around with me

And name some things that start with *G*?

*Elizabeth McKinnon*

## "H" Makes Me Happy

*H* is for hair and *H* is for hand,
  *(Point to hair, then hand.)*
*H* is for heels on which we stand.
  *(Stand back on heels.)*
*H* is for houses here and there,
  *(Gesture to left, then to right.)*
*H* is for hats seen everywhere.
  *(Stand hands on top of head.)*
*H* is for hearts and horses too,
  *(Touch chest, then gallop in place.)*
*H* makes me happy, how about you?
  *(Point to others.)*

*Elizabeth McKinnon*

## The Letter "I"

*I* stands for me when I want it to,

*I* is for ink and for ice cream too.

*I* is such a simple letter,

There's no other that I like better.

*Elizabeth McKinnon*

## A Journey to Japan

I'm taking a journey to Japan,
My jet is leaving in June.
I'm packing up my *J* things,
You'd think I was off to the moon.

I'm taking a jack-o'-lantern
And plenty of juice and Jell-O.
Of course, I will take my jewelry
And my jacket that's sort of yellow.

I'm planning to take my jellyfish,
Who speaks perfect Japanese.
He taught me how to jitterbug,
Jeepers, that jars the knees!

I packed a jigsaw puzzle
And a book about how to juggle.
I didn't forget my jack rabbit,
The bed toy I love to snuggle.

Now I'll just pack my jump rope
And a jar of jam, if I can.
Then I think I'll have all my *J* things
For my journey to Japan.

*Susan M. Paprocki*

## "K" Is for King

*K* is for king,
*K* is for key,
And *K* is for all
The kites we see.

*Elizabeth McKinnon*

## In My Lap

Put a leaf in my lap,
    *(Do actions as rhyme indicates.)*
Then everybody clap
For the leaf that I have
In my lap.

Repeat, substituting words such as *lid,
lemon,* or *leash* for *leaf.*

*Elizabeth McKinnon*

## The "M's" Are Marching

Here come the *M*'s, hurray, hurray!
    *(March.)*
They're marching around in a big parade.
A monkey, a mitten, a mouse, and more,
All are marching around the floor.

*Jean Warren*

## "N" Is for Nuts

N is for nuts that I like to eat,
 *(Form circles with thumbs and fingers.)*
N is for nest where a bird can sleep.
 *(Cup hands together.)*
N is for net to catch a big fish,
 *(Pretend to net fish.)*
N is for noodles, my favorite dish.
 *(Pretend to eat.)*
N is for noise, a very loud sound,
 *(Cover ears with hands.)*
N is for nails that I like to pound.
 *(Pretend to hammer.)*

*Jean Warren*

## The Letter "O"

I just love the letter O,

Here are some O words that I know.

Olive, owl, and octopus too.

Letter O, I love you.

*Jean Warren*

## Paula Had a Party

Paula had a party, and I think you'll agree
That a lot of attention was paid to P.

Poodles and polar bears paraded by.
Pigeons and parakeets came to fly.

Penguins splashed around in Paula's pool.
People drank purple juice just to keep cool.

Peaches and pears were served on plates.
The peanuts and popcorn tasted just great.

Panda played the piano, ever so proud,
Till Paula shouted, "You're playing too loud!"

Then Paula looked around, her place was a mess.
She was tired of P, she needed a rest.

"Please leave my party," Paula said.
Then she turned off the light and went to bed.

*Susan M. Paprocki*

## I Like "Q"

Q is for queen with a crown on her head,

Q is for quilt that covers my bed.

Q is for questions I like asking,

Q is for ducklings' quack-quack-quacking.

Q is for quarter and quick and quill,

I like Q and I always will.

*Elizabeth McKinnon*

## A Rooster, a Rabbit, and a Robin

A rooster, a rabbit, and a robin

Went rowing down the river one day.

They met a friendly rhinoceros,

And asked if she wanted to play.

The rhino loved to play in the water,

She rolled and rolled all around.

But the great big waves she created

Turned the rowboat upside down.

The rooster, the rabbit, and the robin

Then climbed on the rhino's back.

She sailed them way down the river,

And then she sailed them right on back.

*Jean Warren*

## Silly "S" Rhyme

Here's a silly *S* rhyme

Just for you—

A snake and a spoon

Went sailing in a shoe.

*Elizabeth McKinnon*

## Tap Your Toe for "T"

Tap, tap, tap your toe,
　　*(Tap toe.)*

Tap your toe for *T*.

Tap for train and turkey and toy,

Tap, tap. One, two, three.

*Elizabeth McKinnon*

## "U" Is for My Umbrella

U is for my umbrella,

I use it when it rains.

U is for my uncle

Who travels on trains.

U is for a uniform

A soldier would wear.

U is for unicorns

On my underwear.

*Jean Warren*

## The Letter "V"

I love to make the letter *V*
For everyone to see.
    *(Form* V *with two fingers.)*
*V* is for vinegar, *V* is for van,
And *V* is for victory!

*Elizabeth McKinnon*

## "W," We'll Wave Today

Waffles that we love to eat,
Watermelons, oh, so sweet.
*W*, we'll wave today
    *(Wave hand.)*
When we see you come our way.

Worms and wagons here and there,
Walls and windows everywhere.
*W*, we'll wave today
    *(Wave hand.)*
When we see you come our way.

*Elizabeth McKinnon*

## "X's" Mean Kisses

*X*'s mean kisses I like a lot,
*X* is for X-ray and "*X* marks the spot."
*X* is for xylophone I like to play,
*X* is quite extra-special, I'd say.

*Elizabeth McKinnon*

## Young Yolanda

Young Yolanda rides a yak,
Sitting proudly on its back.

Young Yolanda sails a yacht,
Especially when it's very hot.

Young Yolanda does her yoga
In a sunny yellow toga.

Young Yolanda just loves yams,
Served up nicely with canned hams.

Young Yolanda says yogurt's yummy,
Good and healthy in your tummy!

*Susan M. Paprocki*

## There Once Was a Zebra

There once was a zebra
Who lived at the zoo.
All day long
She had zero to do.
So she planted zinnias
And zucchini too,
And watched them grow
All day at the zoo.

*Jean Warren*

## "A, B, C"

*A* is for apples we love to eat,
   *(Form circle with hands.)*
*B* is for boots we wear on our feet,
   *(Point to feet.)*
*C* is for candy that tastes so sweet.
   *(Lick lips.)*

*Elizabeth McKinnon*

## Alphabet Rhyme

*A* is for apple, *B* is for ball,
*C* is for candy, *D* is for doll.

*E* is for elephant, *F* is for frog,
*G* is for goose, *H* is for hog.

*I* is for Indian, *J* is for jam,
*K* is for key, *L* is for lamb.

*M* is for monkey, *N* is for nail,
*O* is for owl, *P* is for pail.

*Q* is for queen, *R* is for rose,
*S* is for scissors, *T* is for toes.

*U* is for umbrella, *V* is for vase,
*W* is for wind that blows in my face.

*X* is for X-ray, *Y* is for you,
*Z* is for zebra in the zoo.

*Marie Wheeler*

## My Little Horn

Watch me play my little horn,

I put my fingers so.
> *(Place fists end to end.)*

Then I lift it to my mouth

And blow and blow and blow.
> *(Bring fists to mouth and toot.)*

*Adapted Traditional*

## My Instruments

I have some rhythm sticks
> *(Hold up pointer fingers.)*

And a sturdy little drum.
> *(Hold up left fist.)*

I play them everyday,

It's a lot of fun.
> *(Nod head.)*

The drum goes "Boom,"
> *(Pound left fist with right fist.)*

The sticks go "Tap."
> *(Tap pointer fingers.)*

And when I cannot play them,

I rest them in my lap.
> *(Fold hands in lap.)*

*Angela Wolfe*

## All Around the Room

All around the room we march,

Beating on our drum.
> *(March and pretend to beat drum.)*

Around we go and back again.

Gee, what fun!

All around the room we march,

Ringing loud our bell.
> *(March and pretend to ring bell.)*

Around we go and back again.

Gee, how swell!

All around the room we march,

Tapping on our sticks.
> *(March and pretend to tap sticks.)*

Around we go and back again.

Gee, what kicks!

*Jean Warren*

## The Finger Band

The finger band is coming to town,
*(March fingers out from behind back.)*
Coming to town, coming to town.

The finger band is coming to town,

So early in the morning.


This is the way they wear their hats,
*(Stand fingers on top of head.)*
Wear their hats, wear their hats.

This is the way they wear their hats,

So early in the morning.


This is the way they beat their drums,
*(Use fingers to beat pretend drum.)*
Beat their drums, beat their drums.

This is the way they beat their drums,

So early in the morning.


This is the way they toot their horns,
*(Use fingers to play pretend horn.)*
Toot their horns, toot their horns.

This is the way they toot their horns,

So early in the morning.


The finger band is going away,
*(March fingers around behind back.)*
Going away, going away.

The finger band is going away,

So early in the morning.

*Adapted Traditional*

## Marching Band

Marching down the street
*(March.)*
Is so much fun.

See our band,

Here we come!


When we march together,

Hear us play.

Won't you march

With us today?

*Jean Warren*

## March Along

We march along,
*(March.)*
We march along,

We lift our feet high off the ground.

We march and sing a happy song,

As we go

A-marching on.

*Diana Nazaruk*

# Movement

## Movement Rhyme

I clap my hands, I touch my feet,
   *(Do actions as rhyme indicates.)*
I jump up from the ground.
I clap my hands, I touch my feet,
And turn myself around.

*Adapted Traditional*

## Watch Out for the Bugs

Clap your hands, stomp your feet,
   *(Do actions as rhyme indicates.)*
Wiggle all around.
Reach your arms high in the air,
Then bend them to the ground.

Nod your head, shake your hips,
Give yourself some hugs.
Lay down flat upon the floor,
But watch out for the bugs!

*Diana Nazaruk*

## Thank You

My hands say thank you
With a clap, clap, clap.
   *(Clap hands.)*
My feet say thank you
With a tap, tap, tap.
   *(Tap feet.)*
Clap, clap, clap.
Tap, tap, tap.
   *(Clap hands, then tap feet.)*
Turn myself around and bow,
Thank you!
   *(Turn around, bow, then smile.)*

*Adapted Traditional*

## Hop One Time

Hop one time,
*(Do actions as rhyme indicates.)*
Hop two.
Hop and hop
Till you get through.

Hop three times,
Hop four.
Hop and hop
And hop some more.

Hop five times,
Hop six.
Do some silly
Hopping tricks.

Hop seven times,
Hop eight.
Hop a lot
Now, that's great!

Hop nine times,
Hop ten.
Hop and hop
And hop again.

*Lois E. Putnam*

## Find a Foot

Find a foot and hop, hop, hop,
*(Do actions as rhyme indicates.)*
When you're tired stop, stop, stop.
Turn around and count to ten,
Find a foot and hop again.

*Adapted Traditional*

## A Boy Named Jack

Once there was
*(Jump as rhyme indicates.)*
A boy named Jack.
He loved to jump
Over and back.
He jumped over candles,
He jumped over sticks.
He loved to do
His jumping tricks!

*Jean Warren*

## Two Little Feet Go Tap

Two little feet go tap, tap, tap,
*(Tap feet.)*
Two little hands go clap, clap, clap.
*(Clap hands.)*
A quick little leap up from my chair,
*(Stand up quickly.)*
Two little arms reach high in the air.
*(Stretch arms high.)*

Two little feet go jump, jump, jump,
*(Jump.)*
Two little fists go thump, thump, thump.
*(Pound fists.)*
One little body goes round and round,
*(Twirl around.)*
And one little child sits quietly down.
*(Sit down.)*

*Adapted Traditional*

## Magic Feet

Have you seen my magic feet,
*(Do actions as rhyme indicates.)*
Dancing down the magic street?
Sometimes fast, sometimes slow,
Sometimes high, sometimes low.

Come and dance along with me,
Dance just like my feet you see.
First we'll slide and then we'll hop,
Then we'll spin and then we'll stop.

*Jean Warren*

## Here We Go

Here we go up, up, up,
*(Raise hands high.)*
Here we go down, down, down.
*(Lower hands.)*
Here we go forward,
*(Take one step forward.)*
Here we go backward.
*(Take one step backward.)*
Here we go round, round, round.
*(Turn around once.)*

*Adapted Traditional*

## Let's Ride the Bumps

Let's ride the bumps as we drive in the car.
*(Bounce up and down in chair.)*
Now let's stand and touch a star.
*(Stand up and reach high.)*
Let's be jumping jacks, and then
*(Jump.)*
Let's be still and sit down again.
*(Sit.)*

*Adapted Traditional*

## Around and About

Around and about, around and about.
*(Do actions as rhyme indicates.)*
Over and under, and in and out.
Run through a field, swim in the sea.
Slide down a hill, climb up a tree.

*Adapted Traditional*

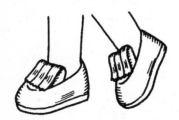

## We Can

We can jump, jump, jump,
　*(Do actions as rhyme indicates.)*
We can hop, hop, hop.

We can clap, clap, clap,

We can stop, stop, stop.

We can nod our heads for yes,

We can shake our heads for no.

We can bend our knees a tiny bit

And sit down slow.

*Adapted Traditional*

## Marching

Marching together one by one,

Marching together, oh what fun!
　*(Have children march in a circle.)*

Marching together two by two,

You march with me, I'll march with you.
　*(Have children march in groups of two.)*

Marching together three by three,

Marching together, look at me!
　*(Have children march in groups of three.)*

Marching together four by four,

Marching together, let's march some more.
　*(Have children march in groups of four.)*

Marching together five by five,

No more children will arrive.
　*(Have children march in groups of five.)*

*Betty Ruth Baker*

## Leap and Fly

Now you're going to learn to leap,

So all get in a line.
　*(Stand in line.)*
First, you run and then you jump,

Then do it one more time.
　*(Run and jump.)*
That is how you learn to leap,

Higher every time.

Keep together in your row,

My, you're doing fine!

Now you're going to learn to fly,

It really is quite grand.
　*(Stand in open space.)*
Just move your arms while you leap,

And watch out how you land.
　*(Flap arms while running and jumping.)*
Up and up and up you go,

Flying all around.

Careful now—come back down

And land upon the ground!

*Jean Warren*

## Getting Ready for Snacks

Let's get ready for snacks today,

Listen to our teacher, what does she say?
*(Cup hand behind ear.)*

"Wash your hands until they're clean,

All around and in between.
*(Pretend to wash hands.)*

Sit down quietly in your seats.

Now you're ready for your good treats!"
*(Sit down.)*

*Florence Dieckmann*

## Snack Attack

A snack attack! It's time to eat.

A snack attack! Let's sit in our seats.

Peanuts or raisins or cheese would be great,

Even bananas, we can't wait.

A snack attack! We're ready for treats.

A snack attack! Now let's eat!

*Carol Kyger*

## At Our Snack Table

At our snack table in the morning,

We eat good foods for our day—
*(Pretend to eat.)*

Foods we need to help us grow,

Foods we need to help us play.

*Sr. Linda Kaman, R.S.M.*

## Time to Stop Playing

It's time to stop playing,
 *(Do actions as rhyme indicates.)*
I'll pick up my toys.
Then I'll come to the circle
With the other girls and boys.

*Elizabeth McKinnon*

## Tiptoe to Our Circle

Let's all tiptoe to our circle,
 *(Walk on tiptoe.)*
Let's all tiptoe after me.
Let's all tiptoe to our circle,
And see how quiet we can be.

*April Brown*

## How Quiet Can You Be?

How quiet can you be
 *(Do actions as rhyme indicates.)*
As you tiptoe after me?
I come to the circle without a sound,
I cross my legs and then sit down.

*April Brown*

## Come Around

Joseph and Libby, come around,

Peter and Becky, sit on the ground.

Abby and Tommy will sit next to you,

Kerri, Billy, and Kim will too.

Andrew, Andrew is the last one,

Now we're ready to have some fun!

Substitute the names of your children for those in the rhyme.

*Krista Alworth*

## Ready to Listen

Let your hands go clap,
 *(Clap hands.)*
Let your fingers go snap,
 *(Snap fingers.)*

Let your lips go up and down,
 *(Open and close mouth.)*
But don't make a sound.
 *(Shake head.)*

Fold your hands and close your eyes,
 *(Fold hands, then close eyes.)*
Take a breath and softly sigh.
 *(Inhale deeply, then exhale.)*

*Adapted Traditional*

## And Quiet Be

Let your little hands go clap, clap, clap,
*(Clap hands.)*
Let your little feet go tap, tap, tap.
*(Tap feet.)*
Then fold your arms,
*(Fold arms.)*
Close your eyes,
*(Close eyes.)*
And quiet be.
*(Put finger to lips and say, "Shhh.")*

*Adapted Traditional*

## Our Quiet Sound

Stretch and make a yawn so wide,
*(Do actions as rhyme indicates.)*
Drop your arms down to your sides.

Close your eyes and help me say

Our very quiet sound today—

"Shhh."

*Adapted Traditional*

## Room Cleanup

We're cleaning up our room,
*(Do actions as rhyme indicates.)*
The job will be done soon.

It's fun to put the toys away

While we sing a happy tune.

*Susan Burbridge*

## Rested

Raise your head, look and see,
*(Do actions as rhyme indicates.)*
Take a deep breath, one, two three.

Smile and put your hands in your lap,

Make believe you've had a nap.

Now you're rested from your play,

It's time to work again today.

*Adapted Traditional*

## End of Our Day

Now it is time

To end our day.

We pick up our toys

And put them away.

*Author Unknown*

## Going Home Rhyme

Now our day is done,

We've all had lots of fun.

Tomorrow is another day,

And we'll be coming back to play.

*Kerry L. Stanley*

## Outside Play

Let's all go outside and play.

The sun is shining,

It's a beautiful day.

We're sure to have a lot of fun.

We'll hop and skip

And dance and run.

*Patricia Coyne*

## Blowing Bubbles

Blowing bubbles every day,

I blow them all around.
    *(Blow.)*

Then I watch them float up high

Or pop upon the ground.
    *(Clap once.)*

*Jean Warren*

## Bubbles

Bubbles, bubbles everywhere,
    *(Make floating movements with hands.)*
Bubbles floating through the air.

Some are oval, some are round,
    *(Form shapes with fingers.)*
They very seldom touch the ground.

*Angela Wolfe*

## Blow, Blow, Blow

Blow, blow, blow, blow,
    *(Blow into cupped hands.)*
I blow and then I stop.
    *(Open hands wider.)*
For if I keep on blowing,
    *(Open hands still wider.)*
My bubble will surely pop!
    *(Clap once.)*

*Jean Warren*

## Watch Me Blowing Bubbles

Watch me blowing bubbles

Pretty bubbles in the air.

They float so high

They reach the sky,

But then they fall

And fade and die.

Watch me blowing bubbles,

Pretty bubbles here and there.

*Jean Warren*

## Seesaw

Seesaw, seesaw,
*(Stretch arms out to sides.)*
Up and down we go.
*(Rhythmically bend left and right.)*
Seesaw, seesaw,

High and then down low.

Seesaw, seesaw,
*(Continue bending left and right.)*
Fun as it can be.

Seesaw, seesaw,

Seesaw-see.

*Adapted Traditional*

## The Slide

Climb up the ladder,
*(Climb fingers up arm.)*
Hang on to the side.
*(Grasp arm with fingers.)*
Sit down at the top,
*(Place fist at top of arm.)*
Then down you slide.
*(Slide fist down arm.)*

*Adapted Traditional*

## My Turn to Slide

Climbing, climbing up the ladder,
*(Do actions as rhyme indicates.)*
Sliding, sliding down the slide.

Now I stop with a bump

On my feet, and up I jump.

Running, running round the side,

Now I'll wait my turn to slide.

*Adapted Traditional*

## On the Playground

Playing on the playground is a treat,

Swinging and sliding can't be beat.
*(Make swinging and sliding motions with hands.)*
The playground is where we like to play,

We run and skip and hop each day.
*(Run, skip, and hop fingers.)*

*Judy Hall*

My School

## Our Playground

Climb the ladder and down we slide,
*(Swoop hand downward.)*

Then on the teeter-totter we ride.
*(Move hand like a teeter-totter.)*

Swinging, swinging, way up high,
*(Swing hand back and forth.)*

Swinging, swinging, to the sky.
*(Swing hand high.)*

Round we go on the merry-go-round,
*(Move hand in a circle.)*

We have fun on our playground.
*(Nod head.)*

*Adapted Traditional*

## Going for a Walk

Going for a walk is so much fun,
*(Walk around.)*

We look at all the lovely trees.
*(Cup hand above eye.)*

We don't hurry, we don't run,
*(Shake head.)*

We watch for birds and watch for bees.
*(Flap arms, then make buzzing sounds.)*

*Adapted Traditional*

## To Our School

Over the bridges and through the streets,
  *(Pretend to drive bus.)*
It's to our school we go.
The drivers always know the way
As they drive us, safe and slow.

Over the bridges and through the streets,
In rain and sleet and snow.
They drive with care, they get us there,
As through the town we go.

*Judy Hall*

## Walking Down the Stairs

When we walk down the stairs,
  *(Do actions as rhyme indicates.)*
We walk next to the wall.
We hold on to the handrail,
So that we won't fall.

We never push or shove—
It's not the thing to do.
We walk the stairs so carefully,
And hope that you do too.

*Frank Dally*

## Off to School We Go

Off to school we go,
It's off to school we go.
We'll take our lunch
And ride the bus
With everyone we know.

Off to school we go,
It's off to school we go.
We'll learn our ABC's
And more
With everyone we know.

*Judy Hall*

## My Little House

I'm going to build a little house

With windows wide and bright.
*(Stretch arms out to sides.)*

With chimney tall and curling smoke

Rising out of sight.
*(Spiral hand upward.)*

In winter when the snowflakes fall

Or when I hear a storm,
*(Cup hand behind ear.)*

I'll go and sit inside my house

Where I'll be snug and warm.
*(Hug self.)*

*Adapted Traditional*

## Building a House

Building a house is lots of work,
*(Wipe brow.)*

First, you dig up lots of dirt.
*(Pretend to dig.)*

Then you pour a concrete floor,
*(Touch floor.)*

And pound up boards with nails galore.
*(Pretend to hammer.)*

Doors and windows go in fast,
*(Draw squares in air with finger.)*

Now your house is done at last.
*(Clasp hands together above head.)*

*Diane Thom*

## I Will Make a Little House

I will make a little house
*(Form roof shape with fingers.)*

Where two playmates come to hide.
*(Bend thumbs under roof.)*

When I peek in at the door,
*(Peek under roof.)*

They quickly run outside.
*(Pop thumbs back out.)*

*Adapted Traditional*

## A House for Me

Here is a nest for Mrs. Bluebird.
*(Cup hands together.)*

Here is a hive for Mr. Bee.
*(Place fists together.)*

Here is a hole for Bunny Rabbit.
*(Form circle with thumb and finger.)*

And here is a house for me.
*(Form roof shape with fingers.)*

*Adapted Traditional*

## Where Do We Live?

A squirrel lives in a tree,
*(Form tree shape with hands.)*

A snail lives in a shell.
*(Cover fist with opposite hand.)*

A bear lives in a cave,
*(Make fist with thumb inside.)*

It suits her very well.

A fish lives in a fishbowl,
*(Form circle with hands.)*

A bird lives in a nest.
*(Cup hands together.)*

Matthew lives in a house,
*(Make roof above head with arms.)*

He thinks his home is best.

Substitute one of your children's names
for *Matthew*.

*Elizabeth McKinnon*

## Two Little Houses

Two little houses,

Closed up tight.
*(Close fists.)*

Let's open the windows,

And let in some light.
*(Open fists.)*

*Adapted Traditional*

## See the Window

See the window I have here,

So big and wide and square.
*(Draw window in air with finger.)*

I can stand in front of it,

And see the things out there.
*(Point out window.)*

*Adapted Traditional*

## Around the Block

Let's go walking
   *(Walk.)*
Around the block.
We will keep on walking,
Then we'll stop.
   *(Stop.)*

Let's go driving
   *(Pretend to drive car.)*
Around the block.
We will keep on driving,
Then we'll stop.
   *(Stop.)*

*Jean Warren*

## Dial 9-1-1

Dial 9-1-1.
   *(Pretend to dial number.)*
Dial 9-1-1.
You'll hear them say
That help's on the way.
If you need help, you know what to do—
Call the police and the firehouse too.
Just dial 9-1-1, that's what you do.
Dial 9-1-1.

*Sue Brown*

## Seven Little Numbers

Seven little numbers
On my phone,
I learn them together
To call my home.

Seven little numbers,
What are they?
My telephone number
I learned today!
   *(Say telephone number.)*

*Carla Cotter Skjong*

## Building a Skyscraper

Brick by brick
By brick by brick.
My building's so high
It's scraping the sky.
   *(Place fists one on top of the other, going higher each time.)*

Brick by brick
By brick by brick.
My building will sway
When the wind blows this way.
   *(Sway left, then right.)*

Brick by brick
By brick by brick.
Now I'm ready to stop
And a flag goes on top.
   *(Open one fist and wave hand left and right.)*

*Polly Reedy*

## Stop, Look, and Listen

Stop, look, and listen
  *(Do actions as rhyme indicates.)*
Before you cross the street.

First use your eyes and ears,

Then use your feet.

*Adapted Traditional*

## Traffic Light

The red light means stop,
  *(Stand still.)*
The green light means go,
  *(Walk forward.)*
The yellow light means caution.
  *(Walk in place.)*
This you should know.

*Betty Silkunas*

## Red Means Stop

Red means stop.

Green means go.

Yellow means watch out,

You'd better go slow!

*Judy Hall*

## Now You Know

When you see the light is green it means go,
  *(Start driving pretend car.)*
When the light is yellow, caution—please go slow.
  *(Drive pretend car slowly.)*
You must stop if the light is red,
  *(Stop driving pretend car.)*
Yes, that is what I said.

Now you know when to stop, slow down, and go.

*Diane Thom*

## Twinkle, Twinkle, Traffic Light

Twinkle, twinkle, traffic light,
  *(Open and close fingers quickly.)*
Shining brightly day and night.

When it's green we can go.
  *(Walk forward.)*
When it's red we stop, you know.
  *(Stop walking.)*

*Judith McNitt*

## One Little Astronaut

One little astronaut floating out from base,

Hooked to a hose, exploring space.
> *(Pretend to float in space.)*

She thought it was such an amazing trick,

She called another astronaut to join her quick.
> *(Beckon with hand.)*

Two little astronauts floating out from base
> *(Hold hands with second "astronaut.")*

Hooked to a hose, exploring space.
> *(Pretend to float in space.)*

They thought it was such an amazing trick,

They called another astronaut to join them quick.
> *(Beckon with hand.)*

Continue with similar verses until all your children are holding hands.

*Jean Warren*

## The Barber

Snip, snip, clip, clip,
> *(Make snipping movements.)*

The barber cuts your hair.

Short hair, long hair,

In-between hair,

All get special care.

*Betty Silkunas*

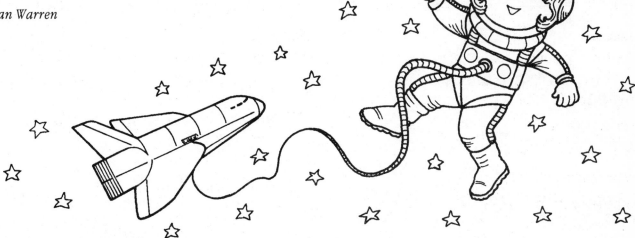

## The Baker

Who makes rolls and bread and cake?
> *(Do actions as rhyme indicates.)*

Who likes to stir and knead and bake?

Who mixes up the dough a lot

And puts it in the oven hot?

Who is the very best muffin maker?

Yes, you guessed, it's our friend the baker!

*Diane Thom*

## The Carpenter

The carpenter's hammer goes rap, rap, rap,
> *(Pretend to hammer.)*

And his saw goes see-saw-see.
> *(Pretend to saw.)*

He hammers and hammers, and saws and saws,
> *(Pretend to hammer, then saw.)*

To build a house for me.
> *(Form roof shape with fingers.)*

*Adapted Traditional*

## I'm a Busy Cobbler

I'm a busy cobbler,

And this is what I do.

I tap, tap, tap, tap,

To mend your shoe.
> *(Pound fist on opposite hand.)*

*Adapted Traditional*

## Dr. Denise, the Dentist

Dr. Denise, the dentist,

Helps me keep my teeth so white.
> *(Point to teeth.)*

Dr. Denise, the dentist,

Teaches me to brush just right.
> *(Pretend to brush teeth.)*

Dr. Denise, the dentist,

Always wears a super smile.
> *(Smile.)*

Dr. Denise, the dentist,

I'll be her friend a long, long while!
> *(Nod head.)*

*Betty Silkunas*

## I'm Happy I'm a Doctor

I'm happy I'm a doctor,

I help make people well.

I'm happy I'm a doctor,

It makes me feel just swell!
> *(Nod head and smile.)*

*Jean Warren*

## Five Little Farmers

Five little farmers

Woke up with the sun,
> *(Hold up five fingers.)*

It was early morning,

There were chores to be done.
> *(Wiggle fingers.)*

The first little farmer

Went to milk the cow,
> *(Point to thumb.)*

The second little farmer

Decided he would plow.
> *(Point to index finger.)*

The third little farmer

Fed the hungry hens,
> *(Point to middle finger.)*

The fourth little farmer

Mended broken pens.
> *(Point to ring finger.)*

The fifth little farmer

Took his vegetables to town,
> *(Point to little finger.)*

Baskets filled with cabbages

And sweet potatoes brown.

*Adapted Traditional*

## Firefighters

Down at the firehouse

Early in the morning,

You can see our clothes

Hanging in a row.

When there is a fire

We can dress real fast.

Boots, jackets,
   *(Touch feet, then shoulders.)*
Hats, gloves,
   *(Touch head, then hands.)*
Off we go!

*Jean Warren*

## Five Friendly Firefighters

Five friendly firefighters standing near the door,
   *(Hold up five fingers.)*
One washes the fire engine, now there are four.
   *(Bend down thumb.)*
Four friendly firefighters waiting patiently,
One fixes the hoses, now there are three.
   *(Bend down pointer finger.)*
Three friendly firefighters have a lot to do,
One climbs up a ladder, now there are two.
   *(Bend down middle finger.)*
Two friendly firefighters exercise and run,
One cooks some dinner, now there is one.
   *(Bend down ring finger.)*
One friendly firefighter—all the work is done,
This one goes to bed, now there are none.
   *(Bend down little finger.)*

*Diane Thom*

## I'm a Garbage Collector

I'm a garbage collector,

I pick up bags and cans.
   *(Make lifting and tossing movements.)*
I help keep our city clean,

And that makes a cleaner land.

*Jean Warren*

## The Grocer

The grocer is the person who
Works at the store where you buy food.
He'll sell you eggs and milk and fish—
Any food that you could wish.
When you push your shopping cart down the aisle,
Be sure to give the grocer a great big smile!

*Diane Thom*

## I'm a Karate Instructor

I'm a karate instructor,
        *(Do actions as rhyme indicates.)*
I wear a suit of white.
I show you how to protect yourself
And how to move just right.

I show you how to stand,
I show you how to defend.
I show you how to jump and yell
And let your body bend.

*Jean Warren*

## I Am a Librarian

I am a librarian,
I check out all the books.
        *(Pretend to stamp books.)*
Come and visit me real soon
And give my books a look.

All the boys and girls can come
And check out books for free.
        *(Hold out hands like an open book.)*
I help them find the books they want
At the library.

*Jean Warren*

## The Mail Carrier

I get to sort the mail,
        *(Pretend to sort and deliver mail.)*
Then carry it to your home
The mail comes from all over,
Like New York, Paris, and Rome.

*Jean Warren*

## I'm a Nurse

I'm a nurse dressed in white,
And I feel just swell.
When you are sick,
I help to make you well.
        *(Nod head and smile.)*

I give you shots,
And if you're afraid,
I'll fix you up
With a big Band-Aid!
        *(Pretend to apply bandage.)*

*Jean Warren*

## I'm a Police Officer

I'm a police officer

With my star,

I help people,

Near and far.

If you have a problem,

Call on me,

And I will be there

One, two, three!
*(Hold up three fingers, one at a time.)*

*Judy Hall*

## If You Get Lost

If you get lost someplace in town,

Don't talk to a stranger.
*(Shake head.)*

Look for a police officer

To keep you out of danger.

Tell her what your name is

And where your house is too.
*(Nod head.)*

She will help you get back home,

Or bring your mom to you.

*Judy Hall*

## I'm a Busy Quilter

I'm a busy quilter,

I sew and sew all day.
*(Pretend to sew.)*

And when my quilts are finished,

I can stop and play.

*Jean Warren*

## Let's Salute the Soldiers

Let's salute the soldiers,
*(Salute.)*

Who protect us night and day.

Let's salute the soldiers,

Whether near or far away.

Let's salute the soldiers

As we work and play.

Let's salute the soldiers.

Hip, hip hurray!

Repeat, substituting other military names,
such as *sailors* or *marines*, for *soldiers*.

*Jean Warren*

## I'm a Teacher

*A, B, C, D, E, F, G,*

I'm a teacher, can't you see?

I plan lessons every day,

And help the children work and play.

*Jean Warren*

## I'm a Veterinarian

I take care of animals,
*(Pretend to treat toy animals.)*
I treat them one by one.
I take care of animals,
I'm a veterinarian.

I give shots,
And sometimes I operate.
I take care of animals,
'Cause I think they're great.

Bring your dogs and cats,
Your hamsters, one by one.
I take care of animals,
I'm a veterinarian.

*Jean Warren*

## The Zookeeper

Down at the zoo
Early in the morning,
You can see the animals
Standing in a row.
You can see me feeding
One and then the other.
I am the zookeeper,
Watch me go.
*(Pretend to feed animals.)*

*Jean Warren*

## Our Country's Workers

We work in the factories,
And in the offices too.
We are the workers
All around you.

We work at the post office,
And we work at the zoo.
Truckers, teachers, bus drivers,
We work hard for you.

*Nancy N. Biddinger and Brian Biddinger*

## Workers of All Kinds

All around us you will find
Working people of all kinds—
Teachers, vets, and dentists who
Have important jobs to do,
Doctors, nurses, firefighters too,
And police officers dressed in blue.

*Lynn Tarleton*

## I'm a Little Airplane

I'm a little airplane
*(Do actions as rhyme indicates.)*
Flying in the sky,
Higher and higher—
See the clouds go by.

I'm a little airplane
Flying all around,
Lower and lower—
Now I'm on the ground.

*Elizabeth McKinnon*

## Flying Fast, Flying Slow

Flying fast, flying slow,
*(Do actions as rhyme indicates.)*
Flying high, flying low.
Swooping and swirling,
I glide through the air.
My special wings
Take me everywhere!

*Jean Warren*

## The Airplane

The airplane has great big wings,
*(Stretch arms out at sides.)*
Its propeller spins around and sings.
*(Move arm around in circle.)*
The airplane goes up,
*(Raise arms.)*
The airplane goes down.
*(Lower arms.)*
The airplane flies high
*(Stretch arms out at sides.)*
Over our town.
*(Turn around.)*

*Adapted Traditional*

## Flying High

Rockets and airplanes flying high,
*(Stretch arms out at sides.)*
Flying fast up in the sky.
*(Pretend to fly around.)*
The Concorde makes a sonic BOOM!
*(Clap once.)*
A rocket flies up to the moon.
*(Thrust arm upward.)*
Maybe someday I'll ride in a jet,
*(Nod head.)*
Or be a pilot, better yet!
*(Pretend to fly plane.)*

*Diane Thom*

## My Little Sailboat

Here's my little sailboat
*(Place elbow in palm of hand.)*
Blowing in the wind.
*(Move arm back and forth.)*
First, it tips this way,
*(Bend arm far to the right.)*
Next, it tips that way.
*(Bend arm far to the left.)*
Then it goes forward,
*(Bend arm forward.)*
Then it goes back.
*(Bend arm back.)*
Now it blows in the wind again.
*(Move arm back and forth.)*

*Polly Reedy*

## Rowing

Waves, waves, back and forth,
*(Move hands like waves.)*
Rock the boat all day.

We row and row so we can go
*(Pretend to row boat.)*
Somewhere far away.

*Jean Warren*

## My Bike

One wheel, two wheels

On the ground,
*(Form two circles with thumbs and fingers.)*
My feet make the pedals

Go round and round.
*(Pretend to pedal bike.)*
The handlebars help me

Steer so straight,
*(Pretend to steer bike.)*
Down the sidewalk

And through the gate.

*Adapted Traditional*

## Bus, Bus

Bus, bus, may I have a ride?
*(Hold up fist and wiggle thumb.)*
Yes, yes, please step inside.
*(Hold up other fist and wiggle thumb.)*
Put in some money.
*(Bend down first thumb.)*
Step on the gas.
*(Bend down other thumb.)*
Chug-a-way, chug-a-way,
*(Pretend to steer bus.)*
But not too fast.

*Adapted Traditional*

## My Little Red Car

Hop aboard my little red car,
*(Pretend to drive car around.)*
Let's drive up and down.

Round and round and round we go,

All around the town.

*Jean Warren*

## The Wheels Go Round and Round

The wheels go round and round,
*(Move arms in circles.)*
As we drive to town.
*(Pretend to steer car.)*
We buckle up so if we stop,
*(Pretend to fasten seat belt.)*
We'll all be safe and sound.
*(Hug self.)*

*Judy Hall*

## When I Get Into the Car

When I get into the car,

I buckle up for near or far.
*(Pretend to fasten seat belt.)*
It holds me in my seat so tight,

I feel so safe, I know it's right.
*(Hug self.)*
I use my seat belt every day

So I'll be safe in every way.
*(Nod head.)*

*Susan Burbridge*

## Car Ride

To go near or to go far,

You can ride inside a car.
*(Pretend to steer car.)*
Give your seat belt a good click,

Now, that ought to do the trick.
*(Pretend to fasten seat belt.)*
It's good to know you're safe and sound

When you're driving round the town.
*(Hug self.)*

*Diane Thom*

## I'm a Windshield Wiper

I'm a windshield wiper,
*(Move upright arm back and forth.)*
Watch me wipe,

First on the left side,

Then on the right.

I just love to wipe

And wipe and wipe.

I can wipe

All day and night.

*Jean Warren*

## Our Windshield Wipers

The windshield wipers on our car
  *(Hold up hands and move them back and forth.)*
Are busy in the rain.

They swing and swing, clup-clup, clup-clup,

Then back and forth again.

*Adapted Traditional*

## Little Red Train

Little red train,

Chugging down the track,

First it goes down,

Then it comes back.
  *(Chug around room.)*
Hooking on cars

As it goes,

Little red train

Just grows and grows.
  *(Have one child hook on behind you.)*

Repeat until all of your children are hooked
onto your little red train.

*Jean Warren*

## I'm a Little Red Train

I'm a little red train
  *(Do actions as rhyme indicates.)*
Chugging down the track,

A little red train

Going up and back.

I travel all day

Going round and round,

Taking goods

From town to town.

I'm a little red train

Going down the track,

Chug-chug-chug.

*Jean Warren*

## The Engineer Rap

Yo, everybody,
*(Clap in rhythm and chug around room.)*
Do the Engineer Rap.
Climb aboard the train,
You don't need a map.

Where will we go?
We'll just follow the track.
Then before you know it,
We'll come back.

Clackety, clack,
Clackety, clack.
Clackety, clackety,
Clackety, clack.

We went on a trip
In our imaginations,
And now we're back
At our own train station.

*Diane Thom*

## I'm a Choo-Choo Train

I'm a choo-choo train,
*(Bend arms at sides.)*
Chugging down the track,
*(Rotate arms in rhythm.)*
First I go forward,
*(Rotate arms forward.)*
Then I go back.
*(Rotate arms backward.)*

Now my bell is ringing,
*(Pretend to pull bell cord.)*
Hear my whistle blow.
*(Toot into closed fist.)*
What a lot of noise I make
*(Place hands over ears.)*
Everywhere I go!
*(Stretch arms out at sides.)*

*Adapted Traditional*

## The Train

The train goes chugging up and down,
*(Chug back and forth.)*
Carrying goods from town to town.

It carries corn and new cars too,

And as it goes, it says "Choo-choo."

*Elizabeth McKinnon*

## Open the Truck Door

Open the truck door,
*(Do actions as rhyme indicates.)*
Climb inside.

I get to help

My mommy drive.

Fasten the seat belt,

Shut the door.

Start the engine,

Hear it roar.

Turn the corner,

Step on the gas.

If the road's clear,

We may pass.

*Adapted Traditional*

# Circus

## Putting Up the Big Top

Everybody circle round,
*(Do actions as rhyme indicates.)*
Lift the canvas off the ground.
Pull and pull and watch it rise,
The Big Top grows before our eyes.

Everybody circle round,
Form a ring upon the ground.
Now we're set to watch the show,
Circus acts both high and low.

Let your children take turns doing circus acts inside their circus ring.

*Jean Warren*

## Under the Big Top

Under the Big Top what do I see?
A great big elephant smiling at me.
*(Smile.)*
Next to the elephant what do I see?
A fuzzy brown bear dancing for me.
*(Dance in place.)*
Next to the bear what do I see?
A lion with a mane roaring at me.
*(Roar.)*
Next to the lion what do I see?
A little seal doing tricks for me.
*(Pretend to balance ball on nose.)*

*Jean Warren*

## Be a Clown

Be a clown, be a clown,
Be a funny clown.
*(Wiggle fingers next to ears.)*
Juggle balls and jump rope,
*(Pretend to juggle, then jump.)*
And fall down on the ground.
*(Sit down on bottom.)*

*Diane Thom*

## If I Were a Circus Clown

If I were a circus clown,
With a red nose big and round,
*(Cover nose with fist.)*
I'd bring a smile to every face
And throw balloons everyplace!
*(Smile and pretend to toss balloons.)*

*Diane Thom*

## A Clown's Nose

Red is a stop sign,
Red is a rose.
Red is an apple
And a funny clown's nose!

*Sue Foster*

## Funny Clowns

Funny clowns, funny clowns,
*(Do actions as rhyme indicates.)*
Jump around, jump around.
Sometimes making faces,
Sometimes running races,
Funny clowns, funny clowns.

Funny clowns, funny clowns,
Spin around, spin around.
Sometimes with a big nose,
Sometimes with two big toes.
Funny clowns, funny clowns.

*Jean Warren*

## The Sad Little Clown

Once there was a little clown
Who looked so very sad.
No matter what trick he did,
It always turned out bad.
*(Pull down corners of mouth.)*

He tried juggling balls
And running up the aisles,
But no matter what he did,
The crowd would never smile.
*(Shake head.)*

Everybody liked him
But he always looked so sad,
Everyone would start to cry,
And for a clown, that's bad.
*(Pretend to cry.)*

Then one day he tried a trick
Of walking upside down.
Soon everyone was laughing
At this funny clown.
*(Laugh silently.)*

He wondered why they all would laugh
When he was upside down.
He didn't know that turned this way,
His face was not a frown.
*(Shake head.)*

For when he stood upon his hands
And walked around a while,
The frown that was upon his face
Turned right into a smile!
*(Pull corners of mouth down, then up.)*

*Jean Warren*

## Little Color Clown

Little clown with a big red nose,
Little clown with funny clothes.

Little clown with a suit of yellow,
Little clown, a happy fellow.

Little clown with a blue pointed hat,
Little clown, short and fat.

Little clown with a fancy green collar,
Little clown wants to be taller.

Little clown with hair orange and bright,
Little clown, a jolly good sight.

Little clown with two purple feet,
Little clown, a real circus treat!

*Jean Warren*

## Five Funny Clowns

Five funny clowns juggling balls galore,
    *(Hold up five fingers.)*
One tripped and fell, then there were four.
    *(Bend down thumb.)*
Four funny clowns up on a trapeze,
One jumped off, then there were three.
    *(Bend down pointer finger.)*
Three funny clowns blowing up balloons,
One ran away, then there were two.
    *(Bend down middle finger.)*
Two funny clowns chewing bubble gum,
One left to get some more, then there was one.
    *(Bend down ring finger.)*
One funny clown having lots of fun,
He left the circus tent, then there were none.
    *(Bend down little finger.)*

*Diane Thom*

## Popcorn Clowns

See the funny popcorn clowns
    *(Do actions as rhyme indicates.)*
Jumping in their pot.

Watch them while they squirm around,

Ouch! It's so hot!

See the kernels jump and squirm,

See them getting hotter.

Watch them as they all explode,

Pop! in the popper!

*Jean Warren*

## The Tightrope Walker

While the band is playing,

Back and forth I go,
    *(Pretend to walk tightrope.)*
High above the people,

Sitting far below.
    *(Cup hand over eye and look down.)*

While the crowd is cheering,

I sway from side to side.
    *(Sway back and forth.)*
Now my act is over,

And down the pole I slide.
    *(Pretend to slide down pole.)*

*Adapted Traditional*

## Five Little Clowns

This little clown is jolly and fat,
    *(Point to thumb.)*
This little clown wears a big red hat.
    *(Point to index finger.)*
This little clown is strong and tall,
    *(Point to middle finger.)*
This little clown likes to fall.
    *(Point to ring finger.)*
And this little clown is wee and small,
    *(Point to little finger.)*
But he does the funniest tricks of all!
    *(Wiggle little finger.)*

*Paula C. Foreman*

## Circus Treats

Out at the circus

Early in the morning,

See the circus vendors

Making things to eat.

See the popcorn vendor

Popping up the popcorn.

Yum, yum, yum, yum,

A circus treat!
    *(Pretend to eat popcorn.)*

Out at the circus

Early in the morning,

See the circus vendors

Making things to eat.

See the hot-dog vendor

Steaming up the hot dogs.

Yum, yum, yum, yum,

A circus treat!
    *(Pretend to eat hot dog.)*

*Jean Warren*

## The Merry-Go-Round

Ride with me on the merry-go-round,
    *(Beckon to other person.)*

Around and around and around.
    *(Move hands in circles.)*

Up, the horses go up.
    *(Raise hands.)*

Down, the horses go down.
    *(Lower hands.)*

You ride a horse that is white,
    *(Point to other person.)*

I ride a horse that is brown.
    *(Point to self.)*

Up and down on the merry-go-round,
    *(Raise and lower hands.)*

Our horses go round and round.
    *(Move hands in circles.)*

*Adapted Traditional*

## Make a Sand Cake

Make a sand cake
In the sand.
Digging and sifting
Just feels grand!

*Betty Silkunas*

## The Sand Castle

Sand castle on the beach,
I built you big and strong.
   *(Raise arms high.)*
A wave washed in upon the sand.
Whoops! You were gone!
   *(Swing hands down, then up.)*

*Saundra Winnett*

## I Like Sand

Sand can be wet,
And sand can be dry.
I like both
And I'll tell you why.

I can make castles
With wet sand.
And pouring it dry
Feels just grand.

*Gayle Bittinger*

## At the Beach

I dig holes in the sand with my fingers,
   *(Wiggle fingers.)*
I dig holes in the sand with my toes.
   *(Wiggle toes.)*
Then I pour some water in the holes,
   *(Pretend to pour water.)*
I wonder where it goes?
   *(Hold hands out to sides, palms up.)*

*Elizabeth McKinnon*

## Let's Play in the Sand

Let's all play in the sand,
   *(Do actions as rhyme indicates.)*
It feels so good on our hands.
We can dig it and sift it
And shake it about,
We can spoon it in pails
And then pour it out.

*Angela Wolfe*

## Shells, Shells, Shells

Giant shells, tiny shells,
*(Form circles with fingers for shells.)*
Shells wherever I look.

There are so very many shells,

I could write a book.

Rainbow shells, purple shells,

Shells that curve around.

I can see the beauty here

Just lying on the ground.

*Jean Warren*

## Ocean Shell

I found a great big shell one day
*(Form cup with two hands.)*
Upon the ocean floor.

I held it close up to my ear
*(Bring hands up to ear.)*
And heard the ocean roar.

I found a tiny shell one day
*(Form cup with one hand.)*
Upon the ocean sand.

The waves had worn it nice and smooth,
*(Rub opposite palm on cupped hand.)*
It felt nice in my hand.

*Adapted Traditional*

## Water, Water

Water, water everywhere,
*(Stretch out arms at sides.)*
On my face and on my hair.
*(Point to face, then hair.)*
On my fingers, on my toes,
*(Point to fingers, then toes.)*
Water, water on my nose!
*(Point to nose.)*

*Jean Warren*

## Beach Play

Seashells, white sand, ocean blue,

Sunshine, cool breeze, sand castles too.

Hear the children laugh and shout,

As they play and run about.

*Angela Wolfe*

## Ocean Breeze Blowing

Ocean breeze blowing,
> *(Wave hands back and forth.)*

Feet kick and splash.
> *(Kick feet.)*

Ocean waves breaking
> *(Swing hands up and down.)*

On rocks with a crash.
> *(Clap once.)*

Girls finding seashells,
> *(Pretend to pick up shells.)*

Boys sifting sand.
> *(Pretend to sift sand.)*

Friends building castles,
> *(Place fists one on top of the other.)*

As high as they can.
> *(Continue with fist movements.)*

I hold my arms out
> *(Stretch arms out at sides.)*

As far as they'll reach.
> *(Stretch arms even wider.)*

Oh my, what fun
> *(Dance in place.)*

On this day at the beach!
> *(Smile.)*

*Adapted Traditional*

# Nature

## Brown Leaves

Brown leaves, brown leaves, all around,

Twirling, swirling to the ground.
*(Twirl around.)*
See them dancing through the air,

See them falling everywhere.
*(Slowly sink to floor.)*

*Jean Warren*

## Falling Leaves

Little leaves falling down,

Red and yellow, orange and brown.
*(Flutter fingers downward.)*
Whirling, twirling round and round,

Falling softly to the ground.
*(Flutter fingers downward in circles.)*

*Adapted Traditional*

## Mother Nature, Did You Sneeze?

Red leaves, yellow leaves,

Orange leaves, brown,

Big leaves, little leaves,

Crinkled on the ground.

Everywhere are falling leaves!

Mother Nature, did you sneeze?

*Pat Cook*

## Leaves, Leaves

Leaves, leaves falling down,

Falling on the ground.
*(Flutter fingers downward.)*
Red, yellow, orange, and brown,

Triangular, oval, and round.
*(Form named shapes with thumbs and fingers.)*

*Susan A. Miller*

## Fall Leaves

Down, down,

Yellow and brown,
*(Flutter fingers downward.)*
Fall the leaves

All over the ground.

Rake them up

In a pile so high,
*(Pretend to rake leaves.)*
They almost reach

Up to the sky.

*Adapted Traditional*

## What the Leaves Say

Autumn leaves twirling, fluttering down,

Orange and scarlet, gold and brown.

Falling to earth

With a whispery sound.

Zachary runs through the leaves on a sunny day,

And makes them speak in a brand-new way.

"Crackle, crackle, crunch, crunch,"

Is what they say.

Substitute one of your children's names for *Zachary.*

*Diane Seader*

## See the Leaves

See the leaves

Falling down,

Twirling round

To the ground,

Drifting softly

Without a sound.
> *(Put finger to lips.)*

*Barbara Paxson*

## Leaves Are Drifting

Leaves are drifting softly down,
> *(Flutter fingers downward.)*
They make a carpet on the ground.
> *(Make spreading movement with hands.)*
Then, swish! the wind comes whistling by,
> *(Swing hands upward.)*
And sends them dancing in the sky!
> *(Dance fingers in air.)*

*Adapted Traditional*

## Leaves

All join hands and circle round

While we watch the leaves fall down.

See them twirling to the ground,

See them dancing all around.

See them skipping here and there,

See them flipping in the air.

Autumn leaves so peacefully

Falling, falling from the tree.

*Jean Warren*

## Autumn Time

The trees are gently dropping,

Dropping all their leaves.
> *(Flutter fingers downward.)*
The flowers are gently nodding,

Nodding in the breeze.
> *(Nod head.)*
The birds are swiftly flying,

Flying to the trees.
> *(Gently flap hands.)*

*Adapted Traditional*

## Jack Frost

Who comes creeping in the night

When the moon is clear and bright?
*(Tiptoe around.)*

Who paints tree leaves red and gold

When the autumn days turn cold?
*(Pretend to paint.)*

Up the hill and down he goes,

In and out the brown corn rows.
*(Run fingers back and forth.)*

Making music crackling sweet

With his little frosty feet.
*(Dance in place.)*

Jack Frost!

*Adapted Traditional*

## Changing Seasons

I'm a little person

Who's aware

Of the changes

In the air.
*(Hold up pointer finger.)*

First the leaves fall,

Orange and brown,

Then the snow comes

Lightly down.
*(Flutter fingers downward.)*

*Barbara Robinson*

## Leaves Are Falling

Leaves are falling round the town,

Watch them drifting to the ground.
*(Flutter fingers downward.)*

Autumn's here, it is true,

Then comes winter, just for you!
*(Point to other person.)*

*Judy Hall*

## I'm an Icicle

I'm a frozen icicle,

Hanging in the sun.
*(Stand straight.)*

First I start to melt,

Then I start to run.
*(Sag body.)*

Drip, drip, drip, drip,

Melting can be fun!
*(Slowly sink to floor.)*

*Donna Mullennix*

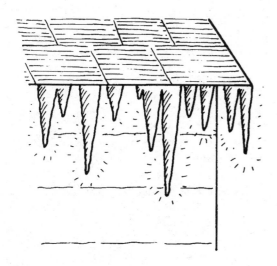

## Icy Winter

Icy you and icy me,

Icy branches on each tree.

Icy patterns on the glass,

Icy steps we have to pass.

Icy walks and roads galore,

Icy wintertime once more.

Icy vines upon the wall,

Icy scenes I now recall.

Help your children discover that
*icy* could also be read as *I see.*

*Jean Warren*

## Ice Cube

I'm a little ice cube,

Frosty and square.
*(Outline square shape with hands.)*

I make things cold

Everywhere.
*(Shiver.)*

If it gets too warm,

I'd better watch out,
*(Fan face with hand.)*

'Cause I will melt,

Without a doubt!
*(Slowly sink to floor.)*

*Gayle Bittinger*

## I Am a Snowman

I am a snowman cold and white,

I stand so still all through the night.
*(Stand straight and tall.)*

I have a carrot nose way up high,

And a lump of coal to make each eye.
*(Point to nose, then to eyes.)*

I have a muffler colored red

And a tall black hat upon my head.
*(Point to neck, then to top of head.)*

*Adapted Traditional*

## The Snowman

I looked out my window,
*(Cup hand above eye.)*
And what did I see?
*(Tilt head to one side.)*
Snowflakes falling
*(Flutter fingers downward.)*
Around every tree.
*(Move hands in circles.)*

I dressed in my warm clothes,
*(Pretend to dress.)*
And ran out to see
*(Run in place.)*
What I could build
*(Make building movements.)*
With the snow around me.
*(Flutter fingers downward.)*

I scooped up an armful,
*(Make scooping movement.)*
And made a snowball,
*(Pretend to roll snowball.)*
Then another and another,
*(Pretend to make two more snowballs.)*
And piled them up tall.
*(Pretend to stack snowballs.)*

And what did I make?
*(Tilt head to one side.)*
Please guess, if you can.
*(Make beckoning motion with hand.)*
You're right if you say
*(Hold up pointer finger.)*
A giant snowman!
*(Raise arms high.)*

*Beverly Qualheim*

## Building a Snowman

First the body, then the head,
*(Pretend to make snowman.)*
A big black hat and a scarf of red.
*(Point to top of head, then to neck.)*
Coal pieces for eyes, a carrot nose,
*(Point to eyes, then to nose.)*
And a mouth made of pebbles in two smiling rows.
*(Smile and point to mouth.)*

*Adapted Traditional*

## I Will Build a Snowman

I will build a snowman,

Make him big and tall.
*(Make stacking movements.)*
See if you can hit him

With a big snowball.
*(Pretend to throw snowball.)*

*Adapted Traditional*

## Snowballs Rolling Down the Street

Great big ball rolling down the street,

Great big ball landing at my feet.
*(Form large circle with arms.)*

How it got here, I don't know,

A great big ball made of snow.


Medium-sized ball rolling down the street,

Medium-sized ball landing at my feet.
*(Form medium-sized circle with arms.)*

How it got here, I don't know,

A medium-sized ball made of snow.


Teeny tiny ball rolling down the street,

Teeny tiny ball landing at my feet.
*(Form small circle with hands.)*

How it got here, I don't know,

A teeny tiny ball made of snow.


Three round balls made of snow,

Now just watch my snowman grow.
*(Pretend to build snowman.)*

Up go the balls, one, two, three,

Now my snowman's as big as me!


*Jean Warren*

## Cute Little Snowman

A cute little snowman

Had a carrot nose.
*(Hold up left fist for snowman.)*

Along came a rabbit,

And what do you suppose?
*(Hold up two fingers of right hand for rabbit.)*

That hungry little rabbit,

Looking for its lunch,
*(Move right hand back and forth.)*

Ate that snowman's carrot nose,

Nibble, nibble, crunch!
*(Lightly pinch left fist with right hand.)*

*Adapted Traditional*


## A Happy, Jolly Fellow

A snowman sits upon the hill,

He's a happy, jolly fellow.

His hat is black, his scarf is red,

And his mittens are bright yellow.

*Nancy K. Hobbs*

## Five Little Snowmen

Five little snowmen happy and gay,
> *(Hold up five fingers.)*

The first one said, "What a nice day!"
> *(Point to thumb.)*

The second one said, "We'll cry no tears."
> *(Point to index finger.)*

The third one said, "We'll stay for years."
> *(Point to middle finger.)*

The fourth one said, "But what happens in May?
> *(Point to ring finger.)*

The fifth one said, "Look! we're melting away!
> *(Point to little finger, then slowly bend down all five fingers.)*

*Adapted Traditional*

## Snowman, Snowman

Snowman, snowman, where did you go?
> *(Cup hand above eye and look around.)*

I built you yesterday out of snow.
> *(Make stacking movements.)*

I made you tall and I made you fat,
> *(Hold arms up, then out at sides.)*

I gave you eyes, a nose, and a hat.
> *(Point to eyes, nose, then top of head.)*

Now you're gone, all melted away,
> *(Make a sad face, then sag body.)*

But it's sunny outside so I'll go and play!
> *(Stand up straight and smile.)*

*Carole Sick*

## I'm a Friendly Snowman

I'm a friendly snowman big and fat,
> *(Stretch arms out at sides.)*

Here is my tummy and here is my hat.
> *(Point to tummy, then top of head.)*

I'm a happy fellow, here's my nose,
> *(Smile, then point to nose.)*

I'm all snow from my head to my toes.
> *(Point to head, then to toes.)*

I have two bright eyes so I can see
> *(Point to eyes.)*

All the snow falling down on me.
> *(Flutter fingers downward.)*

When the weather's cold I'm strong and tall,
> *(Stand up straight.)*

But when it's warm I get very small.
> *(Crouch down low.)*

*Susan M. Paprocki*

## Build a Little Snowman

Build a little snowman

Starting with his feet.
> *(Pretend to roll snowball.)*

Put on lots of snow

And pat it all so neat.
> *(Make patting motions.)*

Make a round snowball

And put it on top.
> *(Pretend to put head on snowman.)*

Then the sun will come out

And make the snowman hot.
> *(Form circle with arms, then sag body.)*

*Judith McNitt*

## Three Little Snowmen

One little, two little, three little snowmen
*(Hold up three fingers, one at a time.)*
Playing in the sun,
*(Dance fingers around.)*
One little, two little, three little snowmen
Having lots of fun.

One little, two little, three little snowmen
*(Hold up three fingers, one at a time.)*
Sliding on the ice,
*(Slide fingers around.)*
One little, two little, three little snowmen
Said, "This is mighty nice!"

One little, two little, three little snowmen
*(Hold up three fingers, one at a time.)*
Looked at the sun up high,
*(Stretch fingers upward.)*
One little, two little, three little snowmen
Each gave a great big sigh.

One little, two little, three little snowmen
*(Hold up three fingers, one at a time.)*
Began to melt away,
*(Slowly bend fingers down into fist.)*
One little, two little, three little snowmen
Said, "We'll be back some winter day!"

*Elizabeth Vollrath*

## Sing a Song of Winter

Sing a song of winter,

Frost is in the air.
*(Hug self and shiver.)*
Sing a song of winter,

There are snowflakes everywhere.
*(Dance fingers in air.)*
Sing a song of winter,

Hear the sleigh bells chime.
*(Cup hand behind ear.)*
Can you think of anything

As nice as wintertime?
*(Tilt head to one side.)*

*Judith McNitt*

## Walking in the Snow

Let's go walking in the snow,
*(Do actions as rhyme indicates.)*
Walking, walking on tiptoe.

Lift your right foot way up high,

Then your left foot—keep it dry!

All around the yard we skip,

Watch your step, or you might slip.

*Adapted Traditional*

## Snowflakes Falling Down

Snowflakes, snowflakes falling down,
 *(Flutter fingers downward.)*
All around on the ground.
 *(Make spreading movement with hands.)*
Get the sled and climb so high,
 *(Walk fingers up arm.)*
Down we'll go, slippety-slide!
 *(Slide hand down arm.)*

*Pat Cook*

## Sledding

Crunch, crunch, crunch, crunch,
Up the hill, so slow.
 *(March fingers up arm.)*
Sliding, sliding, sliding, sliding,
Down the hill we go!
 *(Slide hand down arm.)*

*Judith McNitt*

## Here's a Great Big Hill

Here's a great big hill
With snow all over the side.
 *(Walk fingers up arm.)*
Let's climb on our sleds
And down the hill we'll slide.
 *(Slide hand down arm.)*

*Adapted Traditional*

## Winter Snow

The clouds roll in, the earth grows white,
 *(Roll hands.)*
The snow keeps falling through the night.
 *(Flutter fingers downward.)*
With morning sun the earth starts glistening,
 *(Wiggle fingers in air.)*
And children play, with mothers listening.
 *(Cup hand behind ear.)*
Now inside, all warm and snug,
 *(Hug self.)*
Dad tucks in covers, snug as a bug!
 *(Pretend to tuck in blankets.)*

*Beverly Qualheim*

## Ice and Snow

Ice and snow, cold winds blow,
Hop aboard our sleigh.
Oh, what fun it is to play
Winter games today.

Ice and snow, cold winds blow,
Let's be on our way.
Oh, what fun it is to play
Winter games today!

*Betty Silkunas*

## Spring

Spring is here, spring is here,

Winter days are past.

Little flowers raise their heads,
  *(Lift head high.)*
Snow is gone at last!

See the trees all in green,

Dressed up just for spring.

See the robins fly about,
  *(Gently flap hands.)*
Listen to them sing!

*Susan M. Paprocki*

## March Rhyme

March winds blow the kites around,

Blow them right up off the ground.
  *(Swing hands down, then up.)*
March means spring is almost here,

Sounds of birds you soon will hear.
  *(Cup hand behind ear.)*
Watch the leaves sprout on the trees,

Soon you'll see some honeybees.
  *(Make buzzing sound.)*

*Barbara B. Fleisher*

## Here Comes Spring

Bells all ring,

Children sing

To celebrate the start of spring.

New plants shoot up from the ground,

Blossoms on the trees abound,

The earth awakens all around.

Here comes spring!

*Jean Warren*

## Spring Colors

See the yellow sun up in the sky,

See the bluebird flying by.

See the green grass under my feet,

See the red flowers that smell so sweet.

See the brown tree that grows straight and tall,

See the pink blossoms just starting to fall.

See the orange caterpillar, so soon to be

A white butterfly for the spring world to see!

*Mildred Hoffman*

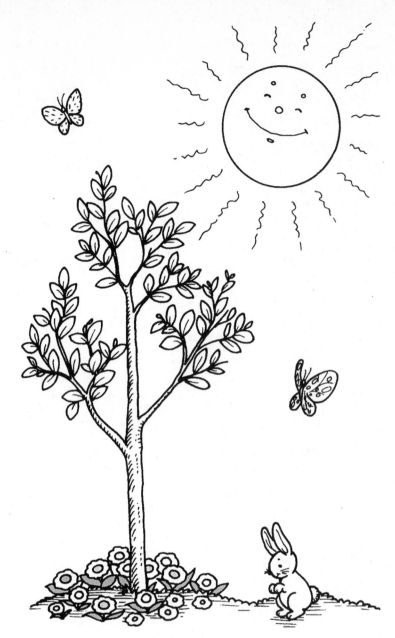

## May Is Here

I see daisies, pretty daisies,

Bloom in May, bloom in May.
  *(Cup hand above eye and look around.)*

May's the month for flowers,

Goodbye, April showers.
  *(Wave goodbye.)*

Hello, May! Hello, May!
  *(Wave hello.)*

*Betty Silkunas*

## Sing a Song of Springtime

Sing a song of springtime,

Bird songs fill the air.
  *(Cup hand behind ear.)*

Plants are sprouting up again,

And the weather's fair.
  *(Hold palms up and smile.)*

The sun is bright and warm,

There are blossoms on the way.
  *(Form small circles with fingers.)*

Isn't it time to enjoy

A wonderful spring day?
  *(Dance and skip.)*

*Elizabeth Vollrath*

## It Is Springtime

It is springtime,

Winter is gone.

Summer is coming,

It won't be long!

*Betty Ruth Baker*

## The Big Round Sun

The big round sun in a springtime sky
  *(Form large circle with arms.)*

Winked at a cloud that was passing by.
  *(Wink eye.)*

The little cloud laughed as it scattered rain,
  *(Flutter fingers downward.)*

Then out came the big round sun again.
  *(Form large circle with arms.)*

*Adapted Traditional*

# Summer

## Summer Day

The summer sun shines overhead,
*(Form circle with arms.)*
And clouds float calmly by.
*(Float hands in air.)*
We lie down on a meadow bed,
*(Lay one hand on top of the other.)*
And watch birds fly in the sky.
*(Gently flap hands.)*

*Beverly Qualheim*

## Sing a Song of Sunshine

Sing a song of sunshine,

Be happy every day.

Sing a song of sunshine,

You'll chase the clouds away.

Be happy every moment,

No matter what you do.

Just sing and sing and sing and sing,

And let the sun shine through!

*Jean Warren*

## Bright Sun

Bright sun shining down,
*(Spread fingers and lower hands slowly.)*
Shining on the ground.

What a lovely face you have,
*(Form circle with arms.)*
Yellow, big, and round!

*Susan A. Miller*

## The Shadow

**S**un is shining, let's go for a walk.

**H**urry outside and around the block.

**A**t your side walks a little friend who.

**D**oes the very same things you do.

**O**pen the door and go inside—

**W**here, oh, where does my shadow friend hide?

*Mildred Hoffman*

## Shadows

Shadows dance upon the wall,

Shadows big and very tall.
*(Raise arms high.)*
Shadows follow me around,

Shadows never make a sound.
*(Put finger to lips and shake head.)*
Shadows down beside my feet,

Shadows everywhere I peek.
*(Point to floor, then peek around.)*

*Gayle Bittinger*

## Four Seasons

Flowers, hot sun, pumpkins, snow
*(Count on fingers.)*
Make the seasons we all know.

Every year they are the same,

And we give them each a name.

Summer, fall, winter, spring,
*(Count on fingers.)*
Watch the changes that they bring.

*Marcia Dean*

## The Seasons

Summer, fall, winter, spring,

Sun, leaves, snow, and rain.

If you watch you will see

The seasons change once again.

*Saundra Winnett*

## Seasons of Beauty

In the winter there are snowflakes,
*(Flutter fingers downward.)*
In the spring raindrops plop.
*(Make tapping sounds with fingers.)*
In the summer there are flowers,
*(Slowly open closed fists.)*
In the fall the leaves all drop.
*(Float hands downward.)*

Four seasons are so lovely,

I want to learn them all.

Winter, spring, summer,

And finally there's fall.
*(Do actions described above as each season is named.)*

*Beverly Qualheim*

## Winter, Spring, Summer, Fall

There are seasons, four in all,

Winter, spring, summer, fall.
*(Count on fingers.)*
The weather changes, sun or snow,

The leaves fall down or flowers grow.

There are seasons, four in all,

Winter, spring, summer, fall.
*(Count on fingers.)*
Look outside, what will it be?

Just what season do you see?

*Judy Hall*

# Pets

## Who Am I?

Soft fur, paws, and a little pink nose,

Do you know who has all those?

Pretty whiskers and a long tail,

Could it be a little snail?

Try again, take one more guess.

Did you say a kitten? Yes!

*Becky Valenick*

## My Kitty Cat, Puff

I have a kitty cat named Puff,

She's round and soft as a ball of fluff.
> *(Bend down fingers of left hand and hold up thumb.)*

Each day she laps up all her milk,

And her fur is soft as silk.
> *(Stroke left hand with right hand.)*

When she's happy you will know,

For her tail swings to and fro.
> *(Wiggle little finger of left hand.)*

*Adapted Traditional*

## Soft Kitty, Warm Kitty

Soft kitty, warm kitty,

Little ball of fur.
> *(Form fist with one hand.)*

Pretty kitty, sleepy kitty,

Purr, purr, purr.
> *(Stroke fist with other hand.)*

*Adapted Traditional*

## My Kitten

I have a little kitten,

She's black and white and gray.

When I try to cuddle her,

She always wants to play.
> *(Pretend to cuddle kitten.)*

So I drag a piece of yarn

Across the kitchen floor.

She thinks it is a little mouse,

And always asks for more.
> *(Pretend to drag yarn across floor.)*

*Elizabeth Vollrath*

## Five Little Kittens

Five little kittens

Sleeping on a chair,
> *(Hold up five fingers.)*

One rolled off,

Leaving four there.
> *(Bend down thumb.)*

Four little kittens,

One climbed a tree

To look in a bird's nest,

And that left three.
> *(Bend down pointer finger.)*

Three little kittens

Wondered what to do,

One ran after a mouse,

And that left two.
> *(Bend down middle finger.)*

Two little kittens

Playing near a wall,

One little kitten

Chased a red ball.
> *(Bend down ring finger.)*

One little kitten

With fur soft as silk,

Left all alone

To drink a dish of milk
> *(Wiggle little finger.)*

*Adapted Traditional*

## There Once Were Some Kittens

There once were some kittens

Who lost their mittens
> *(Hold up both hands and shake head.)*

And they began to cry,

"Boohoo, boohoo,

Boohoo, boohoo,

Now we shall have no pie."
> *(Pretend to cry.)*

Then all the kittens

Found their mittens
> *(Hold up both hands and nod head.)*

And they began to cry,

"We found our mittens,

We're good little kittens,

Now we can have our pie!"
> *(Nod head and smile.)*

*Jean Warren*

## Color Cats

When the cat that is red
Is finally fed,
He raises his head
And says, "Meow!"

When the cat that is blue
Has nothing to do,
He comes up, too,
And whispers, "Meow!"

When the cat that is yellow
Is feeling mellow,
He tends to stretch
And bellow, "Meow!"

When the cat that is green
Is finally seen,
You'll know what I mean
When I say he can really "Meow!"

Okay, little cats,
Let's hear some "Meows,"
*(Make meowing sounds.)*
And now it's time
For curtsies and bows.
*(Curtsey and bow.)*

*Susan M. Paprocki*

## Little Puppy

Little puppy, happy and gay,
*(Bend down fingers of one hand.)*
Won't you please come out to play?
*(Hold up thumb.)*
Lick my face,
*(Stroke face with thumb.)*
Wag your tail.
*(Hold up little finger and wiggle it.)*
We'll have fun that will not fail!

*Betty Silkunas*

## My Dog Buffy

My little dog Buffy
Has quite a loud bark.
She barks in the yard
And she barks in the park.
*(Hold hands over ears.)*

Her favorite toy
Is an old tennis shoe.
Just toss it—she'll catch it
And bring it to you!
*(Pretend to pet dog.)*

*Marion Scofield*

## Five Little Puppy Dogs

Five little puppy dogs by the kennel door,
*(Hold up five fingers.)*
One left the crowd, then there were four.
*(Bend down thumb.)*
Four little puppy dogs running round a tree,

Mother called one home, then there were three.
*(Bend down pointer finger.)*
Three little puppy dogs playing with a shoe,

One ran after a cat, then there were two.
*(Bend down middle finger.)*
Two little puppy dogs having so much fun,

One went to find a bone, then there was one.
*(Bend down ring finger.)*
One little puppy dog sitting in the sun,

She went in the kennel, then there were none.
*(Bend down little finger.)*

*Adapted Traditional*

## My Little Puppy

I had a little puppy,

Her coat was silver gray.
*(Hold up fist.)*
One day I thought I'd bathe her

To wash the dirt away.

I washed my little puppy,

Then dried her with a towel.
*(Rub and pat fist with other hand.)*
My puppy seemed to like her bath,

She didn't even growl!

*Adapted Traditional*

## Call the Dog

Call the dog,
*(Cup hands around mouth.)*
Give him a bone,
*(Extend hand.)*
Take him for a walk,
*(Pretend to hold leash.)*
Then put him in his home.
*(Form roof shape with fingers.)*

*Adapted Traditional*

## Puppies and Kittens

One little, two little, three little kittens

Were napping in the sun.
*(Hold up three fingers of left hand.)*
One little, two little, three little puppies

Said, "Let's have some fun."
*(Hold up three fingers of right hand.)*
Up to the kittens the puppies went creeping

As quiet as could be.
*(Creep right-hand fingers up to left hand.)*
One little, two little, three little kittens

Went scampering up a tree!
*(Climb left-hand fingers quickly upward.)*

*Adapted Traditional*

## My Five Pets

I have five pets I'd like you to meet
   *(Hold up five fingers.)*
They live with me on Mulberry Street.

This is my chicken, the smallest of all,
   *(Point to little finger.)*
He comes running whenever I call.

This is my duckling who says, "Quack, quack,"
   *(Point to ring finger.)*
As she shakes the water off her back.

This is my rabbit, he runs from his pen,
   *(Point to middle finger.)*
Then I must put him back again.

This is my kitten, her coat is black and white,
   *(Point to index finger.)*
She loves to sleep on my pillow at night.

And this is my puppy who has lots of fun,
   *(Point to thumb.)*
He chases the others and makes them run.
   *(Wiggle thumb, then fingers.)*

*Adapted Traditional*

## Love Your Pets

Love your pets, love your pets,

Love them every day.

Give them food and water too,

Then let them run and play.

*Elizabeth McKinnon*

# Farm Animals

## In the Barnyard

Out in the barnyard

Early in the morning,

See the yellow chicks

Standing in a row.
*(Hold up fingers of left hand.)*

See the busy farmer

Giving them their breakfast,
*(Make scattering movements with right hand.)*

Cheep, cheep, cheep, cheep,

Off they go.
*(Walk left-hand fingers away.)*

*Jean Warren*

## Little Chick

Snuggled down inside
*(Do actions as rhyme indicates.)*

An egg that was white,

Was a tiny little chick

With its head tucked in tight.

Then it lifted its head,

Tapped the egg with its beak,

And quickly popped out,

Cheep, cheep, cheep!

*Colraine Pettipaw Hunley*

## Little Chicken

When a little chicken eats,

She scampers all around,

Picking up here and there

Dinner from the ground.
*(Make pecking movements with head.)*

When a little chicken drinks,

She stands very still,

While water trickles down

Through her upturned bill.
*(Hold head back and stroke throat.)*

*Adapted Traditional*

## Chicks' Nap Time

"Come, little children," calls mother hen,
*(Beckon with left hand.)*

"It's time to take your nap again."

Then under her feathers the small chicks creep,
*(Creep fingers of right hand into folded left hand.)*

And she clucks a song until they fall asleep.

*Adapted Traditional*

## Little Cow

This little cow eats grass,
*(Point to thumb.)*
This little cow eats hay.
*(Point to index finger.)*
This little cow drinks water,
*(Point to middle finger.)*
This little cow runs away.
*(Point to ring finger.)*
And this little cow does nothing at all
*(Point to little finger.)*
But chew her cud all day.

*Adapted Traditional*

## Cows

Here is the barn,
So big, don't you see?
*(Form roof shape with fingers.)*
In walk the cows,
One, two three.
*(Hold up three fingers, one at a time.)*
Soon there'll be milk
For you and for me.
*(Point to other person, then to self.)*

*Adapted Traditional*

## Little Yellow Ducks

We're little yellow ducks
Who love to see the rain,
*(Waddle like a duck.)*
Little yellow ducks,
Now we will explain.
We love to see the rain come down,
Making puddles all over town.
*(Flutter fingers downward.)*

We're little yellow ducks
Who love to swim and splash,
*(Pretend to swim like a duck.)*
We wish the rain
Would last and last and last.
We love to see the rain come down,
Then we can swim all over town.
*(Nod head and smile.)*

*Jean Warren*

## When a Yellow Duck

When a yellow duck walks down the street,
*(Hold up hand.)*
Quack! goes his bill.
*(Open and close thumb and index finger.)*
Waddle! go his feet.
*(Waddle hand back and forth.)*
He comes to a puddle and with a bound,
*(Form circle with opposite arm.)*
In goes the yellow duck and swims around.
*(Jump hand into circle and move it around.)*

*Adapted Traditional*

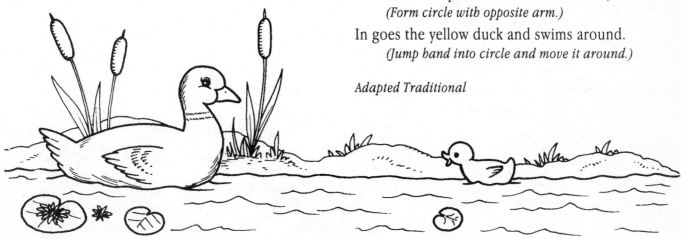

## The Little Ducklings

All the little ducklings
    *(Do actions as rhyme indicates.)*
Line up in a row.
Quack, quack, quack,
And away they go.

They follow their mother
Waddling to and fro.
Quack, quack, quack,
And away they go.

Down to the big pond
Happy as can be.
Quack, quack, quack,
They are full of glee.

They jump in the water
And bob up and down.
Quack, quack, quack,
They swim all around.

All the little ducklings
Swimming far away.
Quack, quack, quack,
They'll play another day.

*Elizabeth Vollrath*

## Little White Goat

Here's a little white goat
    *(Do actions as rhyme indicates.)*
Who found a little snack.
She bends down her front legs
But not the ones in back.

She's very, very busy
Gobbling up her treat.
That little white goat
Just loves to eat and eat!

*Judy Slenker*

## Color Hens

Out in the barnyard by the big corn sack,
Stood a little hen that was colored black.

Out in the barnyard by the kitten's bed,
Stood a little hen that was colored red.

Out in the barnyard by the iron bellow,
Stood a little hen that was colored yellow.

Out in the barnyard by the wagon for town,
Stood a little hen that was colored brown.

Down at the barnyard by the lantern bright,
Stood a little hen that was colored white.

*Jean Warren*

## My Horse

Trot, trot, my little horse,
Trot, trot, on the course.
    *(Trot fingers.)*
Canter, canter, nice and slow,
Canter, canter, off we go.
    *(Canter fingers.)*
Gallop, gallop, speed along,
Gallop, gallop, all day long.
    *(Gallop fingers.)*

*Carla Cotter Skjong*

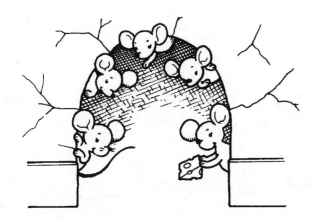

## Clippity, Clippity, Clop

Clippity, clippity, clop,
    *(Gallop hands in rhythm.)*
The horses go clip, clop.

They gallop and gallop,

They start and they stop.

Clippity, clippity, clop.

*Sue Brown*

## Five Little Mice

Five little mice

On the pantry floor,
    *(Hold up five fingers.)*
This little mouse

Peeked around the door.
    *(Wiggle thumb.)*

This little mouse

Nibbled on some cake,
    *(Wiggle pointer finger.)*
This little mouse

Not a sound did make.
    *(Wiggle middle finger.)*

This little mouse

Took a bite of cheese,
    *(Wiggle ring finger.)*
This little mouse

Heard the kitten sneeze.
    *(Wiggle little finger.)*

"Ah-choo!" sneezed the kitten

And "Squeak!" they cried,
    *(Jump fingers high.)*
As the mice found a hole

And ran inside.
    *(Run fingers behind back.)*

*Adapted Traditional*

## Little Mice

Softly, softly,

At the close of day,

Little mice come creeping

From their homes to play.
  *(Creep fingers around.)*

No one hears their padded feet

As they pitter-pat.

Mother mouse has warned them

About the family cat.
  *(Put finger to lips and say, "Shhh.")*

*Adapted Traditional*

## A Little Mouse

A little mouse ran up the clock,

He thought that it was fun.

But when he reached the very top,

The clock struck one.
  *(Hold up one finger.)*

Another mouse ran up the clock,

In tiny shoes of blue.

And when she reached the very top,

The clock struck two.
  *(Hold up two fingers.)*

Another mouse ran up the clock

To see what he could see.

And when he reached the very top,

The clock struck three.
  *(Hold up three fingers.)*

Another mouse ran up the clock

And found a little door.

And when she reached the very top,

The clock struck four.
  *(Hold up four fingers.)*

*Jean Warren*

## This Little Mousie

This little mousie peeked in the door,
  *(Point to thumb.)*
This little mousie jumped to the floor.
  *(Point to index finger.)*
This little mousie came out to play,
  *(Point to middle finger.)*
This little mousie ran away.
  *(Point to ring finger.)*
This little mousie said, "Dear me,
  *(Point to little finger.)*
Dinner is over and it's time for tea!"

*Adapted Traditional*

## Piglets

Out in the barnyard

Early in the morning,

You can hear the piglets

Squealing up a storm.

Here comes the momma pig,

She will feed her babies.

Oink, oink, oink, oink,

On the farm.

*Judy Hall*

## Pigs on the Farm

Down on the farm we love to play

In the mud all through the day.
*(Pretend to play in mud.)*

That is why we love to spy

Great big rain clouds in the sky.
*(Point upward.)*

Down in the mud we make a hole

Where we like to roll and roll.
*(Roll around on floor.)*

That is why we shout "Hurray!"

Every time it rains today.
*(Shout "Hurray!")*

*Jean Warren*

## Five Little Ponies

Five little ponies all dapple gray,
*(Hold up five fingers.)*

Down in the meadow not far away.
*(Gesture with hand.)*

The first one said, "Come on, let's run!"
*(Wiggle thumb.)*

The second one said, "Oh, that's no fun."
*(Wiggle pointer finger.)*

The third one said, "I'm going to neigh."
*(Wiggle middle finger.)*

The fourth one said, "I'd like some hay."
*(Wiggle ring finger.)*

The fifth one said, "Here comes a Jeep."
*(Wiggle little finger.)*

So the five little ponies away did leap.
*(Jump all five fingers behind back.)*

*Adapted Traditional*

## Ponies in a Meadow

Ten little ponies in a meadow green,
*(Hold up ten fingers.)*

Friskiest ponies I've ever seen.
*(Wiggle fingers.)*

They go for a gallop, they go for a trot,
*(Gallop fingers, then trot them.)*

They come to a halt in the big feed lot.
*(Stop finger movements.)*

Ten little ponies fat and well fed,
*(Bring fingertips of hands together.)*

Curl up together in a soft straw bed.
*(Close fingers and bring fists together.)*

*Adapted Traditional*

## The Rooster

The rooster crows each morning

To say the day is new.

We all know just what he'll say,

It's "Cock-a-doodle-doo!"
*(Flap hands at sides and crow.)*

*Judy Hall*

## A White Sheep

There once was a white sheep,

And this is the way

The farmer cut off

Its wool one day.
*(Pretend to shear sheep.)*

The wool was spun

Into thread so fine,

And made into cloth

For this coat of mine.
*(Place hands on shoulders.)*

*Adapted Traditional*

## I Love Sheep

I love sheep,

I count them in my sleep.

They jump all night over fences high,

They jump so high they reach the sky.

They help me sleep and that is why

I love sheep!

*Jean Warren*

## All Around the Barnyard

All around the barnyard

The animals are fast asleep.

Sleeping cows and horses,

Sleeping pigs and sheep.
   *(Rest cheek on folded hands.)*

Here comes the cocky rooster

To sound his daily alarm.

"Cock-a-doodle-doo!

Wake up, sleepy farm!"
   *(Flap arms at sides and crow.)*

*Pat Beck*

## The Puppy and the Chicken

All around the barnyard

The puppy chased the chicken.
   *(Chase left hand with right hand.)*

He thought it was a lot of fun

Until the chicken pecked him!
   *(Peck right hand with left hand.)*

*Saundra Winnett*

## To the Farm

Horses, donkeys, cows that moo,
   *(Make mooing sound.)*

Chickens, kittens, piglets too.
   *(Make oinking sound.)*

Fish that swim down in the pond,
   *(Make swimming movements.)*

Ducklings quacking all day long.
   *(Make quacking sound.)*

All these animals you can see
   *(Cup hand above eye.)*

If you go to the farm with me.

*Beverly Qualheim*

## Farm Animals

This is hungry Piggy Snout,
   *(Point to thumb.)*

He'd better stop eating or his tail will pop out.

This is busy Mother Hen,
   *(Point to index finger.)*

She likes to scratch for her chickens ten.

This is patient Friendly Cow,
   *(Point to middle finger.)*

She likes to eat from a big haymow.

This is Baa-Baa, the woolly sheep,
   *(Point to ring finger.)*

His wool keeps me warm while I'm asleep.

And this is little Fuzzy Cat,
   *(Point to little finger.)*

She likes to chase a mouse or rat.
   *(Run fingers away.)*

*Adapted Traditional*

## In the Farmyard

In the farmyard at the end of day,

Listen to what the animals say.

The cow says, "Moo,"

The pigeon, "Coo."

The sheep says, "Baa,"

The lamb says, "Maa."

The hen, "Cluck, cluck,"

"Quack," says the duck.

The dog, "Bow-wow,"

The cat, "Meow."

The horse, "Neigh,"

The pig grunts, "Oink."

Then the barn is closed up tight,

And the farmer says, "Goodnight."
*(Rest cheek on folded hands.)*

*Adapted Traditional*

## Our Farm Friends

The big horse is so good to me,

He gives me a ride, as you can see.
*(Pretend to ride horse.)*

The hen lays eggs for us to eat,

The cow gives milk so fresh and sweet.
*(Pretend to drink.)*

On our farm are many friends,

And upon these animals we depend.
*(Point to pretend animals.)*

*Carol Metzker*

## Spring Babies

Baby bunny in your hutch,

I like you so very much.
*(Nod head.)*

With furry coat and ears that flop,

And a little hop, hop, hop.
*(Hop.)*

Baby duck with feathery back,

I can hear you quack, quack, quack.
*(Cup hand behind ear.)*

You swim in the pond nearby,

Soon you'll fly up to the sky.
*(Flap arms at sides.)*

Fluffy little yellow chick,

You'll grow up so very quick.
*(Nod head.)*

Pecking here and pecking there,

Cheeping, cheeping everywhere.
*(Make cheeping sound.)*

*Diane Thom*

## Out in the Garden

Out in the garden

Where the cabbages grow,
*(Gesture to one side.)*

Happy little Cottontails

Are hopping to and fro.
*(Hop fingers of left hand.)*

Along comes Puppy Dog

Looking for some fun,
*(Creep out right hand.)*

"Bow-wow-wow," he barks,

And off the bunnies run.
*(Hop left-hand fingers away.)*

*Adapted Traditional*

## The Bear

Here is a cave,
*(Make a fist.)*
Inside is a bear.
*(Put thumb inside fist.)*
Now he comes out
To get some fresh air.
*(Pop out thumb.)*

He stays out all summer
In sunshine and heat.
He hunts in the forest
For berries to eat.
*(Move thumb in circle.)*

When snow starts to fall,
He hurries inside
His warm little cave,
And there he will hide.
*(Put thumb back inside fist.)*

Snow covers the cave
Like a fluffy white rug.
Inside the bear sleeps
All cozy and snug.
*(Cover fist with other hand.)*

*Author Unknown*

## Time for Sleeping

Now it's time for sleeping,
The bears go in their caves,
Keeping warm and cozy,
Time for lazy days.
*(Creep fingers under opposite hand.)*

When the snow is gone
And the sun comes out to play,
The bears will wake up from their sleep
And then go on their way.
*(Creep fingers out from under hand.)*

*Terri Crosbie*

## Bears Are Sleeping

Bears are sleeping
In their lairs.
*(Pretend to sleep.)*
Soon it will be springtime,
Wake up, bears!
*(Pretend to wake up.)*

*Joyce Marshall*

## A Little Brown Bear

A little brown bear

Went in search of some honey.
*(Cup hand above eye.)*

Isn't it funny,

A bear wanting honey?
*(Tilt head to one side.)*

He sniffed at the breeze

And he listened for bees.
*(Sniff, then cup hand behind ear.)*

And, would you believe it,

He even climbed trees!
*(Make climbing movements.)*

*Adapted Traditional*

## Little Deer

Out in the forest

Early in the morning,

See the little deer

Prancing to and fro.
*(Prance.)*

First she eats some leaves,

Then she eats some berries.
*(Pretend to eat like a deer.)*

Munch, munch, crunch, crunch,

Off she goes.
*(Turn, then leap away.)*

*Jean Warren*

## Five Funny Frogs

Five funny frogs fretting on the floor,
*(Hold up five fingers.)*

One jumped away, and that left four.
*(Bend down thumb.)*

Four funny frogs frolicking in a tree,

One jumped down, and that left three.
*(Bend down pointer finger.)*

Three funny frogs, just a friendly few,

One flipped out, and that left two.
*(Bend down middle finger.)*

Two funny frogs having froggy fun,

One hopped away, and that left one.
*(Bend down ring finger.)*

One funny frog, thinking he's a hero,

He left to tell his tale, and that left zero.
*(Bend down little finger.)*

*Susan M. Paprocki*

## Listen to the Frog

Listen to the frog,
*(Cup hand behind ear.)*

Croaking on a log.

He croaks about this

And he croaks about that.

It seems very clear

That he needs to chat.

Ribbet, ribbet, ribbet.

*Susan M. Paprocki*

## Froggy Catch a Fly

Can your froggy catch a fly?
*(Open and close thumb and fingers of right hand.)*
Yes he can, watch him try.
*(Snap hand at pointer finger of left hand.)*
Can the fly reach the sky?
*(Raise pointer finger high.)*
Can your froggy jump that high?
*(Jump up right hand.)*
Oh my, nice try!.
*(Catch pointer finger with right hand.)*
Bye, bye, little fly!

*Polly Reedy*


## A Little Frog

A little frog in a pond am I,
Hippity, hoppity, hop.
*(Hop fist up and down.)*
Watch me jump in the air so high,
Hippity...hoppity...hop!
*(Hop fist as high as possible.)*

*Adapted Traditional*

## Five Little Lizards

One little lizard all alone,

Lying on a smooth, flat stone.
*(Place right index finger on left palm.)*

Two little lizards side by side,

They play peekaboo, then they hide.
*(Place two fingers under left hand.)*

Three little lizards beneath a tree,

They run away when they see me.
*(Run three fingers behind back.)*

Four little lizards having fun,

Chasing one another in the sun.
*(Wiggle four fingers back and forth.)*

Five little lizards lie so still,

Snoozing on my windowsill.
*(Rest five fingers on left hand.)*

*Lois E. Putnam*


## The Lonely Porcupine

Once there was a porcupine
Who lived beneath a tree.
Everyone would run from her,
What could the matter be?

She was lonely all the time,
No one stayed to play.
Why did everyone she meet
Have to run away?

*Jean Warren*

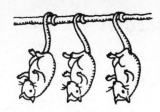

## Three Little Possums

Three little possums

Up in a tree,

Swinging by their tails,

Happy as can be.
*(Hang three fingers on opposite pointer finger.)*

Little possum one

Drops to the ground,
*(Unhook one finger.)*

Chases his tail

Around and around.
*(Move finger in circle.)*

Little possum two

Drops to the ground,
*(Unhook second finger.)*

Chases her tail

Around and around.
*(Move finger in circle.)*

Little possum three

Drops to the ground,
*(Unhook third finger.)*

Chases her tail

Around and around.
*(Move finger in circle.)*

Three little possums,

Tired as can be,
*(Move three fingers slowly.)*

Climb back up

Into the tree.
*(Climb fingers up onto opposite hand.)*

*Margo S. Miller*

## Fluffy Rabbit

See the fluffy rabbit as it hops,
*(Hold hands at sides of head for ears.)*

One ear up while the other one flops.
*(Bend down one hand.)*

He's a gentle fellow with a twitchy nose,
*(Wiggle nose.)*

He's all furry from his ears to his toes.
*(Wiggle rabbit ears, then toes.)*

*Susan M. Paprocki*

## The Rabbit

Can you make a rabbit

With two ears so very long?
*(Hold up two fingers of one hand for rabbit.)*

And let him hop and hop about

On legs so small and strong?
*(Hop hand up and down.)*

He nibbles, nibbles carrots

For his dinner every day.
*(Nibble with thumb and pointer finger.)*

As soon as he has had enough,

He scampers far away.
*(Hop hand behind back.)*

*Author Unknown*

## Little Rabbit

Here's a little rabbit head,

So soft and round to see.
*(Form circle with arms.)*

And here's a rabbit body,

As fluffy as can be.
*(Fan arms at sides.)*

Here are hoppy legs and feet

For jumping all around.
*(Hop while holding up hands like paws.)*

And here are big long rabbit ears

For hearing every sound.
*(Hold hands at sides of head and wiggle them.)*

*Barbara Paxson*

## Little Rabbits

Watch the little rabbits

Peeking through the grass.
*(Peek through fingers.)*

When they see me,

They duck down fast!
*(Crouch down to floor.)*

*Polly Reedy*

## Here Is a Bunny

Here is a bunny with ears so funny,
*(Hold up two fingers of right hand.)*

And here is his hole in the ground.
*(Form circle with left hand.)*

When a noise he hears, he pricks up his ears,
*(Extend first two fingers.)*

And hops in his hole in the ground.
*(Hop fingers into left-hand circle.)*

*Adapted Traditional*

## Raccoon, Raccoon

Raccoon, raccoon,

High up in the tree,

You wear a mask,

But you can't fool me.
*(Form circles around eyes with fingers.)*

I know who you are,

Hiding in that tree!

*Bonnie Woodard*

## A Little Skunk

There is an animal

We know well.

It's black and white

With quite a smell!
*(Hold nose.)*

It's all furry

With a bushy tail.

It's a little skunk,

Could you tell?
*(Tilt head to one side.)*

*Judy Hall*

## Don't Scare a Skunk

If you see a skunk,
*(Cup hand above eye.)*

Take it from me,
*(Point to self.)*

Be sure not to scare him,
*(Shake head.)*

Or sorry you'll be!
*(Hold nose.)*

*Betty Silkunas*

## Five Furry Squirrels

One furry squirrel dashes by,
*(Move one finger through air.)*
Two furry squirrels are way up high.
*(Raise two fingers above head.)*

Three furry squirrels some nuts do hide,
*(Creep three fingers under opposite hand.)*
Four furry squirrels all play outside.
*(Wiggle four fingers around.)*

Five furry squirrels chase round and round,
*(Move five fingers in circle.)*
Scattering acorns on the ground.
*(Flick fingers.)*

*Lois E. Putnam*

## A Little Squirrel

I saw a little squirrel,

A-picking up acorns.
*(Open and close thumb and index finger.)*
I saw a little squirrel,

She ran up a tree.
*(Run fingers up arm.)*
She ran up and ran down,

She ran up and ran down.
*(Run fingers up and down arm.)*
A busy little squirrel,

As busy as could be.
*(Run fingers in circle.)*

*Becky Valenick*

## The Squirrel

These are the brown leaves fluttering down,
*(Flutter fingers downward.)*
And this is the tall tree, bare and brown.
*(Hold up left arm.)*
This is the squirrel with eyes so bright,
*(Hold up right fist.)*
Hunting for nuts with all his might.
*(Move fist in circle.)*

This is the hole where day by day,
*(Form circle with left hand.)*
Nut after nut he stores away.
*(Poke right pointer finger into left-hand hole.)*
When winter comes with its cold and storm,
*(Wave hands back and forth.)*
He'll sleep curled up, all snug and warm.
*(Cover right fist with left hand.)*

*Adapted Traditional*

## Little Turtle

Little turtle in your shell,

Slowly you do go.
> *(Cover right hand with left hand.)*

Slowly creeping, slowly crawling,

Slow is nice, you know!
> *(Creep hands along slowly.)*

*Betty Silkunas*

## Here Is My Turtle

Here is my turtle,
> *(Form fist and extend thumb.)*

He lives in a shell.
> *(Put thumb inside fist.)*

He likes his home

Very well.
> *(Nod head.)*

He pokes his head out
> *(Pop out thumb.)*

When he wants to eat.
> *(Circle thumb around.)*

And pulls it back in

When he wants to sleep.
> *(Put thumb back inside fist.)*

*Adapted Traditional*

## The Turtle

The turtle wears a shell on her back,

She walks so very slow.
> *(Walk hand slowly.)*

But put her in the water and watch—

She can really go!
> *(Swim hand quickly.)*

*Judy Hall*

## Snapping Turtle

He snaps in the morning,
> *(Snap with hand.)*

He snaps at night.

He snaps at the bugs

As he takes each bite.

He snaps so much,

He's quite a sight.

Snap! Snap! Snap!

*Jean Warren*

## Coral

In the tropical ocean
You'll find coral growing,
Building their homes
Without ever slowing.
    *(Wiggle fingers up and outward.)*

They live together
And grow so tall,
They form a reef
That's like a wall.
    *(Stretch hands high, then wide.)*

*Gayle Bittinger*

## A Crab

Along the beach, by the sea,
Search as you walk by.
    *(Cup hand above eye.)*
If you look quite carefully,
A crab you'll surely spy.
    *(Move hands like crab claws.)*

*Susan Peters*

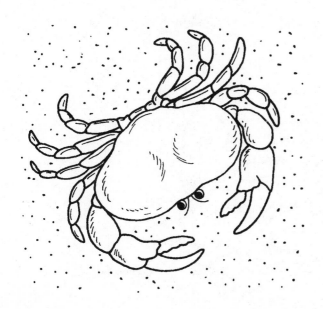

## Five Little Crabs

One little crab, lonely and blue,
    *(Hold up one finger.)*
It met another crab, then there were two.
    *(Hold up two fingers.)*
Two little crabs living near the sea,
Out crawled another, then there were three.
    *(Hold up three fingers.)*
Three little crabs went off to explore,
They soon found another, then there were four.
    *(Hold up four fingers.)*
Four little crabs, glad to be alive,
They found a new friend, then there were five.
    *(Hold up five fingers.)*
Five little crabs went for a walk,
And all at once they spied a rock.
    *(Walk five fingers up to opposite hand.)*
Now five little crabs are happy as can be,
Underneath the rock by the deep blue sea.
    *(Creep fingers under hand.)*

*Marie Wheeler*

## Little Orange Crabs

We're little orange crabs
Who live down by the sea,
And wherever we go
We're quick as quick can be.
    *(Open and close hands like claws.)*

We're little orange crabs
Who like to run and hide,
And when you see us walking by
It's always side to side.
    *(Walk hands along sideways.)*

*Jean Warren*

## I'm a Little Fishy

I'm a little fishy, I can swim,

Here is my tail, are my fins.
*(Swim hand in air.)*

When I want to have fun with my friends,

I wiggle my tail and dive right in!
*(Wiggle hand, then dive it downward.)*

*Lynn Beaird*

## Five Little Fish

Five little fish swimming by the shore,
*(Hold up five fingers.)*

One got caught and then there were four.
*(Bend down thumb.)*

Four little fish swimming in the sea,

One got caught and then there were three.
*(Bend down pointer finger.)*

Three little fish swimming in the blue,

One got caught and then there were two.
*(Bend down middle finger.)*

Two little fish swimming in the sun,

One got caught and then there was one.
*(Bend down ring finger.)*

One little fish swimming for home,

Decided it was best to never roam.
*(Bend down little finger.)*

*Jean Warren*

## Like a Fish

I hold my fingers like a fish,
*(Place one hand on top of the other.)*

And I wave them as I go.
*(Wave hands up and down.)*

See them swimming with a swish,
*(Swim and flip hands in air.)*

So swiftly to and fro.
*(Swim hands back and forth.)*

*Adapted Traditional*

## The Jellyfish

The jellyfish lives in the ocean,

The jellyfish lives in the sea.

The jelly fish looks so transparent,

Please, jellyfish, just swim past me!

*Susan Peters*

## The Lobster's Claws

The lobster opens its big claws
*(Open and close fingers.)*

Then closes them tight in a bunch.

The lobster opens its big claws

And tries to catch its lunch.

*Susan A. Miller*

## Little Lobster

She has two claws in the front,
  *(Do actions as rhyme indicates.)*
They help her to eat.
She crawls along the ocean floor
With her many feet.

Little lobster crawls around,
Digging in the sand.
Opening her claws so wide
And catching all she can.

*Judy Hall*

## Once I Saw an Octopus

Once I saw an octopus
In the deep blue sea.
  *(Point downward.)*
I called, "Mr. Octopus,
Won't you swim with me?"
  *(Cup hands around mouth.)*

Then out came his tentacles,
So very long and straight,
  *(Extend eight fingers.)*
One and two and three and four,
Five and six and seven and eight.
  *(Count on fingers.)*

*Sue Schliecker*

## Eight Arms

Once I saw an octopus,
Deep down in the sea.
  *(Clasp hands together with thumbs inside.)*
Out came her eight tentacles
To play and swim with me.
  *(Extend and wiggle eight fingers.)*

*Sue Schliecker*

## Inside an Oyster's Shell

Inside an oyster's pretty shell
And tucked away from sight,
  *(Form closed shell with hands.)*
You might be lucky enough to find
A pearl that's big and white!
  *(Open hands and look surprised.)*

*Judy Hall*

## A Little Shark

Down in the ocean,
Miles from the shore,
There lives a little shark,
Swimming near the floor.
  *(Swim right hand around near floor.)*

When his friends see the shark,
They all come and play,
Down in the ocean,
Far, far away.
  *(Swim fingers of left hand up to right hand.)*

*Judy Slenker*

## I Am a Sea Star

I am a sea star, not a fish.

I'll tell you the difference, if you wish.

Fish have fins and swim in schools,

While I have feet to wade in tide pools.

Yes, indeed, sea star's my name.

Ask me again, and I'll tell you the same.

Fish can swim and splash all day,

But stuck to a rock I'd rather stay.

*John M. Bittinger*

## Five Little Sea Stars

One little sea star so bright and blue,
 *(Hold up one finger.)*
Along came another, then there were two.
 *(Hold up two fingers.)*
Two little sea stars, all that I could see,

Along came another, then there were three.
 *(Hold up three fingers.)*
Three little sea stars on the ocean floor,

Along came another, then there were four.
 *(Hold up four fingers.)*
Four little sea stars, as sure as I'm alive,

Along came another, then there were five.
 *(Hold up five fingers.)*

*Ione Sautner*

## Big Gray Whale

I swim in the ocean,

I swim in the sea.

I'm a big gray whale,

Come and watch me.
 *(Cup hands above eyes.)*

I love to spray water

Up through my spout.

If you get any closer,

You'd better watch out!
 *(Thrust arms up and make whooshing sound.)*

*Jean Warren*

## Five Big Whales

Five big whales in the sea offshore,
 *(Hold up five fingers.)*
One swam up to spout, and that left four.
 *(Bend down thumb.)*
Four big whales in the deep blue sea,

One swam up to spout, and that left three.
 *((Bend down pointer finger.)*
Three big whales in the sea so blue,

One swam up to spout, and that left two.
 *(Bend down middle finger.)*
Two big whales having lots of fun,

One swam up to spout, and that left one.
 *(Bend down ring finger.)*
One big whale longing for the sun,

It swam up to spout, and that left none.
 *(Bend down little finger.)*

*Elizabeth McKinnon*

## Whales

Whales are very big,
(*Stretch arms out at sides.*)
They live under the sea,
(*Duck down while holding nose.*)
Swimming happily round and round
(*Make swimming movements.*)
With friends and family.
(*Hug self.*)

*Laurie W. Mason*

## I'm a Great Big Whale

I'm a great big whale,
Watch me as I swim.
(*Pretend to swim.*)
Here is my blowhole,
(*Point to top of head.*)
Here are my fins.
(*Wave hands against body.*)
See me flip my tail
As down I go,
(*Pretend to dive.*)
Then up I come
And "Whoosh!" I blow.
(*Thrust arms up and out.*)

*Elizabeth McKinnon*

## The Ocean Below

Down in the ocean,
(*Pretend to swim underwater.*)
The ocean below,
That's where the sharks live
And where they all grow.
You will see whales
And white oysters too.
There's a world underwater
Just waiting for you!

*Judy Hall*

## So Far Below

Down in the ocean, so far below,
(*Cup hands around eyes and look downward.*)
Live many animals that we know.
Fish and crabs and oysters too,
I see them all in the ocean blue.

Oh, oh, watch them go,
(*While looking down, move head back and forth.*)
Some are fast and some are slow.
Down in the ocean, so far below,
Live many animals that we know.

*Pat Beck*

## Deep Down in the Ocean

Deep down in the ocean
Live creatures of every size.
Whales, fish, crabs, and oysters
Live side by side.

*Pat Beck*

## Alligator, Alligator

Alligator, alligator,

Long and green,
*(Form alligator with four fingers and thumb.)*

Alligator, alligator,

Teeth so mean.
*(Open and close fingers and thumb.)*

Snapping at a fly,

Snapping at a bee,
*(Snap with fingers and thumb.)*

Snapping at a frog,

But you can't catch me!
*(Continue snapping, then shake head.)*

*Jean Warren*

## The Elephant

Big and slow, hear him go,
*(Stomp around slowly.)*

He makes a sound like thunder.

See his trunk? He's an elephant.
*(Hold arms together and swing them like a trunk.)*

How big is he, I wonder?

*Cynthia Walters*

## Five Little Elephants

Five little elephants rowing toward the shore,
*(Hold up five fingers.)*

One fell in the water, and that left four.
*(Bend down thumb.)*

Four little elephants climbing up a tree,

One slid down the trunk, and that left three.
*(Bend down pointer finger.)*

Three little elephants living in the zoo,

One walked out the gate, and that left two.
*(Bend down middle finger.)*

Two little elephants having lots of fun,

One went to take a bath, and that left one.
*(Bend down ring finger.)*

One little elephant sitting in the sun,

She fell sound asleep, and that left none.
*(Bend down little finger.)*

*Adapted Traditional*

## What a Nose!

Elephants are tall and fat,
*(Stretch arms up, then out.)*
They stomp around this way and that.
*(Stomp back and forth.)*
Elephants have big ears and toes,
*(Point to ears, then toes.)*
And goodness, gracious, what a nose!
*(Hold arms together and swing them like a trunk.)*

*Becky Valenick*

## I'm a Big Giraffe

I'm a big giraffe stretching way up high,
*(Do actions as rhyme indicates.)*
A big, tall giraffe, I almost reach the sky.

I eat the leaves from the tallest trees,

And when I run, I can move with ease.

I'm a big giraffe stretching way up high.

Way ... up ... high!

*Judy Hall*

## I Know a Giraffe

I know a giraffe

With a neck that's so high,

She stretches and stretches it

Up to the sky.
*(Stretch head high.)*

She lives on the plains

With her family too,

But you also might see her

When you visit the zoo.
*(Point to others.)*

*Judy Hall*

## Hippo

Here is an animal that we know,

H-I-P-P-O.
*(Extend arms, one on top of the other, to form hippo mouth.)*

She eats a lot of vegetables,

And chews them just like so.
*(Open and close arms.)*

She's very big, her skin is gray,

She swims around in the water all day.
*(Make large swimming movements.)*

She is an animal that we know,

H-I-P-P-O.

*Debra Lindahl*

## I'm a Kangaroo

Oh, I'm a kangaroo,
  *(Jump around rhythmically.)*
I live down at the zoo.
I carry a baby in my pouch,
  *(Place hands on tummy.)*
How about you?

*Jean Warren*

## Kangaroo

Jump, jump, jump,
Goes the big kangaroo.
  *(Hop right fist up and down.)*
I thought there was one,
But I see there are two
  *(Hold up one finger, then two.)*

The mother takes her baby
Along in a pouch,
  *(Slip left thumb into right fist.)*
Where he can nap
Like a baby on a couch.
  *(Rest cheek on folded hands.)*

*Adapted Traditional*

## Kangaroo, Kangaroo

Kangaroo, kangaroo,
  *(Hop hand around.)*
How you love to hop.
Going this way, going that,
Don't you ever stop?

*Susan M. Paprocki*

## I Am a Koala

I am a koala,
Yes, it's true.
I am not a bear,
Did I fool you?
  *(Tilt head to one side.)*

One of my cousins
Is the kangaroo.
I carry my baby
In a pouch too.
  *(Place hands on tummy.)*

*Gayle Bittinger*

## I'm a Lion

I love to sleep out in the sun,
  *(Rest cheek on folded hands.)*
And chase other animals just for fun.
  *(Run in place.)*
In all the jungle, I'm Number One.
  *(Hold up pointer finger.)*
I'm a lion!
  *(Make roaring sound.)*

*Jean Warren*

## I'm a Little Monkey

I'm a little monkey, watch me play,
*(Hop around near floor.)*
Munching on bananas every day.
*(Pretend to eat banana.)*
I have monkey friends who play with me,
*(Point to others.)*
See us climb right up the tree.
*(Make climbing movements.)*

*Carla Cotter Skjong*

## Monkey See, Monkey Do

Monkey, monkey in the tree,
Can you jump around like me?
*(Jump around.)*
Monkey see, monkey do,
Little monkey in the zoo.

Monkey, monkey in the tree,
Can you swing your tail like me?
*(Swing arm back and forth behind back.)*
Monkey see, monkey do,
Little monkey at the zoo.

*Jean Warren*

## Little Monkeys

Little monkeys swinging in the tree,
*(Join hands with others and swing arms up and down.)*
All hold hands and swing with me.
Swing up high and swing down low,
Swing in the tree, now don't let go!
Swing, swing, like I do,
Swing like monkeys in the zoo.

*Jean Warren*

## Six Little Penguins

Six little penguins off an iceberg did dive,
*(Hold up six fingers.)*
One bumped his head, then there were five.
*(Hold up five fingers of one hand.)*
Five little penguins swam the ocean floor,
One saw a whale, then there were four.
*(Bend down thumb.)*
Four little penguins twirled around, wheee!
One spun off, then there were three.
*(Bend down pointer finger.)*
Three little penguins with nothing to do,
One went fishing, then there were two.
*(Bend down middle finger.)*
Two little penguins having lots of fun,
One slid away, then there was one.
*(Bend down ring finger.)*
One little penguin, when day was done,
Went home to sleep, then there were none.
*(Bend down little finger.)*

*Nancy J. Smith*

## Waddling Penguins

Penguins, penguins having fun,
*(Waddle around like a penguin.)*
Waddling in the winter sun.

Waddling fast and waddling slow

Waddling to and waddling fro.

Penguins, penguins having fun,

Waddling in the winter sun.

*Bonnie Woodard*


## The Penguin

The penguin wears a black-and-white suit

And waddles around on the snow.
*(Waddle.)*
She swims in water as cold as ice

And lives where freezing winds blow.
*(Hug self and shiver.)*

*Sue Brown*


## The Polar Bear

The polar bear lives where it snows,
*(Flutter fingers downward.)*
He never gets cold in a storm.
*(Shake head.)*
When he swims in the icy cold water,
*(Make swimming movements.)*
His heavy white coat keeps him warm.
*(Hug self.)*

*Marie Wheeler*


## I'm a Little Seal

I'm a little seal,

I'm lucky, I suppose.

I can catch a big round ball

Upon my little nose!
*(Pretend to balance ball on nose.)*

*Sue Brown*


## Snakes

Snakes slither on the ground,

Snakes slither all around.
*(Make slithering motion with hand.)*
Some are short, some are long,
*(Hold hands close together, then far apart.)*
Some have fangs, some have none.
*(Point to eye-teeth, then shake head.)*

*Carla Cotter Skjong*

## The Tiger

Orange and black,

Great big cat.

Four big paws,

Long sharp claws.

Through the jungle running,

Do you see her coming?

What a sight!

Will she bite?

*Cynthia Walters*

## I'm a Little Zebra

I'm a little zebra,

White and black,

With a bushy mane

Running down my back.
   *(Run hand down back of head and shoulders.)*

I like to gallop

And run and play

Out on the grassy plains

All day.
   *(Gallop around.)*

*Jean Warren*

## Zebra Black, Zebra White

Zebra black, zebra white,

Stripes from head to toe.

What a special kind of horse

For everyone to know!

*Betty Silkunas*

## Zoo Fun

As we go walking through the zoo,
  *(Make appropriate movements for each
    named animal.)*
This is what we'll see,
Elephants and hippos,
And monkeys in a tree.

Tigers roaring loudly,
Giraffes who stand so high,
Dolphins swimming freely,
And parrots in the sky.

So let's all go walking,
Having fun the whole day through,
As we go on our field trip
To the friendly city zoo!

*Beverly Qualheim*

## Going to the Zoo

If you're going to the zoo,
  *(Make appropriate sounds for each named animal.)*
Think about who will greet you.
Monkeys, bears, and elephants
Will all be there to meet you.
Then you'll see the king of all,
Lion is his name.
I'm sure the many animals
Will all be glad you came!

*Judy Hall*

## Zoo Train

Boarding the train,
Next to the zoo,
On came an animal,
Do you know who?
  *(Walk in circle.)*

We picked up a kangaroo,
And what do you know,
This is the way
The train started to go.
  *(Start to hop.)*

Hopping, hopping, watch us go,
Hopping fast, hopping slow.
Hopping down, hopping back
All around the zoo-train track.
  *(Hop around circle.)*

Repeat, each time naming a different zoo
animal and appropriate movement.

*Jean Warren*

## Two Little Blackbirds

Two little blackbirds

Sitting on a hill.
> *(Hold up both pointer fingers.)*

One named Jack,
> *(Wiggle one finger.)*

One named Jill.
> *(Wiggle other finger.)*

Fly away, Jack,
> *(Hide first finger behind back.)*

Fly away, Jill.
> *(Hide second finger behind back.)*

Come back, Jack,
> *(Return first finger to front.)*

Come back, Jill.
> *(Return other finger to front.)*

*Adapted Traditional*

## Little Bluebird

Little bluebird,
> *(Do actions as rhyme indicates.)*

Fly around—

Up to the sky,

Down to the ground.

Little bluebird,

Flap your wings.

Open your beak

And sweetly sing.

Little bluebird,

Fly to your nest.

Now it is time

To take a rest.

*Susan M. Paprocki*

## Five Big Crows

Five big crows sitting by the door,
> *(Hold up five fingers.)*

One flew away, then there were four.
> *(Bend down thumb.)*

Four big crows cawing in the tree,

One flew away, then there were three.
> *(Bend down pointer finger.)*

Three big crows wanting pastures new,

One flew away, then there were two.
> *(Bend down middle finger.)*

Two big crows having lots of fun,

One flew away, then there was one.
> *(Bend down ring finger.)*

One big crow feeling lonesome for her son,

She flew away, then there were none.
> *(Bend down little finger.)*

*Adapted Traditional*

## Three Geese in a Flock

Blar, lar, limberlock,

Three geese in a flock.
> *(Hold up three fingers.)*

One flew east, one flew west,
> *(Gesture right, then left.)*

And one flew over the cuckoo's nest.
> *(Fly right hand over left fist.)*

*Author Unknown*

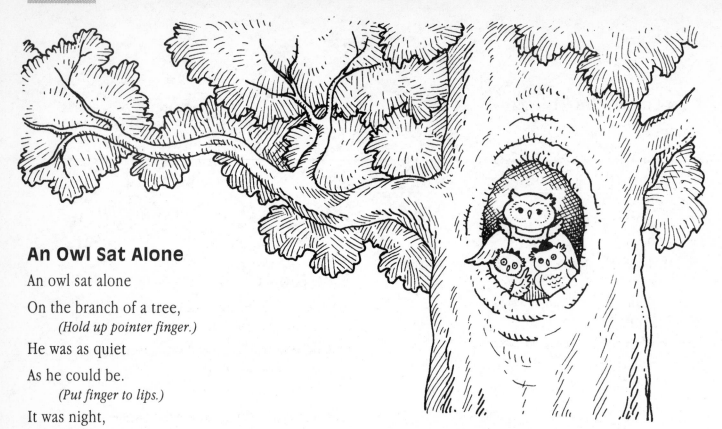

## An Owl Sat Alone

An owl sat alone

On the branch of a tree,
> *(Hold up pointer finger.)*

He was as quiet

As he could be.
> *(Put finger to lips.)*

It was night,

And his eyes were round like this.
> *(Circle eyes with thumbs and fingers.)*

And when he looked around,

Not a thing did he miss.
> *(Move head from side to side.)*

*Adapted Traditional*

## Little Owl

Little owl in the tree,

He is winking down at me.
> *(Wink eye.)*

As he winks all through the night,

Little owl is quite a sight!


Little owl in the tree,

He is hooting down at me.
> *(Make hooting sound.)*

As he hoots all through the night,

Little owl is quite a sight!

*Jean Warren*

## Little Night Owl

Once there was a night owl

Who lived up in a tree.

She could often spot things

That others couldn't see.

Little night owl, answer me,

What do you see

As you sit alone at night

Up in the tree?

*Jean Warren*

## Wise Old Owl

Wise old owl

In the tree,

Whoo-oo are you winking at?
> *(Wink eye.)*

Is it me?

*Jean Warren*

## I Am a Peacock

I am a peacock

With feathers bright and gay,

I strut around and spread my tail.
>    *(Strut.)*

I'm beautiful all day.

*Carla Cotter Skjong*


## Little Quail

Little quail, little quail,

Feathered head, feathered tail.

I like to watch you strutting by,
>    *(Strut.)*

Or flapping as you start to fly.
>    *(Fan arms at sides.)*

Little quail, little quail,

Feathered head, feathered tail.

*Jean Warren*


## Mother Quail

Out in the forest

Early in the morning,
>    *(Gesture to one side.)*

See the little mother quail

Walking to and fro.
>    *(Hold up right thumb for mother quail.)*

See her little babies

Get in line behind her.
>    *(Hold up other four fingers.)*

Peep, peep, peep, peep,

Off they go.
>    *(Holding fingers up, move hand to the left.)*

*Elizabeth McKinnon*


## Little Robin Redbreast

Little robin redbreast

Comes to our town,
>    *(Fly hand through air.)*

She flies to the treetops,

Then to the ground.
>    *(Fly hand up, then down.)*

She goes away in winter,
>    *(Hide hand behind back.)*

She comes back in spring.
>    *(Return hand to front.)*

"Chirp, chirp, chirp,"

Is the song she sings.
>    *(Fly hand around while making chirping sound.)*

*Sue Schliecker*

## Come Watch the Robin

Come watch the robin,
   *(Do actions as rhyme indicates.)*
With a red breast,
Working so hard
To build a new nest.

Come watch the eggs
Deep in the nest
Starting to open,
Each with a guest.

Come watch the babies
Filling the nest,
Crying for food.
Poor robin—no rest!

Come watch the babies
Perched on the nest,
Giving their wings
A last-minute test.

Come watch the babies
Fly from the nest,
Each strong and healthy,
Each with a quest.

Come watch the robin,
Alone in its nest,
Feathers all puffed up,
Singing its best.

*Jean Warren*

## Five Little Robins

Five little robins waiting for spring.
   *(Hold up five fingers.)*
The first little robin started to sing,
   *(Point to thumb.)*
The second little robin flapped its wings.
   *(Point to index finger.)*
The third little robin said "Tweet tweet, tweet,"
   *(Point to middle finger.)*
The fourth little robin sang so sweet.
   *(Point to ring finger.)*
The fifth little robin said, "It's a beautiful day,"
   *(Point to little finger.)*
Then all five robins flew away.
   *(Fly hand behind back.)*

*Allyson G. Baernstein*

## When a Robin Cocks Her Head

When a robin cocks her head

Sideways in a flower bed,
*(Tilt head to one side.)*

She can hear the tiny sound

Of a worm beneath the ground.
*(Make crawling movements with finger.)*

*Adapted Traditional*


## Little Sea Gulls

Down at the seaside

Early in the morning,
*(Gesture to one side.)*

See the little sea gulls

Sitting in a row,
*(Hold up fingers of left hand.)*

Waiting for a fish

To jump out of the water.
*(Jump up pointer finger of right hand.)*

Gulp, gulp, yum, yum,

Down it goes!
*(Grasp pointer finger with fingers of left hand.)*

*Pat Beck*


## Woodpecker, Woodpecker

Wood-peck-er, wood-peck-er,
*(Tap out rhythm with rhythm sticks.)*

Tap, tap, tap, tap, tap.

Wood-peck-er, wood-peck-er,

Don't you ever nap?


Wood-peck-er, wood-peck-er,

Up high in a tree.

Wood-peck-er, wood-peck-er,

I can tap too. See?


Wood-peck-er, wood-peck-er,

Click, click, click, click, click.

I can tap just like you

With my rhythm sticks.

*Diane Thom*

## Two Young Birds

Way up high
In a big old tree,
Two young birds
Smiled at me.

The first one said,
"Let's fly away."
The second one said,
"I think I'll stay."

So the first flew off
Way up high,
To look for rainbows
In the sky.

The second bird stayed
And built a nest.
She loved the tree,
She thought it best.

Each was happy
In its own way.
One chose to go,
One chose to stay.

We each must choose
Which way to go,
We each must choose
Which way to grow.

So smile at the birds
You happen to see,
Knowing that each
Is happy and free.

*Jean Warren*

## If I Were a Bird

If I were a bird
I'd sing a song
And fly around
The whole day long.
    *(Hook thumbs together and wave hands like wings.)*
And when it was dark
I'd go to rest
Up in my cozy
Little nest.
    *(Cup hands together to form nest.)*

*Adapted Traditional*

## Flying in the Blue

One little bird flying in the blue,
    *(Hold up one finger.)*
Along comes another, now there are two.
    *(Hold up two fingers.)*
Two little birds perched up in a tree,
Along comes another, now there are three.
    *(Hold up three fingers.)*
Three little birds, see them swoop and soar,
Along comes another, now there are four.
    *(Hold up four fingers.)*
Four little birds, through the skies they dive,
Along comes another, now there are five.
    *(Hold up five fingers.)*

*Diane Thom*

## Little Birds

Out in the garden

On a winter morning,
*(Gesture to one side.)*

See the little birds

Playing in the snow.
*(Hop hands around.)*

See them eat the crumbs

We put out for their breakfast.
*(Make pecking movements with hands.)*

Peck, peck, tweet, tweet,

Off they go.
*(Fly hands behind back.)*

*Elizabeth McKinnon*


## Once I Saw a Little Bird

Once I saw a little bird

Go hop, hop, hop.
*(Hop hand.)*

And I called, "Little Bird,

Will you stop, stop, stop?"
*(Cup hands around mouth.)*

I was opening the window

To say "How do you do,"
*(Make opening movement with hands.)*

But he shook his little tail

And far away he flew.
*(Fly hand away.)*

*Adapted Traditional*


## Building Nests

The birds are building nests today
*(Move hand in circle.)*

With twigs, grass, mud, and string.
*(Open and close thumb and index finger.)*

The birds are building nests today,
*(Move hand in circle.)*

They're using everything!
*(Hold hands out, palms up.)*

*Dorothy Samorajski*


## Little Birds Without Any Home

Five little birds without any home,
*(Hold up fingers of left hand.)*

And five little trees in a row.
*(Hold up fingers of right hand.)*

Come build your nests in our branches tall.
*(Interlace fingers of both hands to form nest.)*

We'll rock you to and fro.
*(Sway hands back and forth.)*

*Adapted Traditional*

## Two Birds on a Wire

Two tall telephone poles,
*(Hold up both pointer fingers.)*

Between them a wire is strung.
*(Form wire by placing thumb tips together.)*

Two little birds hopped on the wire,
*(Lower tips of middle fingers to thumbs.)*

And swung and swung and swung.
*(With fingers in position, swing hands back and forth.)*

*Adapted Traditional*

## Color Birds

Yellow bird, yellow bird,

High in a tree,

How many yellow things

Can you see?
*(Name yellow objects.)*

Blue bird, blue bird,

High in a tree,

How many blue things

Can you see?
*(Name blue objects.)*

Red bird, red bird,

High in a tree,

How many red things

Can you see?
*(Name red objects.)*

*Jean Warren*

## Five Little Birds

Five little birds peeping at the door,
*(Hold up five fingers.)*

One flew away, and that left four.
*(Bend down thumb.)*

Four little birds sitting on a tree,

One flew away, and that left three.
*(Bend down pointer finger.)*

Three little birds looking at you,

One flew away, and that left two.
*(Bend down middle finger.)*

Two little birds sitting in the sun,

One flew away, and that left one.
*(Bend down ring finger.)*

One little bird left all alone,

It flew away, and that left none.
*(Bend down little finger.)*

*Adapted Traditional*

## The Beehive

Here is the beehive,
*(Make a fist.)*
Where are the bees?
*(Tilt head to one side.)*
Hidden inside where nobody sees.

Here they come buzzing out of the hive,
*(Slowly begin to open fist.)*
One, two, three, four, and five!
*(Raise fingers one at a time.)*

*Adapted Traditional*

## Bumblebee

I'm a little bumblebee, watch me go,
*(Place index finger on arm, then fly it upward.)*
Buzz, buzz, buzz, buzz, to and fro.
*(Fly finger back and forth.)*
When I find a flower blooming nearby,
*(Fly finger down into cupped hand.)*
I drink its nectar, then away I fly.
*(Fly finger up and away.)*

*Sally Braun*

## Bumblebee, Bumblebee

Bumblebee, bumblebee,
*(Using finger for bee, do actions as indicated.)*
Landing on my toes.

Bumblebee, bumblebee,

Now he's on my nose.

On my arm, on my leg,

Now on my elbow.

Bumblebee, oh, bumblebee,

You land and then you go!

*Jean Warren*

## Six Buzzing Bumblebees

Six buzzing bumblebees flying round the hive,
*(Hold up six fingers.)*
One buzzes off, and that leaves five.
*(Hold up five fingers of one hand.)*
Five buzzing bumblebees flying near my door,

One buzzes off, and that leaves four.
*(Bend down thumb.)*
Four buzzing bumblebees flying round a tree,

One buzzes off, and that leaves three.
*(Bend down pointer finger.)*
Three buzzing bumblebees in the sky so blue,

One buzzes off, and that leaves two.
*(Bend down middle finger.)*
Two buzzing bumblebees flying by the sun,

One buzzes off, and that leaves one.
*(Bend down ring finger.)*
One buzzing bumblebee looking for some fun,

It buzzes off, and that leaves none.
*(Bend down little finger.)*

*Susan M. Paprocki*

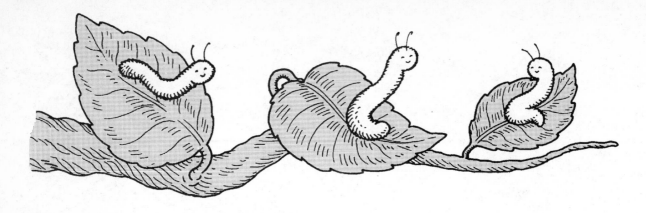

## Caterpillar

Caterpillar creeping,
> *(Do actions as rhyme indicates.)*

Caterpillar crawl.

Caterpillar climbing

All along the wall.

Caterpillar spinning,

Caterpillar snug.

Caterpillar changing,

What have you become?
> *(Say, "A butterfly!" and pretend to fly around room.)*

*Beverly Qualheim*

## The Fuzzy Little Caterpillar

The fuzzy little caterpillar

Curled up on a leaf,
> *(Make self small.)*

Spun her little chrysalis

And then fell fast asleep.
> *(Rest cheek on folded hands.)*

While she was sleeping,

She dreamed that she could fly,
> *(Smile.)*

And later when she woke up,

She was a butterfly!
> *(Pretend to fly around room.)*

*Elizabeth McKinnon*

## Fuzzy Wuzzy Caterpillar

Fuzzy wuzzy caterpillar

Into a corner will creep,
> *(Creep hand.)*

She'll spin herself a blanket

And then go fast asleep.
> *(Close eyes.)*

Fuzzy wuzzy caterpillar

Will wake up by and by,
> *(Open eyes.)*

To find that she has grown two wings,

Now she's a butterfly!
> *(Wave arms at sides.)*

*Adapted Traditional*

## Pretty Butterfly

Here comes a butterfly and lays an egg,
> *(Fly fingers onto opposite palm.)*

Out comes a caterpillar with many legs.
> *(Crawl fingers on palm.)*

Now see the caterpillar spin and spin
> *(Circle fingers on palm.)*

A little chrysalis to sleep in.
> *(Close fingers and rest hand on palm.)*

Then from the chrysalis, my oh my,
> *(Open fingers slowly.)*

Out comes a beautiful butterfly!
> *(Fly fingers away.)*

*Stella Waldron*

## Flutter, Flutter, Butterfly

Flutter, flutter, butterfly,
  *(Wave arms at sides and float like butterfly.)*
Floating in the summer sky.

Floating by for all to see,

Floating by so merrily.

Flutter, flutter, butterfly,

Floating in the summer sky.

*Bonnie Woodard*

## Butterfly, Butterfly

Butterfly, butterfly,

Dancing all around.
  *(Fly fingers up and down.)*
Butterfly, butterfly,

Now you're on the ground.
  *(Lower fingers to opposite palm.)*
In a tree, hard to see,

Now you've flown away.
  *(Fly fingers up, then behind back.)*
Butterfly, oh, butterfly,

Please come back some day.
  *(Fly fingers to front.)*

*Gee Gee Drysdale*

## Color Butterflies

The first to come to the garden bed
Is a lovely butterfly of brilliant red.

Then in comes another and that makes two,
Fly right in, my friend of blue.

"The garden is fine, the best I've seen,"
Says the butterfly of springtime green.

Our garden needs a sunshiny fellow,
Fly in, butterfly with wings of yellow.

Little friend of purple, fly in too,
This garden is waiting for a color like you.

Orange, orange, you've waited so long,
Fly right in where you belong.

Butterflies, butterflies, you're such a sight,
Flying together—a springtime delight!

*Susan M. Paprocki*

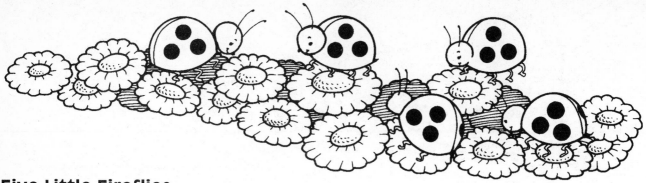

## Five Little Fireflies

One little firefly shines very bright,
> *(Hold up one finger.)*

Poppity-pop-pop, on-off goes its light.

Two little fireflies suddenly spark,
> *(Hold up two fingers.)*

Poppity-pop-pop, they glow in the dark.

Three little fireflies flicker and fly,
> *(Hold up three fingers.)*

Poppity-pop-pop, oh, watch them pass by.

Four little fireflies glimmer and glow,
> *(Hold up four fingers.)*

Poppity-pop-pop, just look at them go.

Five little fireflies blink in the night,
> *(Hold up five fingers.)*

Poppity-pop-pop, my, what a sight!

*Lois E. Putnam*

## I'm a Little Ladybug

I'm a little ladybug on the go,
> *(Fly finger around.)*

Landing on an arm, then an elbow.
> *(Touch arm, then elbow with finger.)*

See me fly around and around your hand,
> *(Circle hand with finger.)*

Then watch as on your thumb I land.
> *(Rest finger on thumb.)*

*Susan M. Paprocki*

## Five Little Ladybugs

Five little ladybugs sitting in a tree,
> *(Hold up five fingers.)*

The first one said, "I'm glad I'm me."
> *(Wiggle thumb.)*

The second one said, "I feel great too,"
> *(Wiggle pointer finger.)*

The third one said, "How about you?"
> *(Wiggle middle finger.)*

The fourth one said, "It's time to fly away,"
> *(Wiggle ring finger.)*

The fifth one said, "We'll talk another day."
> *(Wiggle little finger.)*

*Rita Galloway*

## Little Spider

See the little spider

Climbing up the wall,
> *(Crawl fingers up opposite arm.)*

See the little spider

Stumble and fall.
> *(Drop fingers quickly down arm.)*

See the little spider

Tumble down the street,
> *(Jump fingers down leg.)*

See the little spider

Stop down at my feet.
> *(Rest fingers on foot.)*

*Author Unknown*

## The Teeny Tiny Spider

The teeny tiny spider
> *(Crawl fingers for spider as rhyme indicates.)*

Began to crawl on me.

I found him on my leg,

To be exact, my knee.


The teeny tiny spider

Crawled up onto my chest.

This was such a long trip,

He took a little rest.


The teeny tiny spider

Headed for my arm.

It tickled quite a bit,

But I knew he meant no harm.


The teeny tiny spider

Crawled up on my finger.

He landed on my thumb,

But he didn't want to linger.


I helped him to my face

And placed him on my nose.

Then he lost his balance

And fell down to my toes.


The teeny tiny spider

Went upon his way.

He'd clearly had enough

Of his crawling for today.


*Susan M. Paprocki*

## I'm a Little Spider

I'm a little spider,
> *(Move hand around in ever smaller circles.)*

Watch me spin,

If you'll be my dinner,

I'll let you come in.

Then I'll spin my web

To hold you tight,

And gobble you up

In one big bite!
> *(Close hand quickly.)*

*Sue Brown*


## The Eeensy Weensy Spider

The eensy weensy spider

Went up the water spout.
> *(Crawl fingers up high.)*

Down came the rain

And washed the spider out.
> *(Drop fingers quickly.)*

Out came the sun

And dried up all the rain.
> *(Form circle with arms.)*

And the eensy weensy spider

Went up the spout again.
> *(Crawl fingers back up high.)*

*Adapted Traditional*

## Little Worm

Slowly, slowly turn around,
  *(Turn around.)*
Right behind you on the ground
  *(Look down.)*
You will see a little worm.
  *(Wiggle finger.)*
Careful now, he'll make you squirm!
  *(Squirm.)*

*Mildred Claus*

## Wiggle Worm

One day while I was playing,

I met a tiny worm.

Instead of going straight,

He squirmed and squirmed and squirmed.
  *(Lie on floor and squirm.)*

Here, now, let me show you

How he got around.

He wiggled, wiggled, wiggled

All across the ground.
  *(Wiggle across floor.)*

*Jean Warren*

## Crawly Bug

See the little crawly bug

Walk across the floor.
  *(Crawl fingers across floor.)*
See the little crawly bug

Walk right up the door.
  *(Crawl fingers up pretend door.)*

See the little crawly bug—

I hope he doesn't fall!—
  *(Stop fingers for a moment.)*
Walk across the ceiling,

Then down the other wall.
  *(Crawl fingers across pretend ceiling, then down wall.)*

See the little crawly bug

Creep out in the sun.
  *(Crawl fingers away.)*
Come again, crawly bug,

Watching you is fun!
  *(Nod head and smile.)*

*Beverly Qualheim*

## A Bug on Me

One, two, three,

There's a bug on me!
  *(Pretend to brush bug off shoulder.)*
Where did it go?
  *(Cup hand above eye and look around.)*
I don't know!

*Adapted Traditional*

## Great Big Dinosaurs

Great big dinosaurs
*(Stomp around.)*
Lived so long ago.
They roamed the earth in search of food,
But now they're gone, you know.

Great big dinosaurs,
Some could even fly.
But now there are no dinosaurs,
I often wonder why.

*Angela Wolfe*

## Dinosaurs

Dinosaurs
Lived long ago.
Some walked,
*(Stomp in place.)*
Some swam,
*(Pretend to swim.)*
Some flew, you know.
*(Flap arms at sides.)*
Some were big,
*(Hold hand high.)*
Some were small.
*(Hold hand low.)*
Some were gigantic—
*(Stretch arms out wide.)*
V-e-r-y tall!
*(Stretch arms up high.)*

*Diane Thom*

## The Dinosaur Who Couldn't Roar

Once there was a dinosaur,
Who tried and tried, but couldn't roar.

He would open up his mouth real wide,
But all he found were giggles inside.

He couldn't be mean, he couldn't be gruff,
He couldn't roar, he couldn't be tough.

"I wish I could roar," the dinosaur said,
Every night as he went off to bed.

And what do you know, one day he could roar,
He roared all day till his throat was sore.

But when he looked, he was all alone,
No one had liked his roaring tone.

Being tough wasn't much fun,
If it meant you were the only one.

So the next time the dinosaur went out to play,
He took his roar and threw it away.

Then he opened up his mouth real wide,
And shared again the giggles inside.

So, if you think you need to roar,
Just remember the dinosaur.

It's better to have a lot of fun,
Than to be the only roaring one.

*Diane Thom and Jean Warren*

## The Spotted Owl

Spotted owl has lost his home
In an old dead tree.
His home has been cleared away
To plant more trees, you see.

It's not that he's so fussy,
Any old tree would do.
It's just that he can't manage
When all the trees are new.

So let's remember the spotted owl,
Old trees, let's leave a few.
Then he'll have a place to live—
It's the least that we can do.

*Jean Warren*

## Let's Protect All Creatures

Let's protect all creatures,
    *(Make appropriate movements for each
    animal named.)*
Whether big or small.
Let's protect the ocean whales,
And tiny worms that crawl.

Let's protect the eagles
That soar across the sky.
Let's protect the pandas,
With black around their eyes.

Let's protect the tigers
That through the jungles crawl.
Let's protect the gorillas,
We need them, one and all.

*Jean Warren*

## It's Up to You

Pandas, rhinos, and elephants,
Whales and gorillas too—
These animals are endangered,
And here's what you can do.

Don't throw litter,
Keep our waters clean.
Value every creature,
Even ones you haven't seen.

Pandas, rhinos, and elephants,
Whales and gorillas too—
These animals are endangered,
Now it's up to you.

Repeat, substituting the names of other
endangered animals for those in the rhyme.

*Jean Warren*

## Let's Share the Earth

Let's share the earth with the animals,
Let's give them all a home.
Let's leave some trees to nest in,
Let's leave some space to roam.

Let's share the earth with the animals,
Let's make a better land.
Let's clean up all our litter,
Let's give the world a hand.

*Jean Warren*

## I See Three

I see three,

One, two, three,
> *(Hold up three fingers.)*

Three little kittens

All wearing mittens.

I see three,

One, two, three,
> *(Bend down three fingers.)*

Three little fishes

Swimming in dishes.

I see three,

One, two, three,
> *(Hold up three fingers.)*

Three little ducks

Riding on trucks.

I see three,

One, two, three,
> *(Bend down three fingers.)*

Three little bears

Going upstairs.

*Adapted Traditional*

## So Many Animals

Birds fly high and bees fly low,
> *(Fly hand up, then down.)*

Caterpillars creep and crawl like so.
> *(Crawl hand.)*

Cats meow and cows go "Moo,"
> *(Meow, then moo.)*

Puppies bark and pigeons coo.
> *(Bark, then coo.)*

So many animals to see and hear,
> *(Pretend to count on fingers.)*

I use my eyes and I use my ears.
> *(Point to eyes, then ears.)*

*Barbara Robinson*

## I Can Be Any Animal

I can hop like a rabbit,
> *(Do actions as rhyme indicates.)*

I can jump like a frog.

I can waddle like a duck,

I can run like a dog.

I can fly like a bird,

I can swim like a fish.

I can be any animal that I wish!

*Adapted Traditional*

## Animal Movements

Worms wiggle, jellyfish jiggle.
> *(Do actions as rhyme indicates.)*

Rabbits hop, horses clop.

Snakes slide, birds glide.

Mice creep, deer leap.

Puppies bounce, kittens pounce.

Lions stalk—but I walk!

*Adapted Traditional*

## Baby Seeds

In their little cradles

Tucked in tight,
*(Cup hands together.)*

Baby seeds are sleeping

Out of sight.
*(Rock hands back and forth.)*

Mr. Wind comes blowing

With all his might.
*(Blow.)*

The baby seeds are scattered

Left and right.
*(Flutter fingers to left, then right.)*

*Adapted Traditional*

## Planting

Plant, plant, plant your seeds,

In a long straight row.
*(Pretend to plant seeds.)*

Attend them well with gentleness

And watch them as they grow.
*(Cup hand above eye.)*

*Shirley M. Harp*

## A Little Seed

A little seed is planted

In the dark, dark ground.
*(Pretend to plant seed inside left fist.)*

Out comes the yellow sun,

Big and round.
*(Form circle with right thumb and finger.)*

Down comes the cool rain,

Soft and slow.
*(Flutter right fingers downward.)*

Up sprouts the little seed,

Grow, grow, grow!
*(Slowly extend pointer finger up from left fist.)*

*Leora Grecian*

## Planting Time

Dig, dig, in the ground,
*(Make digging movements.)*

Then plant seeds in a row.
*(Pretend to plant seeds.)*

A gentle rain
*(Flutter fingers downward.)*

And bright sunshine
*(Form circle with arms.)*

Will help your flowers grow.
*(Extend one arm out at side and move other arm up behind it to represent a growing flower.)*

*Vicki Claybrook*

## Dig a Little Hole

Dig a little hole,
*(Pretend to dig.)*
Plant a little seed.
*(Pretend to drop in seed.)*
Pour a little water,
*(Pretend to pour.)*
Pull a little weed.
*(Pretend to pull up weed.)*

Chase a little bug,
*(Flick hand to one side.)*
Oh! there he goes!
*(Cup hand above eye.)*
Give a little sunshine,
*(Lower spread fingers slowly.)*
Grow a little rose!
*(Pretend to smell sweet flower.)*

*Adapted Traditional*

## Making a Garden

Dig, dig, dig,
*(Do actions as rhyme indicates.)*
Rake just so.

Plant the seeds,

Watch them grow.

Chop, chop, chop,

Pull up weeds.

Sun and rain

My garden needs.

Up, up, up,

Green stems climb.

Open wide,

It's blossom time!

*Adapted Traditional*

## My Garden

This is my garden, I've raked it with care,
*(Do actions as rhyme indicates.)*
And planted my tiny brown flower seeds there.

I patted the earth and smoothed over the bed,

While the warm yellow sun shone high overhead.

Soon raindrops came pattering over the ground,

And warm spring winds blew with a soft gentle sound.

The little seeds woke and pushed up toward the light,

Up, up they grew slowly, by day and by night.

And now, see my garden, so lovely and gay,

With all of the flowers that blossomed today.

*Additional verse:* Substitute *vegetable seeds* for *flower seeds* in line two and change the last line to read, "With all the ripe vegetables growing today."

*Author Unknown*

## Little Plants

Out in the garden early in the morning,
*(Stand straight and tall.)*
See the little plants bending to and fro.
*(Bend body back and forth.)*
See the gentle breeze help them lift their arms,
*(Raise arms out at sides.)*
Swish-swish, swish-swish, wave hello!
*(Wave arms gently up and down.)*

*Jean Warren*

## The Peanut Plant

Up through the ground the peanut plant grows,
*(Crouch down near floor.)*
Peeking out its little green nose.
*(Slowly start to rise.)*
Reaching, reaching for the sky,
*(Raise arms above head.)*
Growing, growing, growing high.
*(Stand on tiptoe.)*
Then the flower starts to grow,
*(Form circle with arms.)*
But it doesn't grow up! Not it! Oh, no!
*(Shake head.)*
Down it goes, sending shoots underground,
*(Bend down and touch floor with fingers.)*
And there grow the peanuts, plump and round!
*(Kneel and pretend to dig up peanuts.)*

*Author Unknown*

## Flowers in a Row

Out in the garden

Early in the springtime,

See the pretty flowers

All in a row.
*(Hold up fingers of left hand.)*
See the little bees

Flying down to greet them,
*(Fly right-hand fingers down to left-hand fingers.)*
Buzz, buzz, buzz, buzz,

Off they go!
*(Fly right-hand fingers away while making buzzing sound.)*

*Jean Warren*

## Growing Things

The flower holds up its little cup,
*(Cup hands together.)*
The tree holds out its leaves.
*(Hold out hands, palms up.)*
That's the way that growing things
Have of saying please.

So, when they are thirsty,
Down come the drops of rain,
*(Flutter fingers downward.)*
And we can watch them pitter-pat
Against the window pane.
*(Rest chin in hands and pretend to look out window.)*

*Adapted Traditional*

## Five Little Potatoes

Five little potatoes
Were growing in the ground,
*(Hold up five fingers.)*
Covered up with rich soil,
Making not a sound.
*(Place other hand over fingers.)*

Down came the rain
One stormy summer day.
*(Flutter fingers downward.)*
The five little potatoes
Slept the day away.
*(Rest cheek on folded hands.)*

Out came the sun,
The farmer came out too.
*(Walk in place.)*
He dug up those potatoes
To give to me and you.
*(Pretend to dig.)*

*Mildred Hoffman*

## Carrots in the Garden

Out in the garden

Under the sun,

Grew some carrots.

Ryan picked one.
> *(Hold up one finger.)*

Out in the garden

Under skies so blue,

Grew some carrots.

Katie picked two.
> *(Hold up two fingers.)*

Out in the garden

Near a big oak tree,

Grew some carrots.

Chris picked three.
> *(Hold up three fingers.)*

Out in the garden

By the back door,

Grew some carrots.

Tyler picked four.
> *(Hold up four fingers.)*

Out in the garden

Near a beehive,

Grew some carrots.

Michelle picked five.
> *(Hold up five fingers.)*

We took those carrots

And washed the whole bunch.

Then we sat down

And ate them for lunch!
> *(Pretend to eat.)*

Substitute the names of your children
for those in the rhyme.

*Jean Warren*

## Color Vegetable Garden

Out in the garden early in the morning,

See the red tomatoes all in a row.

See the happy farmer coming out to pick them,

Pick, pick, pick, pick, off he goes.

*Additional verses:* See the yellow squashes all in a row;
See the blueberries all in a row; See the green string beans
all in a row; See the orange carrots all in a row; See the
purple cabbages all in a row.

*Jean Warren*

## Harvest Time

Harvest time is here again,

In the garden we will dig

Carrots, onions, radishes,

And sweet potatoes, oh, so big!
> *(Pretend to dig up vegetables.)*

*Kristine Wagoner*

## Cherry Blossoms

Little cherry blossoms,

Closed up, oh, so tight.
> *(Lower head and hug self.)*

See them bursting into bloom,

Colored pink and white.
> *(Raise head and open arms wide.)*

Along comes the spring breeze,

Blowing all around.
> *(Wave arms gently.)*

And down fall the petals,

Twirling to the ground.
> *(Flutter fingers downward in circles.)*

*Elizabeth McKinnon*

## What Flower Is It?

Daffy-down-dilly

Has come to town,

In a yellow petticoat

And a green gown.

What flower is it?

Can you guess?

If you said, "Daffodil,"

The answer is yes!

*Adapted Traditional*

## Yellow Daffodils

Out in the garden

Early in the morning,
> *(Gesture to one side.)*

See the little daffodils

All in a row.
> *(Bow head.)*

See them lift their heads

And give their horns a blow.
> *(Lift head and pretend to blow horn.)*

Toot, toot, toot, toot,

Fast and slow!

*Jean Warren*

## Dandelions

One little dandelion had nothing much to do,
> *(Hold up one finger.)*

Out popped another one, then there were two.
> *(Hold up two fingers.)*

Two little dandelions were smiling at a bee,

Out popped another one, then there were three.
> *(Hold up three fingers.)*

Three little dandelions were growing by the door,

Out popped another one, then there were four.
> *(Hold up four fingers.)*

Four little dandelions were glad to be alive,

Out popped another one, then there were five.
> *(Hold up five fingers.)*

Five little dandelions were wearing golden crowns,

They danced in the breeze in green satin gowns.
> *(Dance fingers.)*

*Jean Warren*

## A Rose

My hand is a rosebud closed up tight,

With not a tiny speck of light.
*(Close hand into fist.)*

Then slowly the petals open for me

And here is a beautiful rose, you see!
*(Slowly open hand.)*

*Adapted Traditional*

## I'm a Little Tulip

I'm a little tulip

On my stem,
*(Raise arms high.)*

Here are my green leaves,

See how they bend.
*(Bend down forearms.)*

A tulip all alone

Might droop its head,
*(Bow head and frown.)*

But I'm happy 'cause I'm in

A flower bed!
*(Raise head and arms, then smile.)*

*Susan M. Paprocki*

## Violets in My Garden

One purple violet in my garden grew,
*(Hold up one finger.)*

Up popped another, and that made two.
*(Hold up two fingers.)*

Two purple violets were all that I could see,

But Mommy found another, and that made three.
*(Hold up three fingers.)*

Three purple violets—if I could find one more,

I'd put them in a tiny vase, and that would make four.
*(Hold up four fingers.)*

Four purple violets, sure as we're alive,

Oh, here's another one, now that makes five!
*(Hold up five fingers.)*

*Adapted Traditional*

## Five Little Zinnias

Five little zinnias growing outside my door,
*(Hold up five fingers.)*

I picked one for Grandma, now there are four.
*(Bend down thumb.)*

Four little zinnias, the prettiest I've seen,

I picked one for Grandpa, now there are three.
*(Bend down pointer finger.)*

Three little zinnias, just a lovely few,

I picked one for Mommy, now there are two.
*(Bend down middle finger.)*

Two little zinnias reaching for the sun,

I picked one for Daddy, now there is one.
*(Bend down ring finger.)*

One little zinnia, a colorful little hero,

I picked it just for you, now there are zero.
*(Bend down little finger.)*

*Susan M. Paprocki*

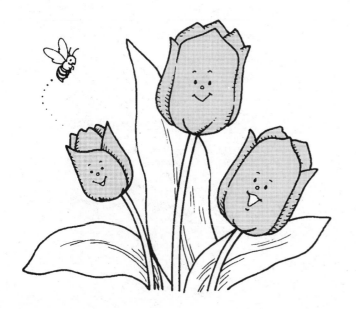

## Purple and White Blossoms

See the purple and white blossoms

In my garden bed.
*(Crouch down beside pretend garden.)*
The daisy spreads its petals wide
*(Hold palm outward, fingers apart.)*
And the tulip bows its head.
*(Close fingers and bend hand down at wrist.)*

*Adapted Traditional*

## Daisies and Sweet Peas

See the rows of daisies

And the rows of sweet peas.
*(Gesture to right, then to left.)*
Water, hoe—grow, grow,

In my garden, please!
*(Pretend to water and hoe garden.)*

*Jean Warren*

## A Little Garden Flower

A little garden flower

Is growing in its bed.
*(Make a fist with left hand.)*
A warm spring sun

Is shining overhead.
*(Form circle with right thumb and finger.)*
Down come the raindrops,

Dancing to and fro.
*(Flutter right fingers downward.)*
The little flower wakens

And starts to grow.
*(Slowly extend pointer finger up from left fist.)*

*Adapted Traditional*

## If I Were a Flower

If I were a little flower

Growing in the ground,
*(Stand straight.)*
I'd stretch my arms
*(Raise arms up and out.)*
And raise my head
*(Lift head.)*
So I could look around.
*(Move head back and forth.)*
Then I'd nod my head and say,

"I'm glad to see you all today."
*(Nod head and smile.)*

*Adapted Traditional*

## Watch It Bloom

Here is a green leaf,
*(Hold out one palm.)*
And here is a green leaf,
*(Hold out other palm.)*
That, you see, makes two.
*(Hold up two fingers.*

Here is a bud,
*(Cup hands together.)*
That makes a flower,
*(Slowly start opening hands.)*
Watch it bloom for you.
*(Open hands wide.)*

*Adapted Traditional*

## Four Little Flowers

Four little flowers I did see,
*(Hold up four fingers.)*
I picked one, then there were three.
*(Bend down one finger.)*
Three little flowers pretty and new,

I picked another, then there were two.
*(Bend down two fingers.)*
Two little flowers out in the sun,

I picked one more, then there was one.
*(Bend down three fingers.)*
One little flower left in the sun,

I picked it too, then there were none.
*(Bend down four fingers.)*

*Jean Warren*

## Color Flowers

We are all such pretty flowers

Growing in Mary's garden bed.

When the rain comes down,

Up come the flowers red.
*(Have children wearing red stand up.)*

We are flowers that have grown

In the warmth of the sun.

Mary tends us gently,

Up come the yellow ones.
*(Have children wearing yellow stand up.)*

We are flowers in the spring,

Glistening in the morning dew.

When the breeze blows soft and warm,

Up come the flowers blue.
*(Have children wearing blue stand up.)*

We are flowers in the garden,

We are Mary's pride and joy.

But if you look more closely,

You'll see we're girls and boys!
*(Smile and wave.)*

*Susan M. Paprocki*

# Trees

## The Chestnut Tree

Once a little chestnut

Was planted in the ground.
*(Crouch low.)*

Down came the raindrops,

Falling all around.
*(Flutter fingers downward.)*

Out came the big sun,

Bright as bright could be.
*(Form circle with arms.)*

And that little chestnut grew up

To be a chestnut tree!
*(Slowly stand, raising arms up and out.)*

*Elizabeth McKinnon*

## Elm Trees

Elm trees stretch and stretch so wide,

Their limbs reach out on every side.
*(Stretch arms out at sides.)*

Pine trees stretch and stretch so high,

They almost reach up to the sky.
*(Stretch arms straight up.)*

Willows droop and droop so low,

Their branches sweep the ground below.
*(Bend over and brush floor with fingers.)*

*Adapted Traditional*

## Maple Tree, Maple Tree

Maple tree, maple tree,

You grow so tall,

And your leaves turn

Gorgeous colors in fall.
*(Stretch arms up and out.)*

Maple tree, maple tree,

Would you give up

Some of your sap

To make maple syrup?
*(Lick lips.)*

*Diane Thom*

## An Oak Tree

Here's a brown acorn on the ground,
*(Crouch down near floor.)*

It's a nut that Mrs. Squirrel found.
*(Pretend to pick up nut with paws.)*

If she doesn't eat it, someday it will be
*(Pretend to nibble nut.)*

A tall and stately old oak tree.
*(Slowly stand, raising arms up and out.)*

*Diane Thom*

## Here Is an Oak Tree

Here is an oak tree straight and tall,
*(Stand straight.)*
And here are its branches wide.
*(Stretch arms up and out.)*
Here is a nest of twigs and moss,
*(Cup hands together.)*
With three little birds inside.
*(Hold up three fingers.)*

The breezes blow and the little leaves play,
*(Flutter fingers.)*
But the branches hold the nest—
*(Cup hands together.)*
As they swing and sway and bob and rock,
*(Gently rock hands back and forth.)*
So the little birds can rest.
*(Rest cheek on folded hands.)*

*Adapted Traditional*

## If I Were a Leaf

If I were a leaf,
*(Do actions as rhyme indicates.)*
I'd jump down from my tree.
I'd dance in the wind,
I'd fly in the breeze.

I'd change to bright colors,
I'd spin in the air.
Then I'd land on the ground—
I just don't know where.

*Diane Thom*

## Plant a Little Tree

Gotta jump down, turn around,
*(Do actions as rhyme indicates.)*
Plant a little tree now.
Jump down, turn around,
Plant a little green.
Gotta jump down, turn around,
Plant a little tree, now.
Gotta jump down, turn around,
Plant a little green!

*Martha Thomas*

Plants & Foods

## I Am a Tall Tree

I am a tall tree,

I reach toward the sky,
*(Raise arms up and out.)*

Where bright stars twinkle

And clouds float by.
*(Wave hands gently overhead.)*

My branches toss this way

As wild winds blow,
*(Wave arms around in air.)*

Then they bend forward,

Laden with snow.
*(Bend arms over and down.)*

When they sway gently,

I like it best.
*(Sway arms back and forth.)*

Then I rock little birds

To sleep in their nest.
*(Cup hands together while swaying arms.)*

*Adapted Traditional*

## Tree Friends

Deep in the forest

With trees so tall,
*(Stretch arms high.)*

I feel so little,

So very small.
*(Make self small.)*

I love to look up

And see the trees bend
*(Cup hand over eye and look up.)*

I know they're saying,

"Let's all be friends."
*(Hug self.)*

*Jean Warren*

## Hug a Tree Today

Why not hug a tree today
*(Do actions as rhyme indicates.)*

Or pat it on its bark?

Give a tree a great big squeeze

At home or in the park.

Find the tree you like the best

And stand beneath its shade.

Stretch your arms around its trunk

And hug until you fade.

Imagine the birds that have lived in your tree,

Imagine the squirrel in its nest.

A tree is a home to all that come,

The perfect place to rest.

So put your arms around your tree,

Whether it's short or tall.

Hug your tree—you'll feel so good,

Winter, spring, summer, or fall.

*Susan M. Paprocki*

## Ten Red Apples

Ten red apples growing on a tree,
*(Hold hands high with fingers extended.)*
Five for you and five for me.
*(Wave one hand, then the other.)*
Help me shake the tree just so,
*(Shake body.)*
And ten red apples fall down below.
*(Lower hands with fingers extended.)*
One, two, three, four, five,
*(Count fingers on one hand.)*
Six, seven, eight, nine, ten.
*(Count fingers on other hand.)*

*Author Unknown*

## Two Green Apples

Way up high

In a tree,
*(Raise arms high.)*
Two green apples

Smiled at me.
*(Smile.)*

So I shook that tree

As hard as I could,
*(Pretend to shake tree.)*
And down fell the apples.

Mmmm, they were good!
*(Rub tummy.)*

*Adapted Traditional*

## Look at the Apple

Look at the apple I have found,

So round and rosy on the ground.
*(Clasp hands to form round apple.)*
Mother will wash it and cut it in two,

Half for me and half for you.
*(Hold out one palm, then the other.)*

*Martha T. Lyon*

## Applesauce

Peel an apple,
*(Do actions as rhyme indicates.)*
Cut it up,

Put it in a pot.

When you taste it,

You will find

It's applesauce

You've got!

*Martha T. Lyon*

## Making a Cake

Mix the batter, stir the batter,
    *(Do actions as rhyme indicates.)*
Shake some flour in.

Mix the batter, stir the batter,
Pour it in a tin.

Sprinkle little raisins on,
Pop batter in to bake.
Then open wide the oven door,
And out comes a cake!

*Adapted Traditional*

## Three Little Carrots

Three little carrots,
    *(Hold up three fingers.)*
What can I make?
I'll use one
To make a carrot cake.
    *(Bend down first finger.)*

Two little carrots,
Just watch my carrot tricks.
I'll chop one
To make some carrot sticks.
    *(Bend down second finger.)*

One little carrot,
Alone in the sink.
I'll blend one
To make a carrot drink.
    *(Bend down third finger.)*

*Jean Warren*

## Five Little Cookies

Five little cookies with frosting galore,
    *(Hold up five fingers.)*
Mother ate the white one, then there were four.
    *(Bend down thumb.)*
Four little cookies, two and two, you see,
Father ate the green one, then there were three.
    *(Bend down pointer finger.)*
Three little cookies, but before I knew,
Sister ate the yellow one, then there were two.
    *(Bend down middle finger.)*
Two little cookies, oh, what fun!
Brother ate the brown one, then there was one.
    *(Bend down ring finger.)*
One little cookie, watch me run!
I ate the red one, then there were none.
    *(Bend down little finger.)*

*Adapted Traditional*

## Making Cookies

I am making cookie dough,
*(Point to self.)*
Round and round the beaters go.
*(Move hands in circles.)*
Add some flour from a cup,
*(Pretend to pour.)*
Stir and mix the batter up.
*(Pretend to stir.)*

Roll them, cut them, nice and neat,
*(Pretend to roll and cut out cookies.)*
Put them on a cookie sheet.
*(Pretend to transfer cookies.)*
Bake them, count them, one, two, three,
*(Pretend to count cookies.)*
Then serve them to my friends for tea.
*(Pretend to pass cookies around.)*

*Adapted Traditional*

## Sweet Corn

Standing in the corn field, out in the sun,
*(Form circle with arms.)*
Picking the corn ears one by one.
*(Pretend to pick corn.)*
Cooking up the yellow corn, boy, what fun!
*(Pretend to drop ears into pot.)*
Munching on sweet corn, yum, yum, yum!
*(Pretend to eat ear of corn.)*

*Jean Warren*

## Here Is a Doughnut

Here is a doughnut,
Big, round, and fat.
*(Form circle with thumb and index finger.)*
And here is the hole,
Now, don't eat that!
*(Point to center of circle.)*

*Adapted Traditional*

## A Little Hot Dog

I had a little hot dog,
*(Do actions as rhyme indicates.)*
I popped it in a bun.
I added some relish—
Hot dogs are fun!

I spread on some ketchup
And mustard, like I should.
Then I popped it my mouth
And said, "Mmmm, good!"

*Janet Graves Wilson*

## Ice-Cream Colors

We have ice cream, the best in town,
Let's begin with chocolate brown.

Now, let's scoop up some bubble-gum pink,
It's sweet and yummy, the best, some think.

Here is ice cream minty and green,
It's the creamiest I've ever seen.

Yellow ice cream is lemony and tart,
We like its taste from the very start.

Scoops of blueberry would make my day,
Look at all this ice cream, hip, hip hurray!

Red ice cream is a strawberry delight,
All these scoops are a heavenly sight.

Vanilla white is a popular flavor,
It tastes very good to an ice-cream craver.

Purple ice cream really gives me a kick,
Good and yummy till the very last lick.

Ice cream, ice cream, what a cool sensation,
We love ice cream in any combination!

*Susan M. Paprocki*

## I'm a Juicy Orange

I'm a juicy orange
Round as you please,
   *(Form circle with arms.)*
A big juicy orange
Waiting for a squeeze.
So if you happen
To come my way,
Give me a hug—
You'll make my day!
   *(Hug self.)*

*Jean Warren*

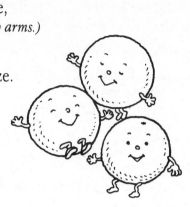

## Mix a Pancake

Stir a pancake,
   *(Do actions as rhyme indicates.)*
Mix a pancake,
Pop it in a pan.
Cook a pancake,
Toss a pancake,
Catch it if you can!

*Adapted Traditional*

## I Love Pasta

I love pasta shapes, yes, I do,
Noodles and twists are but a few.
Then there's spaghetti and bow ties,
Wheels and macaroni, any size.

Cook up the pasta shapes, yum, yum, yum,
I just love pasta in my tum.
Hand out the forks, and now let's eat,
I say pasta is a special treat!
   *(Rub tummy and lick lips.)*

*Gayle Bittinger*

## Pea Soup

One little pea jumped into the pot,

And waited for the soup to get hot.
   *(Cup hand and bend down thumb.)*

Two little peas jumped into the pot,

And waited for the soup to get hot.
   *(Bend down pointer finger.)*

Three little peas jumped into the pot,

And waited for the soup to get hot.
   *(Bend down middle finger.)*

Four little peas jumped into the pot,

And waited for the soup to get hot.
   *(Bend down ring finger.)*

Five little peas jumped into the pot,

And waited for the soup to get hot.
   *(Bend down little finger.)*

Finally, the soup got so very hot,

All the little peas jumped out of the pot!
   *(Quickly open hand.)*

*Jean Warren*

## Peanut Butter

Peanut butter, peanut butter, fun to chew,

Peanut butter, peanut butter, good for you.
   *(Rub tummy and lick lips.)*

Put peanuts in a blender, add oil too,

Then whirl and swirl until it's through.
   *(Move hand around and around.)*

Peanut butter, peanut butter, now it's done,

Making peanut butter was lots of fun.
   *(Nod head and smile.)*

Peanut butter, peanut butter, fun to chew,

Peanut butter, peanut butter, good for you.
   *(Rub tummy and lick lips.)*

*Susan Peters*

## One Whole Pie

One whole pie

Set by the door,

Cut into pieces,

I count four.
   *(Hold up four fingers.)*

Four pieces of pie

All for me,

I ate one piece,

Now there are three.
   *(Bend down one finger.)*

Three pieces of pie

For me too,

I ate another piece,

Now there are two.
   *(Bend down two fingers.)*

Two pieces of pie

Oh! what fun!

I ate another piece,

Now there is one.
   *(Bend down three fingers.)*

One piece of pie

I can't wait!

I ate that piece,

Empty plate!
   *(Bend down four fingers.)*

*Jean Warren*

## Pizza Treat

It's round and made of dough,

Topped with sauce and cheese just so.
> *(Form circle with hands.)*

It's a big round treat

Filled with vegetables and meat.
> *(Rub tummy.)*

It's a pizza cooked just right.

Are you ready? Have a bite!
> *(Pretend to eat pizza.)*

*Diane Thom*

## Popcorn in the Pan

Watch me pop in the pan,
> *(Hop around.)*

Try to catch me, if you can.

While I'm popping to and fro,

Try to catch me as I go.

*Jean Warren*

## See the Little Kernel

See the little kernel

In the pot,
> *(Crouch down.)*

Turn on the heat

And watch it hop.
> *(Hop.)*

When it gets all warmed up,

It will pop.
> *(Jump.)*

Mmmm, it tastes good

When it's hot!
> *(Lick lips.)*

*Neoma Kreuter*

## A Red Tomato

I'm a red tomato growing on the vine,

Ready to be picked, looking, oh, so fine.
> *(Form circle with arms.)*

Now, you can make good things with me,

Soup, juice, pizza, to name just three.
> *(Count on fingers.)*

I'm a big red tomato growing on the vine,

Pick me now!
> *(Form circle with arms.)*

*Jean Warren*

## Color Fruits

One yellow banana extra nice,

Pretty please, give me a slice.
*(Hold up one finger.)*

Two round oranges really sweet,

What a super-duper treat!
*(Hold up two fingers.)*

Three red apples very bright,

Hurry up and take a bite.
*(Hold up three fingers.)*

Four purple plums in a sack,

Make a really special snack.
*(Hold up four fingers.)*

Five ripe pears all so yellow,

Yum, yum, how rich and mellow!
*(Hold up five fingers.)*

Six green melons nice to eat,

A dessert that can't be beat.
*(Hold up six fingers.)*

Seven peaches rather pink,

A good fruit to eat, I think
*(Hold up seven fingers.)*

Eight blueberries firm and good,

Do have some, you really should.
*(Hold up eight fingers.)*

Nine cherries so shiny red,

Try some now, go right ahead.
*(Hold up nine fingers.)*

Ten green grapes so great to munch,

Here, put a few in your lunch.
*(Hold up ten fingers.)*

*Lois E. Putnam*

## Making Fruit Treats

I am an apple

Growing on a tree.
*(Raise arms up.)*

If you want some applesauce,

Just cook me.
*(Make stirring motions.)*

I am a grape

Growing on a vine.
*(Hold arms out at sides.)*

If you want some grape juice,

Smoosh me fine.
*(Stomp and twist feet.)*

I am a strawberry

Growing on the ground.
*(Point downward.)*

If you want some jam,

Mash me around.
*(Make mashing motions with hands.)*

I am an orange

Growing on a tree.
*(Raise arms up.)*

If you want some orange juice,

Just squeeze me.
*(Hug self.)*

*Polly Reedy*

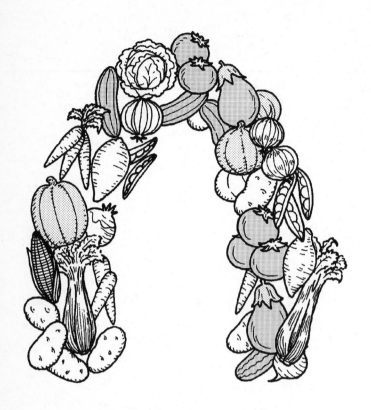

## Carrots and Peas

Carrots and peas,

Carrots and peas,

Where, oh, where

Are my carrots and peas?
*(Tilt head to one side.)*

I went to the garden

And what did I see?

Holes and vines

But no carrots and peas.
*(Shake head.)*

I went to the kitchen

And what did I see?

Pods and tops

But no carrots and peas.
*(Shake head.)*

I went to the stove

And what did I see?

A pan of water

But no carrots and peas.
*(Shake head.)*

I went to the table

And what did I see?

A great big bowl

Full of carrots and peas.
*(Nod head and smile.)*

Carrots and peas,

Carrots and peas,

Will someone please pass

The carrots and peas?
*(Rub tummy and smile.)*

*Jean Warren*

## Vegetables

Vegetables are plants we eat,

They're so good, what a treat!
*(Lick lips.)*

Carrots, beans, and broccoli—

They help us grow so healthily.
*(Rub tummy and smile.)*

*Gayle Bittinger*

## Vegetable Colors

There are many colored vegetables—

They are good for you.

Carrots are orange, I'll eat a few,

Beans are green, I'll try them too.

Repeat, substituting other vegetable names
and colors for those in the rhyme.

*Gayle Bittinger*

# Wind

## I See the Wind

I see the wind when the leaves dance by,
  *(Dance hands around.)*
I see the wind when the clothes wave "Hi!"
  *(Wave hand.)*
I see the wind when the trees bend low,
  *(Bend arms over and down.)*
I see the wind when the flags all blow.
  *(Wave arms high.)*

I see the wind when the kites fly high,
  *(Raise arms high.)*
I see the wind when the clouds float by.
  *(Gently wave hands.)*
I see the wind when it blows my hair,
  *(Lift hair with hands.)*
I see the wind 'most everywhere!
  *(Hold hands out, palms up.)*

*Jean Warren*

## The Playful Wind

The wind came out
To play today.
  *(Dance around.)*
It swept the clouds
Out of its way.
  *(Sweep arms to one side.)*
It blew the leaves,
And away they flew.
  *(Dance fingers to one side.)*
The trees bent low,
And their branches did too.
  *(Bend over and sway arms.)*

*Adapted Traditional*

## Wind Tricks

The wind is full of tricks today,

It blew our newspaper away.
  *(Sweep arms to one side.)*
It chased the trash can down the street,

It almost blew us off our feet.
  *(Stumble and almost fall.)*
It makes the trees and bushes dance,

Just listen to it howl and prance!
  *(Cup hand behind ear.)*

*Adapted Traditional*

## Little Winds

This little wind blows silver rain,
  *(Hold up five fingers and point to thumb.)*
This little wind blows snow.
  *(Point to index finger.)*
This little wind sings a whistly tune,
  *(Point to middle finger.)*
This little wind sighs low.
  *(Point to ring finger.)*
And this little wind rocks baby birds
  *(Point to little finger.)*
So gently to and fro.
  *(Sway cupped hands back and forth.)*

*Adapted Traditional*

## When March Winds Blow

When I hear the March winds blow,
I look up in the sky.
Instead of things like birds or planes,
I watch the hats fly by.

Each one different from the last,
Every color do I see.
Some are big and some are small,
As they fly by me.

Here comes a blue hat flying by,
Now a yellow hat in the sky.
Next, a red hat on its way,
Then a brown hat flies away.

Green and black, orange and white,
Even purple—what a sight!
I like it when there's rain and snow,
But most of all when March hats blow.

*Jean Warren*

## Cold Winds

When cold winds blow
And bring us snow,
    *(Hug self and shiver.)*
At night what I like most,
Is to crawl in bed
    *(Pretend to climb in bed.)*
And hide my head,
And sleep as warm as toast.
    *(Pretend to pull up covers, then close eyes.)*

*Adapted Traditional*

# Rain

## Raindrops

This is the sun

High in the sky.
*(Form circle with arms.)*

Here comes a dark cloud

Sailing by.
*(Sweep hands to one side.)*

These are the raindrops

Pitter-pattering down.
*(Flutter fingers downward.)*

They water the flowers

That grow in the ground.
*(Form flower with cupped hands.)*

*Adapted Traditional*

## Rain, Rain

Rain, rain falling down,

Falling on the ground.
*(Flutter fingers downward.)*

Pitter-patter, pitter-patter,

What a lovely sound!
*(Cup hand behind ear.)*

*Susan A. Miller*

## Pitter-Patter

Pitter-patter falls the rain,
*(Tap fingers in rhythm.)*

On the roof and windowpane.

Softly, softly it comes down,

Pitter-patter all around.

*Adapted Traditional*

## Rain Falling Down

Rain, rain falling down,

Landing all around.
*(Flutter fingers downward.)*

What a lovely sound you make

Splashing on the ground!
*(Cup hand behind ear.)*

*Susan L. Moon*

## Drip-Drop

The rain goes drip-drop,
*(Tap in rhythm.)*

The rain goes drip-drop.

Drip-drop,

How it does plop.

Drip-drop.

*Gayle Bittinger*

## Falling Raindrops

I listen to the raindrops fall

On thirsty trees and flowers.
*(Cup hand behind ear.)*

I hear the pitter-patter sound,

And I'm thankful for the showers!
*(Nod head and smile.)*

*Adapted Traditional*

## Rain on the Green Grass

Rain on the green grass,
*(Flutter fingers down near floor.)*
Rain on the tree.
*(Flutter fingers above head.)*
Rain on the housetop,
*(Form roof shape with fingers.)*
But not on me!
*(Form umbrella above head with arms.)*

*Adapted Traditional*

## Teeny Tiny Raindrops

Teeny tiny raindrops
Are falling from the sky.
*(Flutter fingers downward.)*
They're filling up the puddles
And dropping in my eyes.
*(Blink eyes.)*
Drip, drip, and drop, drop,
I love to hear them fall,
*(Cup hand behind ear.)*
For the teeny tiny raindrops
Mean wet fun for us all!
*(Nod head and smile.)*

*Betty Silkunas*

## Raindrops Falling

Raindrops, raindrops,
*(Tap fingers.)*
Falling all around.
Pitter-patter on the rooftops,
Pitter-patter on the ground.

Here is my umbrella,
*(Form umbrella above head with arms.)*
It will keep me dry.
When I'm walking in the rain,
I hold it up so high.

*Adapted Traditional*

## My Umbrella

My umbrella goes up,
*(Raise arms high, fingers touching.)*
And I go under,
Whenever I hear
The sound of thunder.

It is wild and windy,
*(Move raised arms back and forth.)*
See the weather vane.
My umbrella is pulling
With the blowing rain.

Now it is still,
*(Hold raised arms in place.)*
And I see the sun.
Down comes my umbrella,
*(Lower arms to sides.)*
Time now for fun!

*Susan M. Paprocki*

## Five Umbrellas

Five umbrellas stood by the back door,
*(Hold up five fingers.)*
The red one went outside, then there were four.
*(Bend down thumb.)*
Four umbrellas, pretty as could be,

The blue one went outside, then there were three.
*(Bend down pointer finger.)*
Three umbrellas with nothing to do,

The green one went outside, then there were two.
*(Bend down middle finger.)*
Two umbrellas not having much fun,

The yellow one went outside, then there was one.
*(Bend down ring finger.)*
Just one umbrella alone in the hall,

The purple one went outside, and that was all.
*(Bend down little finger.)*

*Jean Warren*

## Color Umbrellas

We keep our umbrellas so perky and gay,
Ready and waiting for a rainy day.

Here is a green one to keep me dry
When I open it up and hold it high.

Have you seen the umbrella that's ruby red?
It looks so regal held over my head.

The rain can get heavy, oh me, oh my,
But the purple umbrella will keep me dry.

I love the umbrella of sweet sky blue,
It's big enough for both me and you.

The yellow umbrella is bright like the sun,
Jumping puddles with it is ever so fun.

The orange umbrella is saved for showers,
The kind of rain that wakes up the flowers.

Our umbrellas are fun and so nice to see,
Just look at them all, I'm sure you'll agree.

*Susan M. Paprocki*

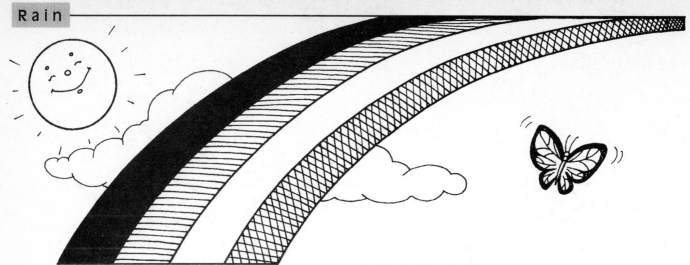

## A Rainbow Fair

When the rain falls from the sky,
  *(Flutter fingers downward.)*
Don't forget to look up high.
  *(Cup hand above eye and look up.)*
If the sun is shining there,
  *(Form circle with arms.)*
You may see a rainbow fair.
  *(Sweep arms in arc above head.)*
Red, orange, yellow, green, and blue,
And you'll see there's purple too.
  *(Count colors on fingers.)*

*Vicki Claybrook*

## Rainbow Colors

Rainbow purple, rainbow blue,
Rainbow green and yellow too.
Rainbow orange, rainbow red,
Rainbow smiling overhead.

Come and count the colors with me,
How many colors can you see?
One, two, three, up to green,
Four, five, six colors can be seen.

*Jean Warren*

## A Rainbow Gay

From big gray clouds
The raindrops fell,
Drip, drip, drip, one day,
  *(Flutter fingers downward.)*
Until the sunlight
Changed them all
Into a rainbow gay.
  *(Form arc above head with arms.)*

*Adapted Traditional*

## Rainbow Over the Waterfall

Rainbow over the waterfall,
  *(Form arc, then dip hands downward.)*
Rainbow over the tree,
  *(Form arc, then a tree shape, with hands.)*
Rainbow over the mountains,
  *(Form arc, then draw mountains in air.)*
Rainbow over the sea.
  *(Form arc, then rock hands like waves.)*

Rainbow over the flowers,
  *(Form arc, then cup hands for flower.)*
Rainbow over the bee,
  *(Form arc, then fly finger around.)*
Rainbow over the dancers,
  *(Form arc, then sway body.)*
Rainbow over me!
  *(Form arc, then point to self.)*

*Jean Warren*

## Snowy Surprise

Sometimes the snow falls when I'm sleeping,
*(Rest cheek on folded hands.)*
I'm so surprised when I awake.
*(Stretch and yawn.)*
I look out at the world around me,
*(Look around.)*
It looks like a frosted birthday cake!
*(Rub tummy and lick lips.)*

*Diane Thom*

## Snow

Snow, snow swirling round,

Falling to the ground.
*(Flutter fingers downward in circles.)*
What a pretty sight you make,

Dancing all around!
*(Dance fingers in air.)*

*Susan L. Moon*

## Snowflakes, Snowflakes

Snowflakes, snowflakes,

Dance around.
*(Dance fingers.)*
Snowflakes, snowflakes,

Touch the ground.
*(Touch floor.)*
Snowflakes, snowflakes,

In the air,
*(Flutter fingers upward.)*
Snowflakes, snowflakes,

Everywhere.
*(Flutter fingers outward.)*

*Jean Warren*

## Falling Snowflakes

Snowflakes falling from the sky

To the earth below,
*(Flutter fingers downward.)*
Watch them as they dance and whirl,

Soft white winter snow.
*(Dance fingers in circles.)*

*Judith McNitt*

## Snowflakes Falling Down

Snowflakes falling down.
*(Flutter fingers downward.)*
Falling to the ground.

Big white fluffy flakes
*(Form circles with thumbs and fingers.)*
That do not make a sound.
*(Put finger to lips and shake head.)*

*Susan A. Miller*

## Snowflakes

Snowflakes falling on the ground,

Snowflakes falling all around.
  *(Flutter fingers downward.)*

I'm bundled up right to my chin,

See my footprints where I've been?
  *(Stomp feet, then look over shoulder.)*

*Frank Dally*

## Snow Is Falling

Snow is falling all around,

Falling, falling to the ground.
  *(Flutter fingers downward.)*

I catch snowflakes on my tongue,

I think snow is so much fun!
  *(Tip head back and stick out tongue.)*

*Susan Nydick*

## It Is Snowing

It is snowing

All around.

Soft, silent snowflakes—

Not a sound.
  *(Put finger to lips and shake head.)*

*Saundra Winnett*

## What's the Weather?

What's the weather, do you know?

Is the sun out?

Is there rain all about?

Or is there snow?

*Gayle Bittinger*

## A Cloud

What's fluffy white and floats up high

Like a pile of cotton in the sky?
    *(Point upward.)*

And when the wind blows hard and strong,

What very gently floats along?
    *(Wave hands up and down.)*

What brings the rain? What brings the snow

That showers down on us below?
    *(Flutter fingers downward.)*

When you look up in the high blue sky,

What is that thing you see float by?
    *(Look upward and say, "A cloud!")*

*Adapted Traditional*

## Clouds

Clouds in the sky, all fluffy and white,

They hide the sun that shines so bright.
    *(Pretend to float like a cloud.)*

They float about the sky so blue,

And form so many fantastic shapes too.
    *(Stretch body into different shapes.)*

*Angela Wolfe*

## When I Look Into the Sky

When I look into the sky,

I can see the clouds go by.
    *(Look upward.)*

They don't ever make a sound

As the winds push them around.
    *(Sweep arms back and forth.)*

Some go fast and some go slow,

I wonder where the clouds all go.
    *(Tilt head to one side.)*

*Frank Dally*

## A Thunderstorm

Boom, bang, boom, bang,
    *(Make sounds with hands and feet.)*

Rumpety, lumpety, bump!

Zoom, zam, zoom, zam,

Clippity, clappity, clump!

Rustles and bustles,

And swishes and zings!

What wonderful sounds

A thunderstorm brings!

*Adapted Traditional*

## No More Pollution

When cars with gasoline go, go, go,

They give off pollution, this we know.
> *(Hold nose.)*

So I'll invent a car some day

That runs on water, and then I'll say,

"Now there's no more pollution in the air,

Because about the earth I care!"
> *(Take a deep breath and smile.)*

Let your children substitute any word they wish
for *water*.

*Gayle Bittinger*

## Cleaning Up Soot

Look, look—soot!
> *(Frown and shake head.)*

The air is filled with soot today,

It covers the buildings, it covers the bay,

I wish pollution would go away.

Look, look—soot!

We can help!
> *(Smile and nod head.)*

We can clean up our air so beautifully

By burning things more carefully

And driving our cars more thoughtfully.

We can help!

*Jean Warren*

## Give a Hoot

This great earth is our home,

It's up to us to care.
> *(Point to self.)*

Woodsy Owl will lead the way,

Come on, let's do our share.
> *(Beckon with hand.)*

"Give a Hoot. Don't Pollute."

Clean land is best, we know.
> *(Nod head and smile.)*

Let's leave a trail that's nice and clean

Wherever we may go.
> *(Walk in circle with others.)*

*Kathleen Cubley*

## Stamp Pollution Out

Give a hoot,
> *(Make hooting sound.)*

Give a shout.
> *(Shout.)*

Look all around,
> *(Move head back and forth.)*

And stamp pollution out!
> *(Stamp feet.)*

*Barbara Fletcher*

## I'm Not a Litterbug

I'm not a litterbug, no, not me!
*(Shake head.)*
I pick up my trash, you see.
*(Point to self and smile.)*

*Elizabeth McKinnon*

## Don't Litter

Please don't litter
Or throw things out.
*(Frown and shake head.)*
Keeping our land clean
Is what it's all about!
*(Smile and nod head.)*

*Angela Wolfe*

## Trash All Around

Trash is blowing all around,
*(Sweep arms back and forth.)*
In the air and on the ground.
*(Move arms high, then low.)*
Let's grab it from the naughty wind
*(Make grabbing motion.)*
And toss it in a big trash bin!
*(Make tossing motion.)*

*Elizabeth McKinnon*

## Pick Up the Trash

Pick up all the trash,
*(Do actions as rhyme indicates.)*
Throw it in a can.
Stoop low to conquer
The litter in our land.

Bend down from your waist,
Grab a piece or two.
Mother Earth needs cleaning up,
And she depends on you!

*Martha Thomas*

## Pick Up Your Litter

The forest is home to lots of critters,
So when you're there, pick up your litter.
*(Pretend to pick up trash.)*
The deer, the beaver, the owl, and the bear,
All will be thankful that you care.
*(Nod head and smile.)*

*Jean Warren*

## A Clean Place to Be

Let's never drop papers or wrappers,
*(Shake head.)*
A garbage can's where they should be.
Let's use and reuse and recycle,
*(Roll hands.)*
Let's make Earth a clean place to be!

*Beverly Qualheim*

## An Earth Day Helper

Be an Earth Day helper,

Do a little bit each day.

Remember not to litter,

But to throw your trash away.
*(Pretend to throw away litter.)*

Be an Earth Day helper

With recycling plans.

Once cleaned, these come back to you—

Bottles, papers, and cans.
*(Hold up three fingers, one at a time.)*

*Ellen Bedford*

## Let's All Recycle

Pretty soon our dumps will all be full,

We'd better figure out something to do.

Let's all recycle, let's use things again

To make new things for me and for you.

*Jean Warren*

## Let's Recycle

Plastic, paper, and aluminum cans—

We have to recycle all we can.
*(Roll hands.)*

If we hope to save our earth,

We cannot bury our trash in dirt.
*(Shake head.)*

Plastic, papers, and aluminum cans—

Let's recycle, I know we can!
*(Roll hands and smile.)*

*Angela Wolfe*

## A Better Land

Let's all recycle,

Let's all give a hand,
*(Roll hands.)*

'Cause if we recycle,

We'll have a better land!
*(Nod head and smile.)*

*Jean Warren*

## Let's Recycle Now

Let's recycle, let's do it now.

Let's recycle, you know how.
*(Point to others.)*

Save your glass and plastic and cans,

Save your newspapers and aluminum pans.
*(Check off named items on fingers.)*

*Martha Thomas*

## My Home, the Earth

I have a home on the planet Earth.

It's here that I was given birth

Along with plants and many trees,

Animals, flowers, birds, and bees.

My home, the earth, needs for me

To watch the sky, to watch the sea.

I must make my home safe and clean

To keep the forests alive and green.

I can do my part to save my home

So future children can play and roam

Upon an earth that shows my care,

Upon a home so clean and fair.

*Susan M. Paprocki*

## It Is Air

You can't see it,
But it's there,
Filling balloons,
Taking up space—
It is air.

You can't see it,
But it's there,
Making things move
When it blows—
It is air.

You can't see it,
But it's there,
Making loud noises
As it rushes by—
It is air.

*Gayle Bittinger*

## Oxygen

People breathe in oxygen
From the air around.
Every time we take a breath,
Oxygen goes down.
	*(Take a deep breath.)*

Oxygen comes from our plants
And goes into the air.
That is why we are so glad
That plants are everywhere!
	*(Hold arms out wide.)*

*Gayle Bittinger*

## The Sea Is Salty

The water in the sea is salty,
As salty as can be.
When sea water dries all up,
A pile of salt you'll see!

*Gayle Bittinger*

## Three Oceans

Three oceans cover the earth, you see.
	*(Hold up three fingers.)*
Can you count them now with me?
Pacific, Atlantic, and Indian make three.
	*(Bend down fingers, one at a time.)*

*Gayle Bittinger*

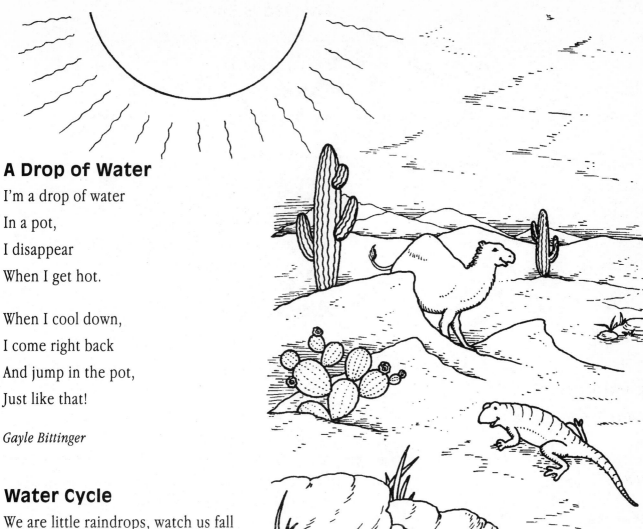

## A Drop of Water

I'm a drop of water
In a pot,
I disappear
When I get hot.

When I cool down,
I come right back
And jump in the pot,
Just like that!

*Gayle Bittinger*

## Water Cycle

We are little raindrops, watch us fall
From clouds to ground, one and all.
Falling together—you will see
A great big puddle is what we'll be.

First we're in puddles, then watch us flow
Into the rivers, now here we go.
We keep on flowing right out to sea,
A part of the ocean we will be.

Now we're in the ocean, oh, so blue,
We float around like raindrops do.
Soon we'll get all warmed up and say goodbye,
Then float back up into the sky.

*Gayle Bittinger*

## The Desert

Hot and cold, hot and cold,
With winds that blow and blow.
    *(Sweep arms back and forth.)*
The desert is hot when the sun is bright.
    *(Brush forehead with hand.)*
It's cold when the sun goes down at night.
    *(Hug self and shiver.)*
And the winds sweep everything out of sight
    *(Sweep arms back and forth.)*
As they blow and blow.

*Gayle Bittinger*

## Sensing the Forest

I love the sounds of the forest,
    *(Cup hand behind ear.)*
The water, the birds, and the leaves.

I also love the silence

That fills my world of trees.

I love the smells of the forest,
    *(Sniff air.)*
The pines and the flowers so sweet.

I love the smells of the forest,

They smell so fresh to me.

I love the feel of the forest,
    *(Pretend to touch with hands.)*
The moss, the ferns, and the trees.

I love the feel of the forest,

It feels just right to me.

I love the sights of the forest,
    *(Cup hand above eye.)*
The streams, the flowers, and leaves.

I love to watch the sunlight

Dancing from tree to tree.

I love the tastes of the forest,
    *(Lick lips.)*
The berries, the honey from bees.

I love the tastes of the forest

At breakfast, dinner, or tea.

*Jean Warren*

## A Friend of Smokey Bear

I am a friend of Smokey Bear,

The best you've ever seen.
    *(Point to self and smile.)*
I want to prevent forest fires

And keep our forests green.
    *(Nod head.)*

Smokey says don't play with matches,

So I never do.
    *(Shake head.)*
I care about our forests—

How about you?
    *(Point to others.)*

Repeat, substituting *lighters* for *matches*.

*Elizabeth McKinnon*

## In the Forest

When animals go walking
Past flowers, grass, and trees,
The fur around their feet
Picks up little seeds.

Then later when the seeds
Fall upon the ground,
That's one way that new plants
Get scattered all around.

*Jean Warren*

## Little Mountains

This little mountain finds the sun,
    *(Hold up one hand and point to thumb.)*
This little mountain drinks the rain,
    *(Point to index finger.)*
This little mountain shades its eyes
And looks out on the plain.
    *(Point to middle finger.)*
This little mountain is ready for bed
With a white nightcap upon its head.
    *(Point to ring finger.)*
And this little mountain is up to its knees
In hundreds of pointed evergreen trees.
    *(Point to little finger.)*

*Adapted Traditional*

## Old Volcano

Old volcano
Is asleep.
    *(Rest cheek on folded hands.)*
Shhh, don't wake him,
Let him sleep.
    *(Put finger to lips.)*

Rumble, rumble,
When will it stop?
    *(Pound feet on floor.)*
Now old volcano
Blows his top!
    *(Thrust arms up and out.)*

*Linda Warren*

## The Sun

Over there the sun gets up
    *(Hold arm straight out at side and point.)*
And marches all the day.
    *(Begin raising arm.)*
At noon it stands just overhead,
    *(Hold arm straight up.)*
And at night it goes away.
    *(Move arm down across body.)*

*Adapted Traditional*

## The Moon

At night when the sun goes down in the sky,
    *(Move right hand up and over left fist.)*
The stars appear real soon.
    *(Hold up hands and wiggle fingers.)*
There also appears a big white ball,
    *(Form ball shape with hands.)*
We call that ball the moon!

*Beverly Qualheim*

## Moon, Moon

Moon, moon,

Up so high,

Big white moon

In the black, black sky.

Moon, moon,

Mighty one,

Following soon

The setting sun.

*Susan M. Paprocki*

## Full Moon

Full moon, oh, so bright,

Shining in the night.
    *(Slowly lower hands, fingers extended.)*
What a lovely face you have,

Big and round and white!
    *(Form circle with arms.)*

*Susan A. Miller*

## Twinkling Stars

At night I see the twinkling stars,
*(Hold up hands and wiggle fingers.)*
And a big white smiling moon.
*(Form circle with arms and smile.)*
Mommy tucks me into bed,
*(Place finger in opposite hand.)*
And sings a goodnight tune.
*(Rock hands gently.)*

*Adapted Traditional*

## Wish on a Star

Starlight, star bright,

First star I see tonight,
*(Point upward.)*
I wish I may, I wish I might,

Have the wish I wish tonight.
*(Make a wish.)*

*Adapted Traditional*

## Stars

I watch the stars

Come out at night,
*(Look upward.)*
I wonder where

They get their light.
*(Tilt head to one side.)*

I don't think

They'll ever fall,
*(Shake head.)*
So I'll reach up

And pick them all.
*(Reach high and pretend to pick stars.)*

*Adapted Traditional*

## A Tiny Little Star

There's a tiny little star

Way up in the sky,
*(Raise fist high.)*
A tiny little star,

Up so very high.
*(Raise fist even higher.)*

She twinkles brightly

Through the night,
*(Open fist and wiggle fingers.)*
But during the day

She's out of sight.
*(Close hand back into fist.)*

*Jean Warren*

## Reach for the Stars

Bend and stretch, reach for the stars,
*(Bend low and stretch high as rhyme indicates.)*
Here comes Jupiter, there goes Mars.

Bend and stretch, reach for the sky,

Stand on tiptoe, oh, so high!

*Adapted Traditional*

## Four Little Stars

Four little stars winking at me,
> *(Hold up four fingers.)*

One shot off, then there were three.
> *(Bend down first finger.)*

Three little stars with nothing to do,

One shot off, then there were two.
> *(Bend down second finger.)*

Two little stars afraid of the sun,

One shot off, then there was one.
> *(Bend down third finger.)*

One little star, alone is no fun,

It shot off, then there were none.
> *(Bend down fourth finger.)*

*Jean Warren*

## A Little Rocket

I'm a little rocket and I'm glad,

Soon I'll blast off from my pad.
> *(Crouch down near floor.)*

When I get all revved up, hear me roar,

Up, up, up I go—watch me soar!
> *(Jump up and pretend to soar.)*

*Jean Warren*

## I Ride in a Spaceship

Outer space is where I like to go,

I ride in a spaceship, just like so.
> *(Pretend to steer spaceship.)*

See me traveling through the stars—

Hello, Jupiter! Hello, Mars!
> *(Wave hand.)*

*Kristine Wagoner*

## Spaceship Ride

Do you want to go with me to the moon?

Let's climb in our spaceship and blast off soon.
> *(Pretend to climb into spaceship.)*

Faster and faster we reach toward the sky,

Isn't it fun to be able to fly?
> *(Slowly stand while raising arms high.)*

We've reached the moon and turned around,

Now it's back to Earth—down, down, down.
> *(Slowly sit while lowering arms.)*

*Adapted Traditional*

## Traveling in Space

I wish I could ride in a spaceship,

It's just what I'd like to do.

I'd travel to Mars and then Neptune—

Would you like to come along too?
> *(Point to other person.)*

*Kathy McCullough*

## Climb Aboard the Spaceship

Climb aboard the spaceship,
> *(Do actions as rhyme indicates.)*

We're going to the moon.

Hurry and get ready,

We're going to blast off soon.

Put on your helmets

And buckle up real tight.

Here comes the countdown,

Let's count with all our might.

10-9-8-7-6-5-4-3-2-1—Blast off!

*Elizabeth McKinnon*

## Ring Around the Spaceship

Ring around the spaceship,
> *(Walk with others in circle.)*

Try to grab a star.
> *(Reach up high.)*

Stardust, stardust,
> *(Wiggle fingers.)*

All fall down.
> *(Drop to floor.)*

*Adapted Traditional*

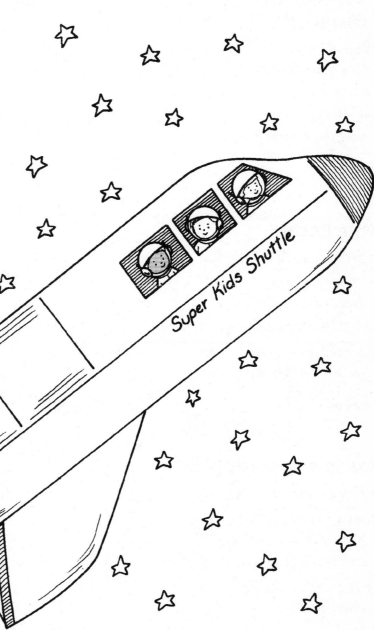

## The Robot

The legs of the robot go up and down,

Up and down, up and down.

The legs of the robot go up and down,

As it walks round the room.
> *(March around like robot.)*

The head of the robot goes side to side,

Side to side, side to side.

The head of the robot goes side to side,

As it walks round the room.
> *(Move head from side to side while marching.)*

*Additional verses*: The arms of the robot go back and forth; The buttons on the robot go beep, beep, beep; The voice of the robot goes "Does not compute."

*Serena K. Butch*

## A Little Robot

I'm a little robot,

Short and strong.

Here are my handles,

Just turn me on.
> *(Pretend to wind self up.)*

When I get all warmed up,

Watch me go,

Sometimes fast

And sometimes slow.
> *(Walk around like a robot.)*

*Jean Warren*

## I'm a Robot

I'm a robot, watch me walk,
> *(Do actions as rhyme indicates.)*
Push my button, now I can talk.

When I get all oiled up I can work,

Even if I have to jerk.

I'm a robot, watch me go,

Sometimes fast, sometimes slow.

When I get all worn out you can see

All I need is a new battery!

*Jean Warren*

# Celebrations & Special People

## Little Black Cat

Little black cat
On Halloween night,
Sits on a fence
In the yellow moonlight.
    *(Sit, holding up hands like paws.)*

Black cat, black cat,
What do you spy
Flying across
The Halloween sky?
    *(Look upward.)*

I see two ghosts
Floating by,
Doing somersaults
In the sky.
    *(Roll hands.)*

Black cat, black cat,
What else do you spy
Flying across
The Halloween sky?
    *(Look upward.)*

I see a black bat
Flying by
The big yellow moon
Up in the sky.
    *(Hook thumbs together and wave hands like wings.)*

*Jean Warren*

## Black Cat

Black cat, black cat,
Up in the tree.
    *(Look upward.)*
Black cat, black cat,
Staring at me.
    *(Form circles around eyes with fingers.)*
Black cat, black cat,
Come down from there.
    *(Beckon with hand.)*
Black cat, black cat,
You gave me a scare!
Boo!

*Karen M. Smith*

## The Ghosts Fly In

The ghosts fly in,
    *(Do actions as rhyme indicates.)*
The ghosts fly out.
The ghosts are certainly
All about.

The ghosts fly high,
And then dive low.
They're always spooky
Wherever they go.

The ghosts fly round,
All dressed in white.
Did you ever see
Such a spooky sight?

*Susan M. Paprocki*

## Ghost Chant

Ghost so scary,
Ghost so white,
Don't scare Jennifer
On Halloween night!

Repeat, each time substituting
one of your children's names
for *Jennifer*.

*Betty Silkunas*

## Little Ghost

Little ghost, little ghost,
    *(Use pointer finger as ghost and act out rhyme.)*
Flying through the air,
Little ghost, little ghost,
Tickling my hair.

Little ghost, little ghost,
Flying way down low,
Little ghost, little ghost,
Tickling my toe.

Little ghost, little ghost,
Circling all around,
Little ghost, little ghost,
Please sit down.

*Betty Silkunas*

## Dancing Ghost

Little ghost, little ghost,
Dressed in white,
See how you dance
On Halloween night!
    *(Dance around.)*

*Additional verses:* See how you
run; See how you hop; See how
you skip; See how you crawl.

*Jean Warren*

## Halloween Goblins

One little goblin standing at the door,
    *(Hold up one finger.)*
Two little goblins dancing 'cross the floor.
    *(Wiggle two fingers.)*
Three little goblins peeking through the latch,
    *(Bring two fingers and thumb together and peek through.)*
Four little goblins, what a happy batch!
    *(Hold up four fingers, then clap hands once.)*
Five little goblins, and more that can't be seen,
    *(Hold up five fingers, then look all around.)*
We're all getting ready for Halloween!

*Author Unknown*

## Five Little Goblins

Five little goblins on Halloween night,
Made a very spooky sight.
    *(Hold up five fingers.)*
The first goblin danced on his tippi-tip-toes,
    *(Wiggle thumb.)*
The second goblin tumbled and bumped his nose.
    *(Wiggle pointer finger.)*
The third goblin jumped high up in the air,
    *(Wiggle middle finger.)*
The fourth goblin walked like a big fuzzy bear.
    *(Wiggle ring finger.)*
The fifth goblin sang a Halloween song,
    *(Wiggle little finger.)*
Then the five little goblins danced the whole night long.
    *(Wiggle all five fingers.)*

*Adapted Traditional*

## Hoot Owl

Hoot owl, hoot owl, sitting in the tree,

Hoot owl, hoot owl, what do you see?

I see black cats running by me,
    *(Run like a cat.)*
All night long as I sit in my tree.


Hoot owl, hoot owl, sitting in the tree,

Hoot owl, hoot owl, what do you see?

I see pumpkins rolling by me,
    *(Roll like a pumpkin.)*
All night long as I sit in my tree.


Hoot owl, hoot owl, sitting in the tree,

Hoot owl, hoot owl, what do you see?

I see spiders crawling by me,
    *(Crawl like a spider.)*
All night long as I sit in my tree.

*Jean Warren*

## Five Little Pumpkins

Five little pumpkins were sitting on the ground.
*(Hold up five fingers.)*

The first little pumpkin was short and round,
*(Point to thumb.)*

The second little pumpkin was happy to be found.
*(Point to index finger.)*

The third little pumpkin had a curly vine,
*(Point to middle finger.)*

The fourth little pumpkin liked sunshine.
*(Point to ring finger.)*

The fifth little pumpkin grew so quick,
*(Point to little finger.)*

Now all five pumpkins are ready to be picked.
*(Wiggle all five fingers.)*

*Diane Thom*

## Pumpkin, Pumpkin

Pumpkin, pumpkin,

Sitting on the wall,
*(Sit on floor.)*

Pumpkin, pumpkin,

Tip and fall.
*(Fall to one side.)*

Pumpkin, pumpkin,

Rolling down the street,
*(Roll on floor.)*

Pumpkin, pumpkin,

Trick-or-treat!

*Author Unknown*

## Five Orange Pumpkins

Five orange pumpkins rolling down a hill,
*(Hold up five fingers.)*

Once they started rolling, they couldn't keep still.

One hit a rock and couldn't roll any more,
*(Bend down thumb.)*

How many pumpkins left? Now there are four.

Four orange pumpkins a-rolling and a-bumping,

I hear them clumping, I hear them thumping.

One fell into a hole next to a tree,
*(Bend down pointer finger.)*

How many pumpkins left? Now there are three.

Three orange pumpkins rolling on the grass,

Watch them tumble and roll so fast.

One rolled until it bumped right against my shoe,
*(Bend down middle finger.)*

How many pumpkins left? Now there are two.

Two orange pumpkins still rolling very fast,

Will they ever slow down and stop at last?

One pumpkin hit a tree, its rolling now is done,
*(Bend down ring finger.)*

How many pumpkins left? Now there is one.

One last orange pumpkin rolling toward me,

Now it's stopped rolling, look and see.
*(Bend down little finger.)*

Now how many pumpkins are rolling in the sun?

Did you guess zero? You're right, there are none.

*Diane Thom*

## There Was a Pumpkin

There once was a pumpkin short and fat,

Alone in the garden, there it sat.
*(Point downward.)*

A little girl picked it from the vine,

Took it home and said, "It's mine!"
*(Pretend to pick pumpkin.)*

She carved a face with a great big smile,

Put in a candle, and after a while,
*(Pretend to put candle inside pumpkin.)*

It wasn't a pumpkin short and fat.

It was a jack-o'-lantern—just like that!
*(Form circle with arms and smile.)*

*Lynne Speaker*

## Three Little Pumpkins

Three little pumpkins sitting very still

In a pumpkin patch high up on a hill.
*(Hold up three fingers)*

The first one said, "I'm very green,

But I'll be orange by Halloween."
*(Wiggle first finger.)*

The second one said, "I'm on my way

To becoming a jack-o'-lantern someday."
*(Wiggle second finger.)*

The third one said, "Oh me, oh my,

Tomorrow I'll be a pumpkin pie!"
*(Wiggle third finger.)*

*Adapted Traditional*

## I'm a Little Pumpkin

I'm a little pumpkin, look at me,

I'm round and cute as I can be.
*(Bend arms out at sides.)*

Carve a face and add a candle bright,

I'll glow and glow all through the night.
*(Form circle with arms and smile.)*

*Deborah A. Roessel*

## The Halloween Surprise

Dad and I shopped for a pumpkin
To carve for Halloween.
The one we bought was round and fat,
The best we'd ever seen.

We took it home, and carefully
My dad cut off the top.
We scooped the gloppy seeds all out
Onto paper—plop, plop, plop!

Next, Dad cut out the eyes and mouth,
Then he cut out the nose.
He winked at me and then he said,
"He'll be bald, I suppose."

I laughed and said, "Oh, Daddy,
Jack-o'-lanterns' heads are bare.
I've never seen a single one
That had a head of hair!"

Then we took our pumpkin outside
With a candle for its light.
Our jolly jack-o'-lantern glowed
So brightly in the night.

Long after I had gone to bed,
Snowflakes began to fall.
They covered up the bushes
And the garden and the wall.

In the morning I ran out to see
If my pumpkin was still there.
I found him sitting on the porch—
But now he had white hair!

*Ellen Javernick*

## Little Pumpkin

I'm a little pumpkin orange and round,
  *(Form circle with arms.)*
When I'm sad, my face wears a frown.
  *(Frown.)*
But when I am happy and all aglow,
  *(Smile.)*
Watch my smile just grow and grow!
  *(Smile even wider.)*

*Barbara Hasson*

## I'm a Jack-O'-Lantern

I'm a jack-o'-lantern, look at me,
I'm as happy as I can be.
  *(Form circle with arms.)*
Put a candle in and light the light,
Don't be frightened—it's Halloween night!
  *(Make a face and say, "Boo!")*

*Betty Ruth Baker*

## Five Stuffed Scarecrows

Five stuffed scarecrows in the corn rows,
  *(Stand straight and tall.)*
The first one said, "Go away, crows!"
  *(Wave arms.)*
The second one said, "I am very small,"
  *(Crouch down low.)*
The third one said, "I am standing tall."
  *(Stand on tiptoe.)*
The fourth one said, "On my head I wear a hat,"
  *(Pretend to put on a hat.)*
The fifth one said, "By my feet runs a cat."
  *(Point downward.)*
Five stuffed scarecrows in the corn rows,
  *(Stand straight and tall.)*
Moving left and right as the autumn wind blows.
  *(Sway back and forth.)*

*Rita Graef*

## Scarecrow, Scarecrow

Scarecrow, scarecrow, what do you see,

Alone at night by the old oak tree?

A ghost and a jack-o'-lantern,

That's what he sees,

Alone at night by the old oak tree.

Repeat, letting your children substitute other
Halloween words for *ghost* and *jack-o'-lantern*.

*Jean Warren*

## Five Little Scarecrows

Five little scarecrows by the old barn door,
  *(Hold up five fingers.)*
One went home and then there were four.
  *(Bend down thumb.)*
Four little scarecrows by the old oak tree,

One went home and then there were three.
  *(Bend down pointer finger.)*
Three little scarecrows with nothing to do,

One went home and then there were two.
  *(Bend down middle finger.)*
Two little scarecrows out in the sun,

One went home and then there was one.
  *(Bend down ring finger.)*
One little scarecrow all alone through the day,

He scared the crows and they all flew away.
  *(Wiggle little finger.)*

*Jean Warren*

## Halloween Is Coming

Halloween is coming, I like it the most.

I'll be a goblin, you can be a ghost.
  *(Point to self, then to other person.)*
When we're all dressed up, we will say,

"Boo! It's trick-or-treat today!"
  *(Make a face.)*

*Becky Valenick*

## Trick-Or-Treaters

Knock, knock, knock.

Sounds like more

Trick-or-treaters at my door.

I open the door and what do I see?

Two funny clowns smiling at me!

Repeat, letting your children complete new endings such as these: A great big _____ smiling at me; A teeny tiny ____ smiling at me; An ugly old ____ smiling at me; A beautiful ____ smiling at me.

*Jean Warren*

## Boo to You

Boo, boo, boo to you,

I'll be a ghost tonight.
    *(Pretend to be a ghost.)*
I will wear a long white sheet

And give you such a fright.

Hee-hee, ha-ha-ha,

Tonight I'll be a clown.
    *(Pretend to be a clown.)*
I will wear a big red nose

And dance all through the town.

Yo-ho, ho-ho-ho,

A pirate I will be.
    *(Pretend to be a pirate.)*
I'll wear a patch across my eye

And sail upon the sea.

*Bobby Lee Wagman*

## Dressed for Halloween

Goblins, ghosts, and black cats too,

The scariest you've ever seen.

Trick-or-treating's what we do,

We're dressed for Halloween.

Jack-o'-lanterns all aglow,

Black bats in the air.

Just be careful where you go

Or you might get a scare.

Boo!

*Judy Hall*

## Don't Be Afraid on Halloween

Listen to the sounds on Halloween
    *(Cup hand behind ear.)*
Listen to the cries and groans.

Listen to the boos and the cackling laughs,

Listen to the sighs and moans.

Don't be afraid on Halloween,
    *(Shake head.)*
Don't worry about what you hear.

For Halloween night is all make-believe,

And you have nothing to fear.

*Jean Warren*

## Halloween Flight

Owls are flying in the sky,
*(Do actions as rhyme indicates.)*
Swooping down, then back up high.

Ghosts are flying by on brooms,

In and out of haunted rooms.

Bats are flying to the moon,

They won't sleep till afternoon.

*Susan A. Miller*

## It's Halloween

Sometimes I like to walk in the dark,

And hiss and groan and scream.
*(Make scary sounds.)*
I sneak behind somebody I know—

Boo! It's Halloween!
*(Make a scary face.)*

*Frank Dally*

## Halloween Fingerplay

Ten big monsters standing in a line,
*(Hold up ten fingers.)*
One stomps away, and that leaves nine.
*(Bend down right thumb.)*
Nine black cats sitting on my gate,

One jumps off, and that leaves eight.
*(Bend down right pointer finger.)*
Eight little ghosts floating in the heavens,

One fades away, and that leaves seven.
*(Bend down right middle finger.)*
Seven grinning goblins doing magic tricks,

One disappears, and that leaves six.
*(Bend down right ring finger.)*
Six tall scarecrows looking so alive,

One falls over, and that leaves five.
*(Bend down right little finger.)*

Five rattling skeletons behind the closet door,

One slides out, and that leaves four.
*(Bend down left thumb.)*
Four black bats flapping round a tree,

One flies away, and that leaves three.
*(Bend down left pointer finger.)*
Three wacky ghouls stirring up a stew,

One falls in the pot, and that leaves two.
*(Bend down left middle finger.)*
Two scary spooks drumming up some fun,

One goes trick-or-treating, and that leaves one.
*(Bend down left ring finger.)*
One jack-o'-lantern in the autumn sun,

It nods off to sleep, and that leaves none.
*(Bend down left little finger.)*

*Susan M. Paprocki*

## Gobble, Gobble

A turkey is a funny bird,

His head goes wobble, wobble.
> *(Wobble head.)*

He knows just one funny word—

Gobble, gobble, gobble!
> *(Speak in warbly voice.)*

*Lynn Beaird*

## My Turkey

I have a turkey big and fat,
> *(Bend out arms at sides.)*

He struts around this way and that.
> *(Strut.)*

His daily corn he would not miss,
> *(Pretend to eat corn.)*

And when he talks, he sounds like this.
> *(Make gobbling sound.)*

*Dee Hoffman and Judy Panko*

## Mr. Turkey

"Gobble-gobble,

Gobble-gobble,"

Says the bird.

Mr. Turkey gobble-gobbles,

While his feet go wobble-wobble.

"Gobble-gobble,

Gobble-gobble,"

Says the bird.
> *(Strut around.)*

*Becky Valenick*

## Strutting Turkey

Mr. Turkey strutting all around,

Pecking at the corn down on the ground.
> *(Strut and make pecking movements.)*

See him walk with a wobble, wobble, wobble,

Hear him talk with a gobble, gobble, gobble.
> *(Speak in warbly voice.)*

*Elizabeth McKinnon*

## Color Turkey Feathers

Mr. Turkey was so sad,

He lost the feathers he once had.

Now he wants us to help him find

All the feathers of his kind.

We will look both high and low,

We will find them, don't you know.

Here's a red one and a blue,

Look, we've found a green one too.

Here's an orange one and a yellow,

Soon he'll be a feathered fellow.

Now we've found the purple one,

Black and white—we're almost done.

If we just look up and down,

I know we'll find the feather brown.

Now Mr. Turkey is so glad,

We found the feathers he once had.

*Gayle Bittinger*

## Handprint Turkey

This isn't just a turkey,

As anyone can see.

I made it with my hand,

Which is a part of me!

It comes with lots of love

Especially to say—

I hope you have

A very happy Thanksgiving Day!

Include this rhyme inside handprint turkey cards that your children make for Thanksgiving.

*Cathy B. Griffin*

## Turkey on the Farm

Turkey, turkey, on the farm,

Are you getting fat?

We are waiting for Thanksgiving,

Now what do you think of that?


Turkey, turkey, on the farm,

Do you ever wonder why

People eat you for Thanksgiving

And not chicken pot pie?

*Debra Lindahl*

## Just Like That

Turkey, turkey,

Big and fat,
*(Bend arms out at sides.)*

I'm going to eat you,

Just like that!
*(Open and close mouth.)*

*Barbara Dunn*


## Turkey, Turkey

Turkey, turkey, look at you,

Please be careful what you do.
*(Shake pointer finger.)*

Thanksgiving Day is almost here,

And we eat turkey every year.
*(Pretend to eat.)*

Go and hide out in the woods,

Then we'll eat pizza, like we should!
*(Pretend to shoo away turkey.)*

*Judy Hall*


## Mr. Turkey, Run Away

Oh, Mr. Turkey,

Run away.
*(Run in place.)*

If you are not careful,

You will be a mouthful
*(Point to mouth.)*

On Thanksgiving Day!

*Margery A. Kranyik*

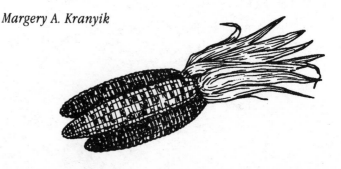

# Five Little Turkeys

Five little turkeys by the front door,
*(Hold up five fingers.)*
One waddled off, then there were four.
*(Bend down thumb.)*
Four little turkeys out under the tree,
One waddled off, then there were three.
*(Bend down pointer finger.)*
Three little turkeys with nothing to do,
One waddled off, then there were two.
*(Bend down middle finger.)*
Two little turkeys in the noonday sun,
One waddled off, then there was one.
*(Bend down ring finger.)*
One little turkey—better run away!
Soon it will be Thanksgiving Day.
*(Bend down little finger.)*

*Jean Warren*

# Do the Turkey Hop

Do the turkey hop,
Do the turkey run,
*(Hop, then run, in place.)*
Do the turkey gobble,
It's a lot of fun.
*(Make gobbling sound.)*

Now flap your wings
Like the turkeys do,
*(Flap arms at sides.)*
Then run from the farmer
Before he catches you!
*(Run away.)*

*Diane Thom*

# Watch Out, Mr. Turkey

Mr. Turkey, you'd better watch out,
Thanksgiving Day is coming.
*(Shake pointer finger.)*
If you're not careful you'll end up
In someone's hungry tummy!
*(Point to tummy.)*

*Maureen Gutyan*

# Mr. Turkey Gobbler

I met a big fat turkey
*(Hold up fists with thumbs facing.)*
When I went out to play.
"Mr. Turkey Gobbler,
*(Move left thumb up and down.)*
How are you today?"

"Gobble, gobble, gobble,
*(Move right thumb up and down.)*
That I cannot say—
Don't ask me such a question
*(Waddle right fist off to side.)*
On Thanksgiving Day!"

*Adapted Traditional*

## Thanksgiving Time

Thanksgiving time is here,

Let's clap and give a cheer

For food and friends and family—

Thanksgiving time is here!
    *(Clap hands and cheer.)*

*Gayle Bittinger*

## It Smells Like Thanksgiving

It smells like Thanksgiving,
    *(Close eyes and sniff.)*
Like it should.
The turkey's in the oven—
Mmmm, it smells good!

It smells like Thanksgiving,
My, oh, my!
What's in the oven now?
Smells like pumpkin pie!

*Elizabeth McKinnon*

## Hurray, It's Thanksgiving Day

The Pilgrims are coming to celebrate,

Hurray, hurray!

The Pilgrims are coming to celebrate

Thanksgiving Day!

The Pilgrims are coming,

So don't be late,

We'll eat and dance

To celebrate,

And we'll all be glad,

So hurry and don't be late!

The Indians are coming to celebrate,

Hurray, hurray!

The Indians are coming to celebrate

Thanksgiving Day!

The Indians are coming,

So don't be late,

We'll eat and dance

To celebrate,

And we'll all be glad,

So hurry and don't be late!

*Jean Warren*

## Hanukkah Candles

Eight little candles in a row,
*(Hold up eight fingers.)*
Waiting to join the holiday glow.
*(Bend fingers down.)*

The first night we light candle number one,
*(Hold up one finger.)*
Hanukkah time has now begun.
*(Bend finger down.)*

The second night we light candles one and two,
*(Hold up two fingers.)*
Hanukkah's here—there's lots to do.
*(Bend fingers down.)*

The third night we light all up to three,
*(Hold up three fingers.)*
Hanukkah's here—there's lots to see.
*(Bend fingers down.)*

The fourth night we light all up to four,
*(Hold up four fingers.)*
Each now a part of the Hanukkah lore.
*(Bend fingers down.)*

The fifth night we light all up to five,
*(Hold up five fingers.)*
Helping our Hanukkah come alive.
*(Bend fingers down.)*

The sixth night we light all up to six,
*(Hold up six fingers.)*
Happy candles—happy wicks!
*(Bend fingers down.)*

The seventh night we light all up to seven,
*(Hold up seven fingers.)*
The glow of each candle reaches to heaven.
*(Bend fingers down.)*

The eighth night we light all up to eight,
*(Hold up eight fingers.)*
Hanukkah's here—let's celebrate!
*(Smile.)*

*Jean Warren*

## Lighting All the Candles

I am lighting all the candles
*(Gradually hold up eight fingers.)*
On this Hanukkah night.
I am lighting all the candles
To see them shining bright.

Flicker, flicker, little candles,
*(Gently flutter upright fingers.)*
Fill me with your glow.
Now it's time to count them,
Ready, set, go!
*(Count to eight on fingers.)*

*Gillian Whitman*

## Eight Candles

Eight candles,
*(Hold up eight fingers.)*
I can't wait.
Hanukkah is here,
Let's celebrate!
*(Nod head and smile.)*

Eight candles,
*(Gently flutter upright fingers.)*
Shining bright.
I can't wait
To count each light.
*(Count fingers.)*

*Susan Peters*

## Eight Little Candles

Eight little candles all in a row,
Waiting to join the holiday glow.
*(Hold up eight fingers.)*
We will light them one by one,
Until all eight have joined the fun.
*(Touch tips of eight fingers, one at a time.)*
Eight little candles burning bright,
Filling the world with holiday light.
*(Gently flutter upright fingers.)*

*Jean Warren*

## Hanukkah Is Coming

Hanukkah is coming soon,
Light each menorah light.
One, two, three, four,
*(Touch tips of four left-hand fingers.)*
Five, six, seven, eight.
*(Touch tips of four right-hand fingers.)*
One for every night.

*Jean Warren*

## Hanukkah Time

In the window of my house,
*(Draw window in air with finger.)*
I see the menorah shine
With eight burning candles—
*(Hold up eight fingers.)*
It must be Hanukkah time!

*Judy Caplan Ginsburgh*

## Counting Candles

One little, two little, three little candles,
*(Hold up fingers one at a time.)*
Four little, five little, six little candles,
Seven little, eight little, nine little candles.
The ninth one is the shammash.

Nine little, eight little, seven little candles,
*(Lower fingers one at a time.)*
Six little, five little, four little candles,
Three little, two little, one little candle
In our Hanukkah menorah.

*Judy Caplan Ginsburgh*

## Five Little Dreidels

Five little dreidels spinning in a row,
*(Do actions as rhyme indicates.)*
The first one spun, oh, so slow.
The second one went round and round,
The third one fell down on the ground.
The fourth one spun like a happy top,
The fifth one said, "I'll never stop!"
Five little dreidels—look and see,
Spinning at Hanukkah for you and me.

*Marjorie Debowy*

## Spin the Dreidel

Spin the dreidel round and round,
*(Do actions as rhyme indicates.)*
It spins and spins and then falls down.
It starts out fast and then spins slow,
Wobble, wobble, down it goes!
Spin the dreidel round and round,
It spins and spins and then falls down.

*Judy Caplan Ginsburgh*

## Spinning Dreidel

I'm a little dreidel spinning round,
*(Do actions as rhyme indicates.)*
Turning, turning, without a sound.
Spin so fast—then slow down,
Slower, slower—fall to the ground.

*Gillian Whitman*

## I'm a Little Dreidel

I'm a little dreidel made of clay,
Spin me around when you want to play.
*(Pretend to spin dreidel.)*
When I fall down, if you don't win,
Just pick me up and spin again.
*(Pretend to spin dreidel again.)*

*Adapted Traditional*

## I Am a Dreidel

I am a dreidel, spin me just right,
*(Clasp hands together.)*
I whirl and whirl with all my might.
*(Roll hands.)*
Now the whirls are out of me,
*(Stop rolling hands.)*
So I will rest as still as can be.
*(Clasp hands in lap.)*

*Adapted Traditional*

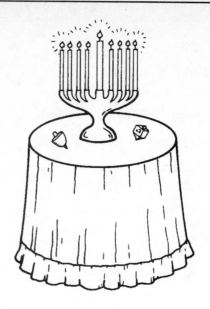

## Celebrating Hanukkah

We're celebrating Hanukkah,

Holiday of light.

We get to light the candles,

One for every night.
*(Pretend to light candles.)*

We gather round the table,

With all our family there.

Holidays are special times

When we get to share.
*(Hold hands in circle with others.)*

*Lynne Copeland*

## Happy Hanukkah

Oh, burn the candles bright,

And dance around the light!
*(Dance fingers in air.)*
Spin the dreidel round,

Then watch it falling down.
*(Make dreidel movements with hand.)*
There are latke treats to eat

And family to greet.
*(Pretend to eat, then hug self.)*
Happy Hanukkah!

*Gillian Whitman*

## Advent

Advent is a time to wait,

Not quite time to celebrate.

Light the candles one by one,
*(Pretend to light four candles.)*
Till this Advent time is done.

Christmas Day will soon be here,

Time for joy and time for cheer!

*Karen Leslie*

## Ring the Bells

Ring, ring, ring the bells,
*(Pretend to ring bell.)*
Ring them loud and clear

To say to people everywhere

That Christmas time is here.

*Karen Vollmer*

## Two Little Bells

Two little bells on the Christmas tree,
*(Use pointer fingers to act out rhyme as indicated.)*
Ringing for you and ringing for me.

One rings high, one rings low.

One rings fast, one rings slow.

Two little bells on the Christmas tree,

Ringing for you and ringing for me.

*Jean Warren*

## My Jingle Bells

Jingle bells, jingle bells,
*(Pretend to shake bells as rhyme indicates.)*
Jingle all the way.

Oh, what fun it is to play

My jingle bells today!

Shake them fast, shake them slow,

Shake them loud and clear.

Oh, what fun it is to shake

My bells for all to hear!

*Jean Warren*

## Little Bell

Little bell, little bell,

If I ask you, will you tell

Why you always seem to chime

When it's close to Christmas time?

*Jean Warren*

## Poinsettia Time

Poinsettia time is here,

Let's clap our hands and cheer.
    *(Clap.)*

Red and green poinsettias say

That Christmas time is near!

*Elizabeth McKinnon*

## Five Little Bells

Five little bells hanging in a row,
    *(Hold up five fingers.)*

The first bell said, "Ring me slow."
    *(Point to thumb.)*

The second bell said, "Ring me fast,"
    *(Point to index finger.)*

The third bell said, "Ring me last."
    *(Point to middle finger.)*

The fourth bell said, "I'm like a chime,"
    *(Point to ring finger.)*

The fifth bell said, "Ring me at Christmas time."
    *(Bend down little finger.)*

*Adapted Traditional*

## Eight Little Reindeer

Eight little reindeer beside Santa's sleigh,

Getting hitched up to be on their way.
    *(Hold up eight fingers.)*

The first one said, "We can't be late."
    *(Wiggle first finger.)*

The second one said, "Christmas won't wait."
    *(Wiggle second finger.)*

The third one said, "The sleigh's full of toys..."
    *(Wiggle third finger.)*

The fourth one said, "For all the girls and boys."
    *(Wiggle fourth finger.)*

The fifth one said, "I'm ready to fly..."
    *(Wiggle fifth finger.)*

The sixth one said, "Across the evening sky."
    *(Wiggle sixth finger.)*

The seventh one said, "Look, it's starting to snow."
    *(Wiggle seventh finger.)*

The eighth one said, "I think it's time to go."
    *(Wiggle eighth finger.)*

"Ready?" asked Santa. "It's almost Christmas Day."

And off they all flew—up, up, and away!
    *(Fly all eight fingers upward.)*

*Jean Warren*

## Christmas Candles

Christmas candles burning bright,
    *(Hold up fingers and gently flutter them.)*

Shining in the winter night.

Shining there for all to see,

Christmas candles, one, two, three.

To use this rhyme for other holidays,
substitute *holiday* for *Christmas*.

*Bonnie Woodard*

## I've Seen a Santa

I've seen a Santa jolly and fat,
*(Hold arms out in front of tummy.)*
He strokes his beard this way and that.
*(Pretend to stroke beard.)*
He puts his pack into his sleigh,
*(Pretend to put pack in sleigh.)*
Then off he goes—up, up, and away.
*(Swing arms upward.)*

*Dee Hoffman and Judy Panko*

## Santa's Elves

We're Santa's little elves,
*(Do actions as rhyme indicates.)*
Making all the toys
That Santa likes to take
To all the girls and boys.

We're Santa's little elves,
Wrapping gifts with bows.
Now the gifts are ready
For Santa when he goes.

We're Santa's little elves,
We're loading up the sleigh.
Christmas is coming,
And Santa's on his way!

*Sharon Engel*

## I Heard Santa Say

Christmas Day is coming soon,

I heard Santa say.
*(Cup hand behind ear.)*
Jingle, jingle, ring the bells

On old Santa's sleigh.
*(Pretend to shake bells.)*
"Ho, ho, ho!" says Santa Claus,

"I'll soon be on my way!
*(Hold arms out in front of tummy.)*
Merry Christmas, everyone,

It's almost Christmas Day!"
*(Wave.)*

*Joan Nydigger*

## Who Is It?

Who laughs this way—"Ho, ho, ho?"
*(Hold arms out in front of tummy.)*
Who drives a sleigh through sleet and snow?
*(Pretend to drive sleigh.)*
Whose hair is white, whose suit is red?
*(Touch hair, then shirt.)*
Who wears a red hat on his head?
*(Touch top of head.)*
Who brings such fun for girls and boys?
*(Tilt head to one side.)*
Yes, it's Santa with the toys!
*(Laugh like Santa.)*

*Debra Lindahl*

## Christmas Eve

When Santa fills my stocking,
*(Pretend to fill stocking.)*
I wish that I could peek.
*(Peek through fingers.)*
But Santa never, ever comes
*(Shake head.)*
Till I am fast asleep.
*(Rest cheek on folded hands.)*

*Author Unknown*

## Santa

Someone's peeking through my window,
*(Peek through fingers.)*
Tapping at my door,
*(Make knocking motion.)*
Sliding down my chimney,
*(Make sliding motion with hands.)*
Landing on the floor.
*(Stamp feet.)*

He's filling all the stockings,
*(Pretend to fill stockings.)*
And looking at the tree.
*(Turn head and widen eyes.)*
He has lots of presents,
*(Pretend to count on fingers.)*
Some for you and some for me.
*(Point to others, then to self.)*

I'm peeking round the doorway,
*(Peek around hand.)*
And, oh, what do I see?
*(Look surprised.)*
The jolly face of Santa
*(Smile.)*
Peeking back at me!
*(Peek through fingers.)*

*Author Unknown*

## Christmas Snowman

I'm a little snowman round and fat,
*(Bend out arms at sides.)*
Here is my scarf, and here is my hat.
*(Touch neck, then top of head.)*
When Christmas comes around, hear me shout,
*(Cup hands around mouth.)*
"Here comes Santa! You'd better watch out!"

*Vivian Sasser*

## Our Christmas Tree

We went out looking for a Christmas tree,
*(Cup hand above eye and start walking.)*
We went to see what we could see.
*(Look all around.)*
The first tree we found was much too small,
*(Lower hand near floor.)*
The second tree we found was much too tall.
*(Raise hand up high.)*
The third tree we found was much too broad,
*(Spread arms out wide.)*
The fourth tree we found was thin as a rod.
*(Hold up one arm.)*

The fifth tree we found looked just about right,
*(Form outline of tree with hands.)*
So we chopped it down with all our might.
*(Pretend to chop down tree.)*
We took our tree home and set it straight,
*(Pretend to set up tree.)*
Everyone thought that it looked just great.
*(Clasp hands and smile.)*
Then we all joined hands and circled round
*(Form circle with others.)*
The beautiful tree that we had found.

*Author Unknown*

## Little Green Tree

I'm a little green tree

By the house.
*(Stand tall.)*

Here is my trunk,
*(Raise arms straight up.)*

Here are my boughs.
*(Hold arms out at sides.)*

Decorate me now

With lights so fine,
*(Move hands back and forth across body.)*

Then plug them in

And watch me shine!
*(Hold arms out at sides and wiggle fingers.)*

*Billie Taylor*

## Little Christmas Tree

I'm a little Christmas tree,

Pretty as can be,
*(Stand with arms out at sides.)*

Standing in the window

For all to see.

Watch my lights twinkling,

Oh, so bright.
*(Wiggle fingers.)*

With my decorations,

I'm a lovely sight!

*Cindy Dingwall*

## Christmas Star

Twinkle, twinkle, Christmas star,
*(Hold hand high and wiggle fingers.)*

Way up high is where you are,

Shining bright for all to see,

On the tiptop of our tree.

*Bonnie Woodard*

## Christmas Bulb

I'm a little Christmas bulb round and bright,
*(Form circle with thumb and fingers.)*
Here is my twinkle, oh, what a sight!
*(Open and close fingers quickly.)*
When Christmas comes around, plug me in,
*(Extend, then retract, thumb and fingers.)*
And watch me blink and blink again.
*(Open and close fingers quickly.)*

*Vivian Sasser*

## Presents Under the Tree

See all the presents under the tree,
*(Make sweeping gesture with hand.)*
Some for you and some for me.
*(Point to others, then to self.)*
Long ones, tall ones, short ones too.
*(Use hand movements to indicate measurements.)*
And here is a round one wrapped in blue.
*(Form circle with arms.)*
Isn't it fun to look and see
*(Nod head and smile.)*
All of the presents under the tree?
*(Make sweeping gesture with hand.)*

*Adapted Traditional*

## Smells Like Christmas

Smells like Christmas, oh, so good,
*(Close eyes and sniff.)*
Smells like Christmas, like it should.
Smells like peppermint and gingerbread too,
Smells like good things for me and you!

*Penny Rover*

## Christmas Time Is Here

Ring, ring, little bell,
*(Pretend to ring bell.)*
Christmas time is here.
Time for wrapping up our gifts,
*(Pretend to wrap presents.)*
Time for yuletide cheer.

Time to put up an evergreen tree,
*(Pretend to stand up tree.)*
Time to make it bright.
Time to have some holiday fun
*(Pretend to decorate tree.)*
On this special night.

*Barbara Paxson*

## Waiting for Christmas

I've been waiting for Christmas,
And it's almost here.
*(Nod head.)*
I've been waiting for Christmas,
Santa's getting near.

I can hear the sleigh bells
And the reindeer up so high.
*(Cup hand behind ear.)*
I can hear the carolers sing
As they walk by.

*Elizabeth Vollrath*

## Love

Love, love, it's all around,
> *(Gesture left, then right.)*

It will grow with you.
> *(Slowly move arms outward.)*

Show it, tell it,
> *(Hold palms out, then point to mouth.)*

Feel it, share it.
> *(Hug self, then hold hands out, palms up.)*

Make it part of you.
> *(Point to others.)*

*Adele Engelbracht*

## I Love You

I love you, you love me,
> *(Point to other person, then to self.)*

We're as happy as can be.
> *(Smile.)*

Here's a great big kiss
> *(Blow a kiss.)*

And a hug from me to you.
> *(Make hugging motion.)*

Won't you say you love me too?
> *(Tilt head to one side.)*

*Lee Bernstein*

## Yes, I Do

I love you,

Yes, I do.

*Je vous aime* means

I love you!

Repeat, substituting the Spanish
*Yo te amo* (yo teh ah-mo), then
the German *Ich liebe dich* (eesh
lee-bah deesh), for the French
*Je vous aime* (juh voo zem).

*Jean Warren*

## My Valentine

It's nice to have a friend like you,
> *(Point to other person.)*

I'll tell you what I'm going to do.
> *(Nod head.)*

Because you make me feel so fine,
> *(Hug self.)*

I'll take you for my valentine!

*Frank Dally*

## Time for Valentines

It's finally time for valentines,

That friendly time of year.

My heart is filled with lots of love

For friends so kind and dear.
> *(Place hand over heart, then point to others.)*

*Susan M. Paprocki*

## Valentine

Valentine, valentine,

Will you be mine?

I'll be your friend forever

If you'll be my valentine.

*Gayle Bittinger*

## Valentine, Valentine

Valentine, valentine,
*(Do actions as rhyme indicates.)*

All dressed in pink,

Won't you be a friend of mine

And share with us a wink?

Valentine, valentine,

Stay for just a while.

Be a kind and loving friend

And share with us a smile.

Valentine, valentine,

Take a loving break.

Show your caring friendship

By sharing a handshake.

Valentine, valentine,

Make a friendship pact.

Give the person next to you

A light pat on the back.

*Susan M. Paprocki*

## Valentines

Valentines,

Pink, white, and blue,

I'll find a pretty one

And give it to you.
*(Pretend to find and give valentine.)*

*Adapted Traditional*

## Happy Little Heart

I'm a happy little heart,

Pink, white, and red.
*(Outline heart in air with hands.)*

I'm a happy little heart

With lace around my edge.
*(Flutter fingers while outlining heart.)*

I have three words

On the front of me.
*(Hold up three fingers.)*

They say, "I love you."

Just look and see!
*(Point to chest and smile.)*

*Gayle Bittinger*

## Five Little Valentines

Five little valentines waiting in the store,
*(Hold up five fingers.)*
Joseph bought one, and then there were four.
*(Bend down thumb.)*
Four little valentines for you and for me,

Katie bought one, and then there were three.
*(Bend down pointer finger.)*
Three little valentines wondering what to do,

Daniel bought one, and then there were two.
*(Bend down middle finger.)*
Two little valentines thinking up some fun,

Teresa bought one, and then there was one.
*(Bend down ring finger.)*
One little valentine said, "Buy me and run!"

Cameron did that, and then there were none.
*(Bend down little finger.)*

Substitute the names of your children for those in the rhyme.

*Mildred Hoffman*

## I'm a Little Valentine

I'm a little valentine

Red and white,

With ribbons and lace

I'm a beautiful sight.

I can say, "I love you,"

On Valentine's Day.

Just put me in an envelope

And give me away!

*Vicki Claybrook*

I LOVE YOU

## Valentine Friends

Five little valentines,
So bright and gay,
Were waiting to be given
On Valentine's Day.
    *(Rest chin on hands.)*

And just when they thought
That their wait would never end,
Each found a way
To make a special friend.
    *(Nod head.)*

The first little valentine,
Lacy and pink,
Told someone "I like you"
With a great big wink.
    *(Wink eye.)*

The second little valentine,
Painted white and red,
Told someone "I like you"
With a pat on the head.
    *(Make patting motion.)*

The third little valentine,
A flowery miss,
Told someone "I like you"
With a great big kiss.
    *(Blow a kiss.)*

The fourth little valentine
Cried, "Take me, take me, please!"
And told someone "I like you"
With a great big squeeze.
    *(Make hugging motion.)*

The fifth little valentine,
The last one in the pile,
Told someone "I like you"
With a great big smile.
    *(Smile.)*

*Vicki Claybrook*

## Lots of Hearts

Lacy hearts, candy hearts,
   *(Outline heart shapes in air with hands.)*
Flowery hearts too.
Hearts of pink, hearts of red,
Hearts of yellow and blue.

Lacy hearts, candy hearts,
Flowery hearts too.
Oh, what fun it is to share
Lots of hearts with you!
   *(Point to others.)*

*Betty Silkunas*

## Little Valentines

One little valentine, colored pink and blue,
   *(Hold up one finger.)*
A second one came, then there were two.
   *(Hold up two fingers.)*
Two little valentines clapping with glee,
A third one came, then there were three.
   *(Hold up three fingers.)*
Three little valentines tapping on the door,
A fourth one came, then there were four.
   *(Hold up four fingers.)*
Four little valentines smiling and alive,
A fifth one came, then there were five.
   *(Hold up five fingers.)*
Five little valentines joined hands to play
And said, "Have a happy Valentine's Day!"
   *(Dance fingers around.)*

*Rose C. Merenda*

## Three Little Valentines

Three little valentines,
Each one with a bow.
Pretty, shiny, lacy,
   *(Hold up three fingers, one at a time.)*
Standing in a row.

*Judith McNitt*

## Valentines I've Made for You

Valentines I've made for you,
Some with hearts and flowers too.
All of them bring love from me,
Each one's special, you will see.
If you promise to be mine,
You can have my valentines.
   *(Pretend to hand out valentines.)*

*Maureen Gutyan*

## Five Red Valentines

Five red valentines from the card store,
    *(Hold up five fingers.)*
I gave one to Matthew, now there are four.
    *(Bend down thumb.)*
Four red valentines, pretty ones to see,

I gave one to Libby, now there are three.
    *(Bend down pointer finger.)*
Three red valentines, pink, red, and blue,

I gave one to Cody, now there are two.
    *(Bend down middle finger.)*
Two red valentines having lots of fun,

I gave one to Christina, now there is one.
    *(Bend down ring finger.)*
One red valentine—my story is almost done,

I gave it to David, now there are none.
    *(Bend down little finger.)*

Substitute the names of your children for those in the rhyme.

*Adapted Traditional*

## Color Valentines

Valentines red,

Valentines blue,

Valentines pink

Say, "I love you."

Valentines yellow,

Valentines green,

Prettiest valentines

I've ever seen!

*Jean Warren*

## Who Sent the Valentine?

I had a valentine sent to me

From somebody—who could it be?
    *(Tilt head to one side.)*
Could it be Nicole? Could that be so?

Could it be Christopher? I do not know!

Substitute the names of your children for those in the rhyme.

*Barbara Robinson*

## Look Who's Coming

Look who's coming down the walk,
  *(Cup hand above eye.)*
Oh, please, mail carrier, won't you stop?
  *(Wave hand.)*
With a knock, knock, knock,
  *(Make knocking motion.)*
Anyone at home?
  *(Cup hand around side of mouth.)*
A valentine for you has come!
  *(Hold up pretend valentine.)*

*Judith McNitt*

## Queen of Hearts

The Queen of Hearts,

She made some tarts

On a winter's day.
  *(Pretend to make tarts.)*
The Knave of Hearts,

He stole those tarts

And quickly ran away.
  *(Make grabbing motion, then run in place.)*

The Queen of Hearts,

She made more tarts,

Then put them safe away.
  *(Pretend to put away tarts.)*
The King of Hearts,

He ate the tarts

And had a happy day!
  *(Pretend to eat.)*

*Jean Warren*

## Eensy Weensy Leprechaun

An eensy weensy leprechaun

Came out St. Patrick's Day

To search for the gold

That was hidden far away.
> *(Cup hand above eye.)*

Look over the rainbow,

Was what he was told.

So with a wink of his eye,

He ran to get the gold.
> *(Wink eye, then run in place.)*

*Sharon Smith*

## Leprechaun March

Leprechauns are marching by,
> *(Do actions as rhyme indicates.)*

See them wave their hands so high.

See them marching two by two,

See them smile and wink at you.

St. Patrick's Day must soon be near

Because the leprechauns are here.

*Margery A. Kranyik*

## I Caught a Leprechaun

Mother, Mother,

What do you say,

I caught a leprechaun

Out at play.
> *(Grasp with hands.)*

Mother, Mother,

What do you say,

That little leprechaun

Ran away.
> *(Run in place.)*

Mother, Mother,

What do you think

He meant when he turned

And gave me a wink?
> *(Wink eye.)*

*Jean Warren*

## Leprechaun, Leprechaun

Leprechaun, leprechaun,

Hiding in the hay.
> *(Hide pointer finger under opposite hand.)*

Leprechaun, leprechaun,

Don't you run away.
> *(Hop pointer finger around.)*

Leprechaun, leprechaun,

Let's go out and play.
> *(Hop both pointer fingers together.)*

Leprechaun, leprechaun,

It's St. Patrick's Day!
> *(Dance pointer fingers up and down.)*

*Karen M. Smith*

## Leprechauns

Leprechauns hiding here and there,

Leprechauns hiding everywhere.
*(Peek through fingers.)*

They don't want us to see them play

When they come out on St. Patrick's Day!
*(Shake head.)*

*Margery A. Kranyik*

## I'm an Irish Leprechaun

I'm an Irish leprechaun tiny and wee,

Hiding in the forest behind a tree.
*(Peek around hand.)*

If you ever catch me, you will see

A wish I'll grant as quick as can be!
*(Snap fingers.)*

*Maureen Gutyan*

## This Little Leprechaun

This little leprechaun slid down the rainbow,
*(Point to thumb.)*

This little leprechaun stayed home.
*(Point to index finger.)*

This little leprechaun picked a shamrock,
*(Point to middle finger.)*

This little leprechaun found some gold.
*(Point to ring finger.)*

And this little leprechaun cried, "See if you can catch me,"
*(Point to little finger.)*

As he ran home.
*(Wiggle little finger.)*

*Diane Thom*

## Little Leprechaun in Green

I'm a little leprechaun dressed in green,

The tiniest man that you ever have seen.
*(Dance in place.)*

If you ever catch me, so it's told,

I'll give you my pot of gold!
*(Point to pretend gold, then wink eye.)*

*Vicki Claybrook*

## Do Your Ears Point Up?

Do your ears point up?
*(Pull on tops of ears.)*

Do you have a lot of luck?
*(Cross fingers.)*

For gold do you dig?
*(Pretend to dig.)*

Can you dance an Irish jig?
*(Dance a jig.)*

If you answered, "Yes,"
*(Nod head.)*

You're a leprechaun, I'd guess!
*(Wink eye.)*

*Diane Thom*

## Tiny Leprechaun

I'm a little leprechaun, can you see?

I'm as tiny as I can be.

I come around just once a year,

When St. Patrick's Day is near.

*Betty Ruth Baker*

## Five Wee Leprechauns

Five wee leprechauns scurrying by my door,
> *(Hold up five fingers.)*

One jumped away, then there were four.
> *(Bend down thumb.)*

Four wee leprechauns climbing in my tree,

One hid in the green leaves, then there were three.
> *(Bend down pointer finger.)*

Three wee leprechauns, just a busy few,

One went for his pot of gold, then there were two.
> *(Bend down middle finger.)*

Two wee leprechauns having lots of fun,

One hopped over the rainbow, then there was one.
> *(Bend down ring finger.)*

One wee leprechaun with all his work done,

He slipped off for a nap, then there were none.
> *(Bend down little finger.)*

*Susan M. Paprocki*

## Can't Pinch Me!

Can't pinch me!

Can't pinch me!

'Cause I'm wearing green,

You see!

*Lois E. Putnam*

## My Shamrock

I have a little shamrock,

It's green as green can be.

Watch me as I count the leaves.

One, two, three.
> *(Count on fingers.)*

*Elizabeth McKinnon*

## Five Little Shamrocks

Five little shamrocks growing outdoors,

Stephanie picked one, and that left four.
> *(Bend down thumb.)*

Four little shamrocks, two and two, you see,

Michael picked one, and that left three.
> *(Bend down pointer finger.)*

Three little shamrocks growing by my shoe,

Amanda picked one, and that left two.
> *(Bend down middle finger.)*

Two little shamrocks nodding in the sun,

Austin picked one, and that left one.
> *(Bend down ring finger.)*

One little shamrock for St. Patrick's Day fun,

Melissa picked it, and that left none.
> *(Bend down little finger.)*

*Elizabeth McKinnon*

## I'm an Easter Bunny

I'm an Easter Bunny, watch me hop,
*(Hop around.)*
Here are my two ears, see how they flop.
*(Hold hands at sides of head and flop them.)*
Here is my cotton tail, here is my nose,
*(Wiggle hips, then point to nose.)*
I'm all furry from my head to my toes.
*(Point to head, then to toes.)*

*Susan M. Paprocki*

## Five Hopping Bunnies

Five hopping bunnies, white is what they wore,
*(Hold up five fingers.)*
One hopped away, then there were four.
*(Bend down thumb.)*
Four hopping bunnies, sweet as they could be,

One hopped around the yard, then there were three.
*(Bend down pointer finger.)*
Three hopping bunnies with so much to do,

One went for Easter eggs, then there were two.
*(Bend down middle finger.)*
Two hopping bunnies playing in the sun,

One hopped down a hole, then there was one.
*(Bend down ring finger.)*
One hopping bunny, cute as a penny,

Hopped into my basket, then there weren't any.
*(Bend down little finger.)*

*Susan M. Paprocki*

## Easter Rabbit

I saw a rabbit,
*(Wiggle two fingers up behind head.)*
I said hello.
*(Wave hand.)*
He didn't stop,
*(Shake head.)*
He went down a hole.
*(Poke finger into opposite fist.)*

Now don't you fret,
*(Shake pointer finger.)*
You might see one too—
*(Nod head.)*
An Easter Rabbit,
*(Wiggle two fingers up behind head.)*
With some eggs for you!
*(Hold out cupped hands.)*

*Adapted Traditional*

## I'm the Easter Bunny

I'm the Easter Bunny, soft and white,
*(Point to self.)*
Here are my ears,
*(Wiggle two fingers up behind head.)*
And my tail so light.
*(Hold fist behind back.)*
I hide Easter eggs all over town,
*(Pretend to hide eggs.)*
Just watch me hop and hop around.
*(Hop.)*

*Judy Hall*

## Easter Bunny

Easter Bunny, soft and white,

Hopping quickly out of sight,
*(Hop.)*

Thank you for the eggs you bring

Every year to welcome spring.
*(Hold out cupped hands.)*

*Irmgard Fuertges*

## Little Easter Rabbit

Little Easter Rabbit goes hip, hop, hip,
*(Hop hand.)*

See how his ears go flip, flop, flip.
*(Hold hands at sides of head and flop them.)*

See how his eyes go blink, blink, blink,
*(Blink eyes.)*

See how his nose goes twink, twink, twink.
*(Wiggle nose.)*

Pet his white coat, so soft and furry,
*(Stroke arm.)*

Hip, hop, hip—he's off in a hurry!
*(Hop hand away.)*

*Author Unknown*

## Easter Rabbits

Five Easter Rabbits standing by the door,
*(Hold up five fingers.)*

One hopped away and then there were four.
*(Bend down thumb.)*

Four Easter Rabbits sitting near a tree,

One hopped away and then there were three.
*(Bend down pointer finger.)*

Three Easter Rabbits looking at you,

One hopped away and then there were two.
*(Bend down middle finger.)*

Two Easter Rabbits enjoying the sun,

One hopped away and then there was one.
*(Bend down ring finger.)*

One Easter Rabbit sitting all alone,

He hopped away and then there were none.
*(Bend down little finger.)*

*Jean Warren*

## The Easter Bunny

The Easter Bunny's ears are floppy,
*(Hold hands at sides of head and flop them.)*

The Easter Bunny's feet are hoppy.
*(Hop feet up and down.)*

His fur is soft and his nose is fluffy,
*(Stroke hand, then touch nose.)*

His tail is soft and powder-puffy!
*(Hold fist behind back and wiggle hips.)*

*Adapted Traditional*

## Easter Eggs

What are oval and painted bright?
*(Make oval shapes with thumbs and fingers.)*
What does the Easter Bunny hide in the night?
*(Poke fingers into opposite fist.)*
What do we love to search around for
*(Cup hand above eye.)*
On Easter morning as we walk out the door?
*(Open pretend door and walk through it.)*
Chickens lay them, and we paint them bright,
*(Pretend to paint.)*
For that old Easter Bunny to hide in the night!
*(Wiggle two fingers up behind head.)*

*Beverly Qualheim*

## Colored Easter Eggs

Easter eggs, Easter eggs,

Eggs of orange and blue—

Here are lots of colored eggs,

All for me and you!
*(Point to self, then other person.)*

Chocolate eggs colored brown,

Jellybean eggs bright green—

Aren't these the most beautiful eggs

You have ever seen?
*(Hold out cupped hands.)*

*Maureen Gutyan*

## Little Egg

Once there was a little egg,
*(Do actions as rhyme indicates.)*
That jumped down to the floor.

It started rolling all around,

Then rolled right out the door.

Little egg, roll, roll, roll,

Roll all around.

Little egg, roll, roll, roll,

All across the ground.

*Jean Warren*

## Hunting for Eggs

Hunting for eggs
*(Do actions as rhyme indicates.)*
Under my bed,
I found one in a slipper,
And the egg was colored red.

Hunting for eggs,
Now I have two,
I found one in the closet,
And the egg was colored blue.

Hunting for eggs,
What a lucky fellow,
I found one in a bucket,
And the egg was colored yellow.

Hunting for eggs
Where none could be seen,
I found one in a shoe box,
And the egg was colored green.

Hunting for eggs,
Quick as a wink,
I found one in the garden,
And the egg was colored pink.

Red and yellow,
Green, pink, and blue.
I found five eggs—
How about you?

*Jean Warren*

## Four Easter Eggs

Blue egg, blue egg,
Oh, what fun!
Blue egg, blue egg,
I found one.
*(Hold up one finger.)*

Green egg, green egg,
I see you.
Green egg, green egg,
Now I've two.
*(Hold up two fingers.)*

Red egg, red egg,
Now I see.
Red egg, red egg,
Now I've three.
*(Hold up three fingers.)*

Yellow egg, yellow egg,
Just one more.
Yellow egg, yellow egg,
Now I've four.
*(Hold up four fingers.)*

*Jean Warren*

## Two Easter Baskets

Two Easter baskets,

Under a tree.

One for you,
> *(Form left fist with thumb inside.)*

And one for me.
> *(Form right fist with thumb inside.)*

I peeked in one basket,

And what did I see?
> *(Look down at left fist.)*

A new baby chick,

Smiling at me!
> *(Pop left thumb out of fist.)*

Then I looked in the other,

And what do you think?
> *(Look down at right fist.)*

Out popped a bunny,

Quick as a wink!
> *(Pop right thumb out of fist.)*

*Jean Warren*

## Easter Time Is Here

Easter time is here,

With flowers everywhere.

We'll decorate some hard-boiled eggs

And hide them far and near.
> *(Pretend to hide eggs.)*

Easter time is here,

With baskets everywhere.

We'll sing and dance in our new hats,

'Cause Easter time is here.
> *(Dance around.)*

*Colraine Pettipaw Hunley*

## Easter Time

Easter time at last is here,

Bunnies, chickies—let us cheer!
> *(Clap and cheer.)*

Easter Bunny hops with joy,

Eggs for every girl and boy.
> *(Hop around like bunny.)*

Easter time at last is here,

Bunnies, chickies—let us cheer!
> *(Clap and cheer.)*

*Ingrid C. Skjong*

## A Happy Easter

Easter time is full of cheer,

It means spring is really here.

Baskets, flowers, fancy hats,

And rabbits too, remember that!

So, now what I would like to say

Is have a happy Easter Day!

*Becky Valenick*

## On Independence Day

Fireworks go snap, snap, snap,

Crack, crack, crack! Zap, zap, zap!
*(Move hands and fingers in rhythm.)*

Fireworks make me clap, clap, clap

On Independence Day!
*(Clap hands.)*

*Barbara Paxson*

## Firecrackers

Firecrackers, firecrackers,
*(Open and close hands quickly.)*

We see them in July,

Like little bursts of diamonds,

Falling from the sky.

Firecrackers, firecrackers,

Exploding, oh, so high,

We can see them bursting

On the Fourth of July!

*Angela Wolfe*

## Fireworks in the Sky

Boom, crack, whistle, pop!
*(Open and close hands quickly.)*

Fireworks in the sky.

See them lighting up the night

On the Fourth of July!

Red, blue, gold, and green,

With fireworks we say,

Happy birthday, America,

It's Independence Day!

*Elizabeth McKinnon*

## Fireworks

Sputter, sputter, up so high,

We can see the lighted sky.
*(Point upward.)*

Illuminations up so high,

Celebrating the Fourth of July.
*(Open and close hands quickly.)*

*Susan Peters*

## July the Fourth Is Coming

July the fourth is coming,

And I can hardly wait!

There'll be lots of fireworks

Set off to celebrate

America's independence—

A very special day.

We'll wave our flags and watch parades.

Happy birthday, U.S.A.!

*Jennifer Wagner*

## Fourth of July

Fourth of July—
Apple pie,
A picnic in the park,
And then, after dark,
Designs in the sky—
Fourth of July!

*Saundra Winnett*

## It's the Fourth of July

Come along and eat the food,
 *(Pretend to eat.)*
It's picnic time once more.
Hot dogs, burgers, and apple pie,
Let's hope the rain won't pour!
 *(Shake head.)*

Come along and play the games,
 *(Pretend to play games.)*
The gang's together now.
Racing, throwing, pitching, rowing,
Let's all take a bow!
 *(Bow.)*

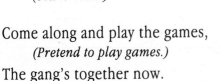

Bang, pop, crackle, hiss!
 *(Open and close hands quickly.)*
The fireworks light the sky.
Come along and celebrate,
It's the Fourth of July!
 *(Give a cheer.)*

*Debra Lindahl*

## Our Nation's Birthday

The Fourth of July
Is my favorite date.
 *(Point to self.)*
It's our nation's birthday—
Let's celebrate!
 *(Give a cheer.)*

*Bonnie Woodard*

## The Fourth Day of July

Picnics, parades,
 *(Pretend to eat, then march in place.)*
Fireworks in the sky.
 *(Open and close hands quickly.)*
This is how we celebrate
 *(Nod head.)*
The fourth day of July!
 *(Give a cheer.)*

*Sue Brown*

## Happy Independence Day

Wave the flag, red, white, and blue,
 *(Pretend to wave flag.)*
Our country belongs to me and you.
 *(Point to self, then to others.)*
So all together, let us say,
 *(Cup hands around mouth.)*
"Happy Independence Day!"

*Barbara Paxson*

## Russian New Year Troika

Troika, troika, one, two, three,

Troika, troika, please pull me

Over ice and over snow,

Ringing sleigh bells as we go.

Troika, troika, one, two, three,

Troika, troika, please pull me!

Have your children line up as if riding in a sleigh. Then let three children at a time be the troika (three-horse team) and lead the others around while everyone recites the rhyme.

*Elizabeth McKinnon*

## Chinese New Year Dragon

There's a great big dragon coming our way,

A great big dragon on this holiday.
*(March with others in a weaving line.)*

Let's grab our lanterns and follow along,

Dancing, waving, and singing a song.
*(Dance and wave while moving in line.)*

There's a great big dragon coming our way,

Hip, hip hurray!
*(Raise arms high.)*

*Jean Warren*

## Passover Is Here

It's time to clean,
*(Pretend to sweep.)*
A meal to make.
*(Pretend to stir.)*
Passover's here,
*(Nod head.)*
Let's celebrate.
*(Smile.)*

*Jean Warren*

## It's Cinco de Mayo Today

It's Cinco de Mayo today,

Let's celebrate this way—

Let's clap our hands and shout, "Olé!

It's Cinco de Mayo today!"
*(Clap hands.)*

*Additional verses:* Let's stomp our feet; Let's twirl around; Let's raise our arms; Let's circle round.

Cinco de Mayo, celebrated on May 5th, is Mexico's Independence Day.

*Elizabeth McKinnon*

## Korean Tano Day Swing

Pump, pump the Tano swing,
*(Swing hands as rhyme indicates.)*
Pump it up so high.

You pump so high you touch the sky,

Then down you come again.

In Korea, in early summer, children celebrate
Tano Day by having swinging contests.

*Jean Warren*

## Swedish Lucia Day Candles

Candles, candles burning bright,

Filling all the world with light.
*(Hold upright fingers around head for candle
crown.)*
Now it is Lucia Day,

Time for us to eat and play.
*(Keeping fingers in place, walk back and forth.)*
Candles, candles burning bright,

Filling all the world with light.
*(Keeping fingers in place, flutter them gently.)*

Lucia Day is celebrated in Sweden on December 13th.

*Elizabeth McKinnon*

## Mexican Christmas Piñata

Here is our piñata,

What a sight to see,
*(Point upward.)*
Filled with treats and goodies

Just for you and me.
*(Point to others, then to self.)*
When it's time to break it,

We will circle round.
*(Form circle with others.)*
Then we'll scramble for the treats

That fall down on the ground!
*(Drop to floor and pretend to search for treats.)*

*Elizabeth McKinnon*

## Kwanzaa Candles

Seven little candles all in a line,

Waiting to be lighted at Kwanzaa time.
*(Hold up seven fingers.)*
Come let's count them—one, two three,

Four, five, six, seven candles to see!
*(Count fingers.)*

Kwanzaa is an African-American celebration that
begins on December 26th and lasts for seven days.

*Elizabeth McKinnon*

## Let's Honor Traditions

Freedom for one,
Freedom for all.
That is our motto,
That is our call.

Let's celebrate now,
We have triumphed at last.
We live in a new world
That honors the past.

Let's open our arms
And embrace one and all.
Let's stand up together,
So no one can fall.

Let's honor traditions
Of all whom we meet.
It will make us strong,
It will keep us unique.

*Jean Warren*

## Come, Let's Celebrate

People all are different,
Each one is unique.
I can tell when I see them,
I can tell when they speak.

That's what's so exciting,
That's why our country's great.
We all are different,
Come, let's celebrate!

*Jean Warren*

## Let's Join Hands

Let's join hands and circle round,
Let's tell the world what we have found.
We're each unique, like our names,
Yet deep inside we're all the same.

Our clothes may be different,
Our skin color too.
But we each have a dream
That's shiny and new—

Where all of us live
Free of the past,
Sharing together
A future at last.

*Jean Warren*

## Families

All families get together,
It's what they like to do—
With lots and lots of relatives,
Or sometimes, just a few.

They like to cook old recipes
And occasionally try things new.
They carry on traditions
That they want to share with you.

Some families like to dance and sing,
Others are quiet and meek.
But that's what makes them special,
That's what makes us all unique.

So learn from your own family,
Learn the old and the new.
Be proud of your own family,
They're a part of you.

*Jean Warren*

## Happy Birthday

Happy birthday, it's your day,
*(Point to birthday child.)*
Hope it's great in every way!
*(Nod head.)*
We will help you celebrate,
*(Hold arms out wide.)*
'Cause we think you're really great!
*(Clap for birthday child.)*

*Rita Galloway*

## My Birthday

Today I have a birthday,
I'm four years old, you see.
*(Hold up four fingers.)*
And here I have my birthday cake,
*(Form circle with hands.)*
Which you may share with me.

First, let's count the candles,
Count them, every one.
One, two, three, four—
*(Hold up four fingers, one at a time.)*
Now our counting's done.

Let's blow out the candles,
Out each flame will go,
"Whh! Whh! Whh! Whh!"
*(Blow four times.)*
As one by one we blow.

Adapt the rhyme to fit the age of the birthday child.

*Adapted Traditional*

## Making a Birthday Cake

Today is Adam's birthday,
*(Point to birthday child.)*
Let's make him a cake.
*(Form circle with hands.)*
Mix and stir, stir and mix,
*(Make stirring motions.)*
Then into the oven to bake.
*(Pretend to put cake in oven.)*

Here's our cake so nice and round,
*(Form circle with hands.)*
We frost it red and white.
*(Pretend to frost cake.)*
We put four candles on it
*(Hold up four fingers.)*
To make a birthday light!
*(Flutter fingers gently.)*

Substitute the name of the birthday child for *Adam* and adjust the number of candles to match the child's age.

*Adapted Traditional*

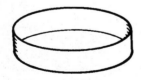

## It's Your Birthday

Jessica, Jessica, hip, hip hurray!
    *(Point to birthday child.)*
We're so glad you're five today!
    *(Hold up five fingers.)*
Please stand up and show us how
You turn around and take a bow!
    *(Have birthday child do actions described.)*

Substitute the name of the birthday child for *Jessica* and the age of the child for *five.*

*Florence Dieckmann*


## Samantha's Fifth Birthday

Samantha had a birthday,
Samantha had a cake.
    *(Form circle with hands.)*
Samantha's mother made it,
Samantha watched it bake.

Frosting on the top,
Frosting in between.
    *(Hold one hand out flat and move other hand up under it.)*
Oh, it was the nicest cake
That you have ever seen!

Samantha had some candles,
One, two, three, four, five.
    *(Hold up fingers, one at a time.)*
Who can tell how many years
Samantha's been alive?

Substitute the name of the birthday child for *Samantha.*

*Adapted Traditional*


## What Am I Making?

Sift the flour and break an egg,
    *(Do actions as rhyme indicates.)*
Add some sugar and a shake of nutmeg.
A pat of butter, a cup of milk,
Stir and beat as fine as silk.
Want to know what I'm going to bake?
Shhh, it's a secret—a birthday cake!

*Adapted Traditional*


## Birthday Party

Oh, welcome to our party,
We're glad you came today!
    *(Beckon to birthday child.)*
Won't you have a cup of tea?
It's made a special way.
    *(Pretend to pour tea.)*

We also have some birthday treats,
We hope you'll have a few.
    *(Hold out pretend plate to birthday child.)*
We're so glad you came today
And that we have friends like you!
    *(Point to birthday child.)*

*Jean Warren*

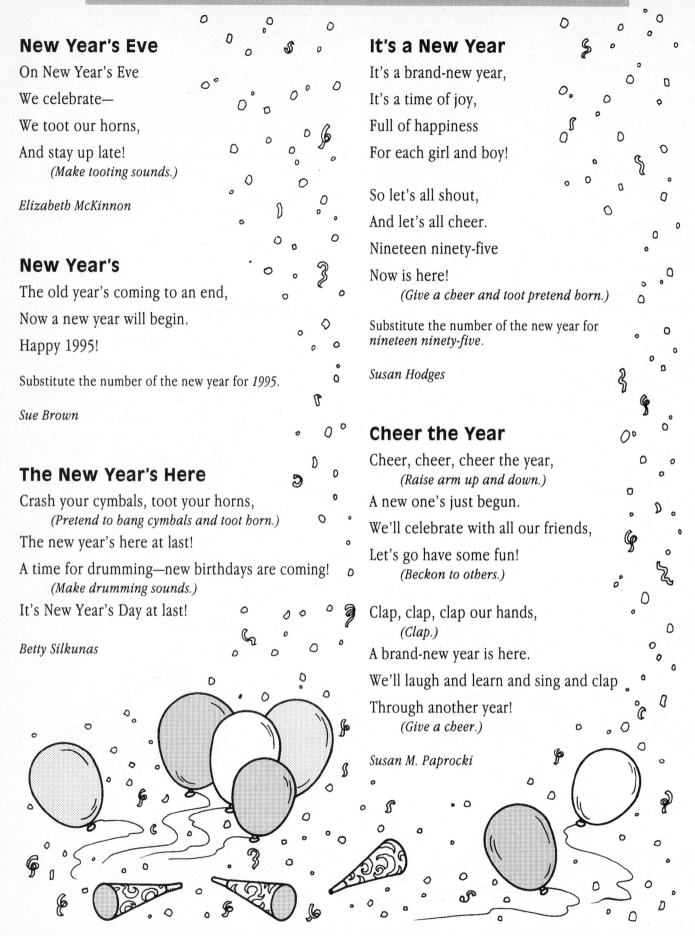

## New Year's Eve

On New Year's Eve
We celebrate—
We toot our horns,
And stay up late!
    *(Make tooting sounds.)*

*Elizabeth McKinnon*

## New Year's

The old year's coming to an end,
Now a new year will begin.
Happy 1995!

Substitute the number of the new year for *1995*.

*Sue Brown*

## The New Year's Here

Crash your cymbals, toot your horns,
    *(Pretend to bang cymbals and toot horn.)*
The new year's here at last!
A time for drumming—new birthdays are coming!
    *(Make drumming sounds.)*
It's New Year's Day at last!

*Betty Silkunas*

## It's a New Year

It's a brand-new year,
It's a time of joy,
Full of happiness
For each girl and boy!

So let's all shout,
And let's all cheer.
Nineteen ninety-five
Now is here!
    *(Give a cheer and toot pretend horn.)*

Substitute the number of the new year for
*nineteen ninety-five.*

*Susan Hodges*

## Cheer the Year

Cheer, cheer, cheer the year,
    *(Raise arm up and down.)*
A new one's just begun.
We'll celebrate with all our friends,
Let's go have some fun!
    *(Beckon to others.)*

Clap, clap, clap our hands,
    *(Clap.)*
A brand-new year is here.
We'll laugh and learn and sing and clap
Through another year!
    *(Give a cheer.)*

*Susan M. Paprocki*

## A Little Groundhog

Way down deep

In a hole in the ground,

Lived a little groundhog,

All furry and round.
>       *(Crouch down near floor.)*

Little furry groundhog

Popped up one day,

Looked all around

And decided to stay.
>       *(Jump up and look around.)*

But just as the groundhog

Started to play,

Out came his shadow

And frightened him away.
>       *(Run in place.)*

Back down his hole

The little groundhog sped,

Back to his home,

Back to his bed!
>       *(Crouch down near floor.)*

*Jean Warren*

## Mr. Groundhog

Mr. Groundhog in the ground,
>       *(Make fist with thumb inside.)*
Pop your head up, look around.
>       *(Pop up thumb and move it in a circle.)*
Look up high, look down low.
>       *(Move thumb up, then down.)*
Will you see your little shadow?
>       *(Tilt head to one side while moving thumb around.)*

*Deborah A. Roessel*

## I'm a Little Groundhog

I'm a little groundhog fat and brown,
>       *(Crouch down near floor.)*
Popping up above the ground.
>       *(Jump up.)*
I sure hope my shadow doesn't show,
>       *(Look for pretend shadow.)*
For if it does, we'll have more snow!
>       *(Frown.)*

*Diane Thom*

## Here's a Little Groundhog

Here's a little groundhog

Furry and brown,
*(Make fist with thumb inside.)*

He's coming up

To look around.
*(Pop up thumb.)*

If he sees his shadow,

Down he'll go,
*(Hide thumb in fist.)*

Then six more weeks of winter—

Oh, no!
*(Shake head and frown.)*

*Nancy N. Biddinger*

## Groundhog, Groundhog

Groundhog, groundhog, popping up today,
*(Do actions as rhyme indicates.)*

Groundhog, groundhog, can you play?

If you see your shadow, hide away,

If there is no shadow, you can stay.

*Jean Warren*

## Little Groundhog

Little groundhog in your hole,

Is it winter, do you know?
*(Look downward.)*

If your shadow chases you,

That means winter is not through.
*(Shake head.)*

If your shadow can't be seen,

Spring is coming, new and green!
*(Nod head and smile.)*

*Diane Thom*

## What April Fools' Is For

April Fools', April Fools',

What a lot of fun!

Everybody's playing tricks

On each and every one.

Men from Mars, falling stars,

Big black bugs and more!

You trick me, I trick you,

That's what April Fools' is for!

*Jean Warren*

## Surprise! It's April Fools'!

All around the town today,

Even here at school,

Everyone is playing tricks—

Surprise! It's April Fools'!
  *(Hold hands out, palms up.)*

*Jean Warren*

## Happy April Fools'

Giant, giant spider,

Crawling up your back.
  *(Creep hand up other person's back.)*

Here, let me help you

Give your back a whack.
  *(Pat person's back once.)*

It was very ugly,

So very mean and cruel.
  *(Make scary face.)*

Aren't you glad I saved you?

Happy April Fools'!
  *(Smile.)*

*Jean Warren*

## April Fool!

Little bears have three feet,
  *(Hold up three fingers.)*
Little birds have four.
  *(Hold up four fingers.)*
Little cats have two feet,
  *(Hold up two fingers.)*
And boys and girls have more.
  *(Hold up five fingers.)*

Do you believe my story?
  *(Point to others.)*
Do you think it's wrong?
  *(Tilt head to one side.)*
I tell it only once a year,
  *(Hold up one finger.)*
When April comes along!
  *(Smile and say, "April Fool!")*

*Adapted Traditional*

## I Saw a Sight Today

I saw a sight today

While on my way to school.

I saw a bee with a shoe on its knee.

Surprise—April Fool!

With your children, make up new third lines like these: I saw a bear who was combing its hair; I saw a cat who was wearing a hat; I saw a fish who was washing a dish.

*Elizabeth McKinnon*

## I'm a Little Basket

I'm a little basket, look at me,
>    *(Point to self.)*
Filled full of flowers pretty as can be.
>    *(Hold arms out in front, fingers touching.)*
Hang me on a friend's door on May Day,
>    *(Pretend to hang basket.)*
Then ring the bell and run away.
>    *(Ring pretend doorbell, then run in place.)*

*Elizabeth McKinnon*

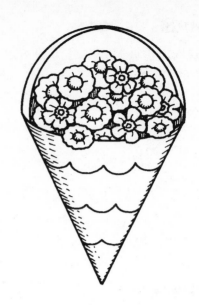

## May Day, May Day

May Day, May Day, how do you do?

I made a basket just for you.
>    *(Hand someone a pretend basket.)*
May Day, May Day, I made one more,

I will hang it on a door.
>    *(Pretend to hang basket.)*
Knock, knock, knock—run, run, run,

May Day is a lot of fun!
>    *(Make knocking motions, then run in place.)*

*Kristine Wagoner*

## May Day's Here

May Day's here,

The sun shines bright.
>    *(Form circle with arms.)*
Birds and butterflies

Are in flight.
>    *(Wave hands gently in air.)*

May Day's here,

Everything feels right.
>    *(Nod head and smile.)*
Flowers are blooming,

What a sight!
>    *(Open cupped hands slowly.)*

*Kristine Wagoner*

## Ring Around the Maypole

Ring around the Maypole,

Pocket full of roses.
>    *(Join hands with others and move in circle.)*
Ribbons, ribbons,

We all fall down!
>    *(Drop to floor.)*

*Toni Lenhardt*

## Happy May Day

Bluebells, tulips, daffodils,

All are blooming today.
>    *(Open cupped hands slowly.)*
What a lovely time of year—

Happy May Day!

*Jean Warren*

## Mommy's Hands

Mommy's hands are soft and warm,
> *(Gently rub hands together.)*
To tuck me in at night.
> *(Pretend to tuck in blankets.)*
Mommy's hands are kind and firm,
> *(Put hands together and squeeze.)*
To hug me snugly tight.
> *(Hug self.)*

*Beverly Qualheim*

## We Love Mothers

We love mothers, yes, we do!
> *(Nod head.)*
Mothers are for hugging,
> *(Hug self.)*
Mothers are for kissing,
> *(Blow a kiss.)*
We love you, yes, we do!
> *(Nod head.)*

*Barbara Fletcher*

## Mommy, Mommy

Mommy, Mommy,

Here are my gifts—

A special hug

And a great big kiss.
> *(Hug self, then blow a kiss.)*

You always love me,

Even when I'm bad.

You always love me,

And never leave me sad.
> *(Shake head and smile.)*

*Patricia Coyne*

## I Love Mommy

I love Mommy,

Yes, I do.
> *(Blow a kiss.)*
And my mommy loves me,

Very much too!
> *(Hug self.)*

*Carla Cotter Skjong*

## A Mom's a Special Lady

A mom's a special lady,

So hug her every day.
*(Hug self.)*

She gives you lots of food to eat

And takes you out to play.
*(Make eating motions, then dance in place.)*

Your mother reads you stories

And buys you sneakers too.
*(Point to mouth, then shoes.)*

Aren't you happy that you have

A mom who loves you?
*(Nod head and smile.)*

*Betty Silkunas*

## On Mother's Day

On Mother's Day I'd like to say

How precious, dear Mother, you are.
*(Blow a kiss.)*

You'll always be, in so many ways,

My very favorite star!
*(Clap hands.)*

*Diane Thom*

## In Mommy's Lap

I love to snuggle in Mommy's lap

And squeeze her tight like this.
*(Hug self.)*

I love to tell her, "I love you so!"

With a great big kiss.
*(Blow a kiss.)*

*Vicki Claybrook*

## Our Country's Flag

Please sit down, everyone,

I'm going to tell a story
*(Point to mouth.)*

About our country's famous flag—

Its nickname is Old Glory.
*(Point to flag.)*

Stars and stripes are on our flag,

They're red and white and blue.
*(Point to flag colors.)*

It tells the world that we are free

And proud to be here too!
*(Nod head.)*

*Sue Brown*

## Stars and Stripes

Wave the flag, wave the flag,
*(Wave arm like a flag.)*

As we march around.

Hold it high to show our pride,

Don't let it touch the ground.

Wave the flag, wave the flag,

Dear red, white, and blue.

Stars and stripes forever bright,

America—here's to you!

*JoAnn C. Leist*

## Our Flag

Stripes and stripes and little stars,
*(Wave arm like a flag.)*

Oh, how beautiful you are!

Red and white and blue, it's true,

Proudly waving for me and you.

*Becky Valenick*

## We Honor You

Oh, red, white, and blue,

We honor you.
*(Salute flag.)*

You have red and white stripes

And fifty stars too.
*(Point to flag's stripes, then stars.)*

*Jennifer Wagner*

## Daddy

Daddy, here's a hug,

And lots of kisses too.
*(Hug self, then blow kisses.)*

Each hug and kiss you get today

Says that I love you!
*(Continue hugging and blowing kisses.)*

*Susan Peters*

## Daddy, Daddy

Daddy, Daddy, I love you,

Yes, oh yes, oh yes, I do!
*(Nod head.)*

I'm so glad that you are mine,

I will love you all the time!
*(Hug self.)*

*Darlene Holaway*

## Daddy Is My Friend

Daddy is my special friend,

The two of us are buddies.
*(Hold up two fingers.)*

I always like the things we do,

I'm thankful for my daddy!
*(Hug self.)*

*Sue Brown*

## Thank You, Daddy

Daddy, it's your special day,

And it's time for me to say

I'm so glad for all you do.

Thank you, Daddy, I love you!
*(Blow a kiss.)*

*Sue Brown*

## Best Daddy

My daddy is the best, you see,

Because he takes good care of me.
*(Nod head.)*

He takes me to the park to play,

Or to the beach on a sunny day.
*(Form circle with arms.)*

At night he tucks me into bed,

Says goodnight, and pats my head.
*(Pretend to tuck in blankets.)*

My daddy's the best in every way,

I love you, Daddy. Happy Father's Day!
*(Hug self.)*

*Nancy K. Hobbs*

## Special Dad

Dad, I'd really like to be

So very much like you.

To grow up strong and caring,

To do the things you do.

When I think of all the fun

And good times we have had,

I must say to everyone

I've got a special dad!

*Diane Thom*

## To My Daddy

I hugged this little card real tight

And kissed it, Daddy, too.

Then I packed it full of love

And sent it off to you!

Include this rhyme inside Father's Day cards that your children make.

*Sharon L. Olson*

## Martin Luther King

Martin Luther King, they say,
*(Nod head.)*
Thought of friendship every day.
*(Clasp hands together.)*
He always wanted you and me
*(Point to others, then self.)*
To live together peacefully.
*(Join hands with others.)*

*June Meckel*

## Dr. King

Dr. King was a man
Who cared for you and me.
He dreamed of a world filled with love
And peace and harmony.
*(Open arms wide.)*

Happy birthday, Dr. King,
Happy birthday to you.
We will work for peace today
To help your dream come true.
*(Nod head and smile.)*

*Debra Butler*

## Peace March

Let's go marching hand in hand
*(Join hands with others and march.)*
Let's march for peace today.
Let's go marching hand in hand,
Let's march and shout "Hurray!"

Let's march like Dr. King today,
Let's make our country strong.
Let's join hands and be as one,
Let's smile and march along!

*Jean Warren*

# Abraham Lincoln

## Abe Lincoln

Abe Lincoln was our president,

Let's shout "Hurray!"
>    *(Cheer.)*

We celebrate his birthday

On Presidents' Day.
>    *(Nod head.)*

Abe lived long ago and he

Wanted all people to be free.
>    *(Open arms wide.)*

*Susan Hodges*

## Honest Abe

His name was Abraham Lincoln,

We see him on our money.

His picture's on the five-dollar bill

And also on the penny.
>    *(Hold up a penny.)*

Honest Abe he was called,

Honest, true, and kind.

He was our sixteenth president,

The best you'll ever find.
>    *(Nod head and smile.)*

*Barbara O'Dowd*

## Abraham Lincoln

Abraham Lincoln

Was our president, you know.

He led our land, America,

A long, long time ago.
>    *(Nod head.)*

He worked to put an end to war,

He worked to make people free.

He made our country a better one

For you and for me.
>    *(Point to others, then self.)*

*Vicki Claybrook*

## A Great Man

A great man you ought to know

Lived a long, long time ago—

Abraham Lincoln, our president,

He gave freedom to each resident.

He made the world a better place

For you and me and the human race.
>    *(Open arms wide.)*

*Carol Metzker*

## Little George

George Washington was very small

When he chopped down a tree.
*(Hold hand low.)*

He took his ax and gave three whacks

And said, "Just look at me!"
*(Make chopping motions.)*

But his father was not pleased

When he saw his cherry tree.
*(Shake head and frown.)*

"I cannot lie," said George at last—

"The chopper, it was me!"
*(Point to self.)*

*Jean Warren*

## Little George Washington

Little George Washington

Chopped down a cherry tree.
*(Make chopping motions.)*

He didn't get in trouble,

He apologized, you see.

He was our first president,

On him we could rely.
*(Hold up pointer finger.)*

We're so very glad that he

Could not tell a lie!

*Jean Warren*

## George and the Cherry Tree

George Washington spied a cherry tree,

His father's pride and joy.

He chopped it down right to the ground,

What a naughty boy!
*(Shake pointer finger.)*

"Who cut this tree, my son, did you?"

His father loudly cried.

"Yes, I did it," said little George,

"I cannot tell a lie!"
*(Shake head.)*

*Betty Ruth Baker*

## George Washington

He said, "Be brave, now don't give up,

We'll build a brand-new country!"
*(Stand straight and tall.)*

He led the soldiers—that was hard,

For they were cold and hungry.
*(Hug self and shiver.)*

The people loved him, one and all,

He worked to make us free.
*(Nod head.)*

Yes, it was George Washington,

First president of our country!
*(Hold up pointer finger.)*

*Vicki Claybrook*

## Clara Barton

There once was a girl named Clara,

Who helped to make people well.

She started the American Red Cross,

And now her story we tell.

Clara Barton cared about people

And was a fine nurse, they say.

Let's always remember Clara Barton,

Let's honor her today!
  *(Clap hands.)*

*Jean Warren*

## George Washington Carver

George Washington Carver liked peanuts,

He thought they were really a treat.
  *(Nod head.)*

He made many products from peanuts,

From peanuts that we love to eat!
  *(Rub tummy and lick lips.)*

*Elizabeth McKinnon*

## Columbus

Christopher Columbus
  *(Rock hands like a ship.)*

Sailed the ocean blue.

He landed in America

In 1492.

*Sue Brown*

## Christopher Columbus

Christopher Columbus

Sailed across the sea

And found a very special land,

Now home to you and me.
  *(Point to others, then self.)*

Christopher Columbus,

We celebrate the day

In fourteen hundred and ninety-two,

When you sailed this way.
  *(Clap hands.)*

*Patricia Coyne*

## Babe Didrikson

Who loved sports?

Babe Didrikson!
 *(Nod head.)*

She loved to play ball,
 *(Toss pretend ball.)*

And she loved to run.
 *(Run in place.)*

She thought that swimming
 *(Make swimming motions.)*

And tennis were fun.
 *(Hit pretend tennis ball.)*

At playing golf,
 *(Hit pretend golf ball.)*

She was number one.
 *(Hold up pointer finger.)*

Babe Didrikson!

*Elizabeth McKinnon*

## Walt Disney

Once there was a man named Walt,

Whose dreams were, oh, so grand.

But he worked and worked and worked,

And now there's Disneyland!

Young Walt Disney had a dream,

A mighty revelation—

Drawings that could move and talk—

We call it animation!

*Jean Warren*

## Lady Liberty

Lady Liberty
 *(Raise arm like Statue of Liberty.)*

Standing tall,

Welcoming the people,

One and all.

Holding her torch

Way up high,

Welcoming all

Who happen by.

*Elizabeth McKinnon*

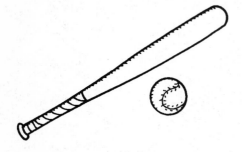

## Jackie Robinson

Jackie Robinson

Went to bat.
 *(Hold pretend bat over shoulder.)*

He hit a home run,

Just like that!
 *(Swing pretend bat.)*

*Elizabeth McKinnon*

## Betsy Ross

Betsy Ross, we thank you,

We thank you, yes we do.
*(Nod head.)*
You made our flag, with its stars and stripes,

Red, white, and blue.
*(Hold up three fingers, one at a time.)*

*Elizabeth McKinnon*

## Sacajawea

Paddle, paddle our canoe,

Let's paddle it this way.
*(Pretend to paddle canoe.)*
Sacajawea will be our guide,

Let's follow her today.

Tramp, tramp through the woods,

Let's tramp our feet this way.
*(Tramp in place.)*
Sacajawea will be our guide,

Let's follow her today.

Climb, climb the mountain high,

Let's climb so high this way.
*(Make climbing movements.)*
Sacajawea will be our guide,

Let's follow her today.

Now it's time to rest,

Let's rest our heads this way.
*(Rest cheek on folded hands.)*
Sacajawea has been our guide,

We followed her today.

*Elizabeth McKinnon*

# First-Line Index

# X

# Y

# Z

# Subject Index

# Contributors

Many of the rhymes and fingerplays in this book were originally submitted by *Totline*® *newsletter* readers. We wish to acknowledge the following contributors.

Krista Alworth, Verona, NJ

Jean Anderson, St. Paul, MN

Allyson G. Baernstein, Newark, DE

Betty Ruth Baker, Waco, TX

Lynn Beaird, Loma Linda, CA

Pat Beck, Red Lion, PA

Ellen Bedford, Bridgeport, CT

Nanette Belice, Kensington, MD

Lee Bernstein, Schererville, IN

Brian Biddinger, Orlando, FL

Nancy N. Biddinger, Orlando, FL

John M. Bittinger, Everett, WA

Janice Bodenstedt, Jackson, MI

Sally Braun, Elmhurst, IL

April Brown, Barnesville, PA

Karen L. Brown, Siloam Springs, AR

Sue Brown, Louisville, KY

Susan Burbridge, Albuquerque, NM

Serena K. Butch, Schenectady, NY

Barbara Butler, Cresskill, NJ

Debra Butler, Denver, CO

Kristina Carle, Kensington, MD

Mildred Claus, Parma, OH

Vicki Claybrook, Kennewick, WA

Pat Cook, Hartford, VT

Lynne Copeland, Poughkeepsie, NY

Patricia Coyne, Mansfield, MA

Terri Crosbie, Oldwick, NJ

Frank Dally, Ankeny, IA

Marcia Dean, Richland, WA

Marjorie Debowy, Stony Brook, NY

Florence Dieckmann, Roanoke, VA

Barbara Dinart, Philipsburg, PA

Cindy Dingwall, Palatine, IL

Gee Gee Drysdale, Syracuse, NY

Barbara Dunn, Hollidaysburg, PA

Sharon Engel, Oshkosh, WI

Adele Engelbracht, River Ridge, LA

Barbara B. Fleisher, Glen Oaks, NY

Barbara Fletcher, El Cajon, CA

Karen Folk, Franklin, MA

Paula C. Foreman, Lancaster, PA

Sue Foster, Mukilteo, WA

Irmgard Fuertges, Kitchener, Ontario

Rita Galloway, Harlingen, TX

Nancy Giles, Key West, FL

Vicki L. Gilliam, Marlin, TX

Judy Caplan Ginsburgh, Alexandria, LA

Rita Graef, New Port Richey, FL

Leora Grecian, San Bernadino, CA

Cathy B. Griffin, Plainsboro, NJ

Lori Gross, Souderton, PA

Maureen Gutyan, Williams Lake, B.C.

Judy Hall, Wytheville, VA

Tami Hall, Owasso, OK

Shirley M. Harp, Columbus, OH

Janet Harris, Annandale, NJ

Barbara Hasson, Portland, OR

Nancy K. Hobbs, Branford, CT

Dee Hoffman, Aitkin, MN

Janet Hoffman, Elmira, NY

Mildred Hoffman, Tacoma, WA

Darlene Holaway, Ventura, CA

Colraine Pettipaw Hunley, Doylestown, PA

Louanne Hutcheson, Carrollton, GA

Ellen Javernick, Loveland, CO

Sr. Linda Kaman, R.S.M., Pittsburgh, PA

Margery A. Kranyik, Hyde Park, MA

Neoma Kreuter, Upland, CA

Carol Kyger, Hood River, OR

JoAnn C. Leist, Smithfield, NC

Toni Lenhardt, Cannon Beach, OR

Karen Leslie, Erie, PA

Debra Lindahl, Libertyville, IL

Martha T. Lyon, Fort Wayne, IN

Joyce Marshall, Whitby, Ontario

Laurie W. Mason, Middletown, NJ
Kathy McCullough, Everett, WA
Judith McNitt, Adrian, MI
June Meckel, Andover, MA
Rose C. Merenda, Warwick, RI
Carol Metzker, Oregon, OH
Margo S. Miller, Westerville, OH
Ruth Miller, San Antonio, TX
Susan A. Miller, Kutztown, PA
Susan L. Moon, Allentown, PA
Donna Mullenix, Thousand Oaks, CA
Teri Muller, Westminster, MD
Diana Nazaruk, Clark Lake, MI
Susan Nydick, Philadelphia, PA
Joan Nydigger, Kent, WA
Ann M. O'Connell, Coaldale, PA
Barbara O'Dowd, Cypress, CA
Sharon L. Olson, Minot, ND
Judy Panko, Aitkin, MN
Susan M. Paprocki, Northbrook, IL
Barbara Paxson, Warren, OH
Susan Peters, Upland, CA
Jeanne Petty, Camden, DE
Lois E. Putnam, Pilot Mt., NC
Beverly Qualheim, Marquette, MI
Polly Reedy, Elmhurst, IL
Barbara Robinson, Glendale, AZ
Deborah A. Roessel, Flemington, NJ
Penny Rover, Jenks, OK
Dorothy Samorajski, Chicago, IL
Vivian Sasser, Independence, MO
Ione Sautner, Minot, ND
Sue Schliecker, Waukesha, WI
Marion Scofield, Spokane, WA
Diane Seader, Maple Valley, WA
Vicki Shannon, Napton, MO
Carole Sick, Hummelstown, PA
Betty Silkunas, Lansdale, PA
Carla Cotter Skjong, Tyler, MN
Ingrid C. Skjong, Tyler, MN
Judy Slenker, York, PA
Karen M. Smith, Bluemont, VA
Nancy J. Smith, Columbus, OH
Sharon Smith, Doylestown, PA

Lynne Speaker, Olympia Fields, IL
Kerry L. Stanley, Centre Square, PA
Priscilla M. Starrett, Warren, PA
Sharon Sweat, Carthage, NC
Lynn Tarleton, Baton Rouge, LA
Billie Taylor, Sioux City, IA
Dawn Thimm, Balsam Lake, WI
Diane Thom, Maple Valley, WA
Martha Thomas, Lake Clear, NY
Cathi Ulbright, Wooster, OH
Becky Valenick, Rockford, IL
Karen Vollmer, Wauseon, OH
Elizabeth Vollrath, Stevens Point, WI
Bobbie Lee Wagman, Milton, WI
Jennifer Wagner, Camarillo, CA
Kristine Wagoner, Puyallup, WA
Stella Waldron, Lincoln, NE
Cynthia Walters, Mechanicsburg, PA
Linda Warren, Newbury Park, CA
Marie Wheeler, Tacoma, WA
Gillian Whitman, Overland Park, KS
Janet Graves Wilson, Windsor, CT
Saundra Winnett, Lewisville, TX
Angela Wolfe, Miamisburg, OH
Bonnie Woodard, Shreveport, LA
Jean Woods, Tulsa, OK